T0315914

The Adolescent Experience

European and American Adolescents in the 1990s

Research Monographs in Adolescence
Nancy L.Galambos/Nancy A.Busch-Rossnagel, Editors

The Adolescent Experience
European and American Adolescents in the 1990s

Françoise D. Alsaker
University of Bergen, Norway
University of Berne, Switzerland

and

August Flammer
University of Berne, Switzerland

In collaboration with:

Nancy Bodmer, *Federal Social Insurance Office, Berne, Switzerland*
Luba Botcheva, *Center for Interdisciplinary Studies, Sofia, Bulgaria*
Benö Csapó, *Attila Jozsef University, Szeged, Hungary*
Connie Flanagan, *Pennsylvania State University, USA*
Nina Gootkina, *Institute of General and Pedagogical Psychology, Moscow, Russia*
Alexander Grob, *University of Berne, Switzerland*
Hania Liberska, *Adam Mickiewicz University, Poland*
Aurora Liiceanu, *Societatae de Educatie Contaceptiva si Sexuala, Rumania*
Petr Macek, *Masaryk University, Brno, Czech Republic*
Peter Noack, *University of Jena, Germany*
Jari Nurmi, *University of Jyväskylä, Finland*
Colette Sabatier, *University of Nanterre—Paris X, France*

Psychology Press
Taylor & Francis Group

New York London

First Published by Lawrence Erlbaum Associates, Inc., Publishers
10 Industrial Avenue
Mahwah, New Jersey 07430

Reprinted 2010 by Psychology Press

This edition published in the Taylor & Francis e-Library, 2009.

To purchase your own copy of this or any of Taylor & Francis or Routledge's
collection of thousands of eBooks please go to www.eBookstore.tandf.co.uk.

Copyright © 1999 by Lawrence Erlbaum Associates, Inc.
All rights reserved. No part of the book may be reproduced in any
form, by photostat, microform, retrieval system, or any other
means, without prior written permission of the publisher.

Cover design by Kathryn Houghtaling Lacey

Library of Congress Cataloging-in-Publication Data

The adolescent experience: European and American adolescents
in the 1990s/[edited by] Françoise D.Alsaker and August
Flammer; in collaboration with Nancy Bodmer...[et al.].
    p. cm.—(Research monographs in adolescence)
    Includes bibliographical references and index.
ISBN 0-8058-2552-5 (cloth: alk. paper)
1. Youth—Europe—Social conditions. 2. Youth—United
States—Social conditions. 3. Adolescent psychology—Eu-
rope. 4. Adolescent psychology—United States. I. Alsaker,
Françoise D. II. Flammer, August. III. Bodmer, Nancy. IV.
Series.
HQ799.E9A325 1998
305.235'094–DC21   98–11809
                                            CIP

ISBN 1-4106-0200-1 Master e-book ISBN

Contents

Series Editors' Foreword

Nancy L.Galambos
University of Victoria
Nancy A.Busch-Rossnagel
Fordham University

Nearly 4 years ago, when we were first approached with the idea of a monograph based on the research of 12 research teams from different nations (the European Network project, or EURONET), we were excited by the prospect of publishing such a work. Perhaps never before in the history of research on adolescence had there been such a massive, collaborative, long-term undertaking. This project was conceived and carried out successfully despite the following: The research teams were from nations differing in sociopolitical, economic, and historical contexts; the collaborators spoke different first languages; and the teams came to the project with differing backgrounds in and perspectives on research and adolescent development. It is manifestly evident in this monograph that the contributors overcame the multiple barriers that stood in their way and that they found common ground for gaining important knowledge about the adolescent experience in the modern world. This product of their cross-national collaboration is a model of the process and value of such an endeavor.

The timing for the appearance of this monograph is just right, as we stand at the edge of new directions in the study of adolescence. Scholars increasingly have recognized that adolescent development is best understood by acknowledging and examining the cultural, social, historical, and political contexts in which adolescents live. The participation of 12 research teams from different nations in a common project exploring adolescent experiences is an explicit attempt to accomplish the goal of understanding young people in their differing contexts. This collaboration also reflects the way that "doing" science is changing, with more emphasis on the establishment of partnerships among multiple research teams located at different geographic sites. Both directions—the exploration of adolescents in context, and multisite research collaborations—are necessary to forge a better understanding of adolescent development.

Our hats go off to the coordinators of this project, Françhise Alsaker and August Flammer, who put their hearts, their heads, and their energies into this large research venture. They showed patience, wisdom, and vision in approaching this collaboration. The individual research teams who conducted studies within their nations and who wrote chapters in this monograph also deserve a great deal of acknowledgment for the thoughtfulness with which they approached their studies and for their willingness to put common goals of the collaborative group at the forefront of their work. All of their efforts have been rewarded, for they—and we—now know infinitely more about adolescence in Europe and the United States than we did prior to the start of this worthwhile project.

Preface

In 1989, a new Europe was born: The iron curtain was lifted and people started to travel from West to East as well as from East to West, eager to see their respective countries, to meet with others, and possibly to learn from one another.

Curiously, the Euronet scientists met in the United States. With the support of the Johann Jacobs Foundation, located in Zürich, Switzerland, Richard M.Lerner set up a postdoctoral training workshop on adolescent psychology for 10 selected American participants and 10 selected European participants. The training staff was also recruited from the United States and Europe. August Flammer was on this training staff and the European participants came up with the idea to extend his study on the perception of adolescents' control in different life domains to their respective countries. Further discussions among this group laid the groundwork for new friendships and the plan to run a simple pilot study in order to become acquainted with international collaboration.

Thus, the Euronet for Research on Adolescence in the Context of Social Change was conceived as a basic description of the perceived living conditions in different countries and cultures, partly using measurement instruments that had already been used by one of the participants or that were at least inspired by their former work and actual interests. One important question was new to all of us—the question of time use by the adolescents. It seemed clear to all of us that we should not go into more theoretical work before having a closer look at the everyday life of the adolescents in each country. We also decided to have our national samples of 14- and 16-year-olds stratified according to the respective country's population in different educational tracks (excluding handicapped adolescents), but not stratified with respect to geographic distribution. The main reason for this was that it was clear that the data collection was to be prepared and conducted without any extra project funding and our first purpose was to exercise intercultural exchange among researchers.

We were indeed a very heterogeneous group. The following countries were represented from the beginning: Bulgaria (Luba Botcheva, then in Sofia), Czechoslovak! an Federal Republic (Petr Macek, Brno; at the time, Czechia and Slowakia were not yet separated), Finland (Jari-Erik Nurmi, then in Helsinki), France (Colette Sabatier, then in Rennes), Germany (Peter Noack, then in Mannheim), Hungary (Benö Csapó, Szeged), Poland (Hanna Liberska, Poznan), Russia (Nina Gootkina, Moscow), Switzerland

(August Flammer, Berne) and the United States (Connie Flanagan, then in Michigan). Some colleagues in other countries were approached, resulting in a few additional country members, that is, Norway (Franchise D.Alsaker, Bergen) and Romania (Aurora Liiceanu, Bucuresti). In some countries, important collaborators were associated, for instance, Erzsébet Czachesz (Hungary) and Alexander Grob and Nancy Bodmer (both Switzerland). The coordination of the entire study was done in Switzerland (Alsaker, Grob, and Flammer).

Those who have experienced cross-cultural research probably would not expect this plan to be pursued basically without funding, to a worthwhile end. Think of the decision of what measures to include, the definitive setup of some new measures, the translations and back translations, the subject sampling, the time coordination of the data collection, the data coding, the consistent pulling together of all the data sets, not to mention the text writing and laborious editing. None of the European participants were native English speakers. But the plan was carried out to a happy and very worthwhile end; this book is the final outcome. Our success was due to many fortunate circumstances, foremost was the enthusiasm and friendship among the participants. Of decisive importance were Alexander Grob's huge effort and competence in data management and first data analysis, and the tenacious and overly time-consuming work of organizing and editing this volume, which was done by Françoise D.Alsaker.

Nevertheless, collaboration and friendship need care and face-to-face contact. We were fortunate to obtain funding from the Swiss National Science Foundation (Project No. 11–33 126.91) for a week-long meeting in Switzerland. This was done in order to bring together and purify our data sets and discuss analytical procedures in 1992. We then received funding from the Johann Jacobs Foundation for more advanced data analyses, the coordination of the project in 1993, and another week-long meeting in order to exchange the initial results from our data analyses; this time we met in Szeged, Hungary, in 1993.

This volume contains the result of our study, offered to all those who have an interest in adolescence and/or an interest in the diversity of Europe, but also to those who are ready to excuse the fact that not all countries are included and the fact that the samples represent the countries only in some selected respects. However, in reading the contributions the reader will learn about hundreds of features of adolescence that are more or less characteristic of the cultures, ages, and genders.

Europe is very diverse; in fact, on average, it is much more diverse in itself than it is different from the United States. These diversities do not make life easy all the time, but most of the time they make it more interesting. We hope that Europe becomes more united without losing the richness of diversity.

—*August Flammer*

The Adolescent Experience
European and American
Adolescents in the 1990s

1

Cross-National Research in Adolescent Psychology: The Euronet Project

Françoise D.Alsaker
University of Bergen, Norway
University of Berne, Switzerland

August Flammer
University of Berne, Switzerland

In the last decade, the role of cultural factors in human development has been increasingly recognized, and the number of studies referring to the possible role of culture has grown rapidly. Frequently, however, possible cultural influences are merely used as alternative explanations for results that depart from mainstream findings (i.e., mostly North American findings). In such cases, the authors rarely offer clear definitions of how they conceptualize cultural effects. Culture becomes merely part of the error variance.

In fact, differences between results of studies conducted in different cultures or countries cannot necessarily be taken as evidence for cultural differences. Cross-cultural research is confronted with a wide range of methodological problems (see, e.g., Berry, Poortinga, Segall, & Dasen, 1992, for a detailed discussion) that may produce differences among samples. In other words, differences or similarities in mean scores may be due to variance in variables other than the cultural context. This particular issue is discussed in more detail chapter 2.

The term *culture* is generally used in a very liberal way. Whereas some authors say that it should be reserved to characterize large units that differ in many ways (e.g., in religion, beliefs, political systems, and traditions), such as the Western versus the Asian culture, others use the term *culture* to describe differences between small units, such as families. In everyday language, we talk about cultural gaps to describe problematic differences between people from different countries, even if the countries belong to the same broad cultural tradition. In doing so, we assume that people raised in a specific context will be bearers of the characteristics of this context and will behave in accordance with the norms, attitudes, and traditions that we call *sociocultural background*. Yet, can we really speak about a German versus

1

a French culture? Are they not both parts of the European culture? How can we define the European culture? Is it so different from the North American culture? Do not both represent the Western culture? So how can we find the boundaries of different cultures?

A German study on attachment (e.g., Grossmann, Grossmann, Spangler, Suess, & Unzner, 1985) is used as an example of the complexity of this issue. It shows clear differences in outcomes between a German sample and a North American sample, with more German infants showing avoidant patterns of reactions than did American infants. The authors explained this difference mainly in terms of the German mothers' higher demands for self-reliance, which was reflected in the way they cared for their children and consequently, in more detached behavior patterns in the children. In what sense are these differences in parental style attributable to cultural differences? One could argue that they are rooted in broader German and North American traditions (LeVine & Norman, 1995), but what if they are not rooted in such long traditions? Could we still speak of two cultural contexts?

Consider another example. Studies on puberty have shown differences, as well as similarities, in the impact of maturational timing in adolescents in different countries (Alsaker, 1995). For example, whereas some North American studies show that as age increases, there is greater dissatisfaction with the adolescents' own body in early maturing girls (e.g., Petersen & Crockett, 1985; Simmons & Blyth, 1987); in Norway, this relation was strongest in younger girls (Alsaker, 1992). In addition, whereas self-esteem seems to be unrelated to pubertal timing in most North American studies, girls who perceived themselves as early maturers had higher self-esteem scores in a German sample (Silbereisen, Petersen, Albrecht, & Kracke, 1989). These differences, too, are explained by broad cultural differences in attitudes toward one's body. Are such attitudinal differences actually substantial enough to be used as cultural indicators? Such questions show that there is a need to clarify what is meant by *culture* before it is used as an explanation. The aim of the following section is to bring some clarity to the definition of *culture* that we use in this volume.

There is another problem related to the use of culture as an explanatory variable, namely, it is difficult not only to identify cultures, but also to know enough about them in order to take advantage of their explanatory power. This volume not only uses cultural knowledge to explain differences among countries, but also contributes new knowledge about cultures. Metatheoretically, this corresponds to the hermeneutic circle in the understanding of historical texts in their historical context. We may say that our point of departure was our knowledge about adolescent development and our search for more differentiation and sophistication of this knowledge. Different cultural backgrounds were seen as opportunities to accomplish this task. In doing so, however, one not only obtains new knowledge about adolescence, but also obtains knowledge about the cultural settings from which the adolescents come. For example, should we find that adolescents more often report to work for money in one country than in others, it might tell us something about the economic conditions or about the general lifestyle of this country. This could push us to look for differences in mean incomes per family, in the way the school day is organized (allowing many or fewer opportunities to work), or in general values. On the other hand, what we already know about one country can help us explain the differences we find in the adolescents' behavioral habits in other countries.

In short, any differences we find expand our knowledge about the cultures and about adolescents. Future research may then start at a higher level of understanding of culture and adolescence, and the circle will develop into a spiral of knowledge acquisition.

WHAT DO WE MEAN BY CULTURE?

Berry et al. (1992) offered a long list of currently used definitions of *culture* and *cross-cultural psychology*. They also offered a short working definition of culture that seems to summarize essential elements; they define *culture* as "the shared way of life of a group of people" (p. 1). According to this definition, the cross-national differences in our earlier examples could definitely be considered as possible effects of cultural differences. However, the same authors also pointed to the fact that *cross-national studies,* defined as studies including samples from countries that are culturally closely related, are usually excluded from the field of cross-cultural psychology "by common consent" (p. 2). In this context, comparative studies between France and Spain are not characterized as cross-cultural studies; France and Spain both derive from the Latin tradition within Europe and, in addition, are geographical neighbors. In our view, the exclusion of such cross-national studies from the cross-cultural field stands in sharp contrast with the working definition proposed by Berry et al. (1992). Countries like Spain and France, although they share something in common, have different languages, histories, political institutions, and climates—they have clear differences in "the shared way of life" of their citizens.

The term *culture* is an anthropological one. Whereas sociologists or social psychologists talk about the members of a group, anthropologists refer more to the culture, in terms of the learned and shared behavior patterns, borne by the members of that group (Seltzer & Seltzer, 1988). Such a use of the term *culture* is very much in line with an early definition given by Kroeber and Kluckhohn (1952), proposing that *culture* consists of patterns, explicit or implicit, of "behavior acquired and transmitted by symbols, constituting the distinctive achievements of human groups, including their embodiments in artifacts; the essential core of culture consists of... traditional ideas and especially their attached values" (p. 181). This implies that people coming from two countries, showing differences in language, political system, historical backgrounds, and so on, are considered as coming from two different cultures. In fact, language is the feature that most anthropologists consider the principal component of culture (Berry et al., 1992).

Naroll (1970) proposed the term *culture bearing unit* (or *cultunit*) to designate groups of people that can be considered to represent, or to be under the influence of, a certain set of cultural variables. He also pointed to difficulties in distinguishing some cultunits from one another when they share several cultural features. We argue that this kind of overlap is a true mirror of our cultural reality in the same way that different languages have common roots, syntactic rules, or expressions, yet still remain different entities. Yet, cultunits also subdivide into cultsubunits, just as languages produce many dialects or sociolects.

Following this argument, one could conceive of culture in a hierarchical manner, starting at the top with very broad categories, such as the Western versus Asian civilization, dividing into large continental units, such as America and Europe, dividing again into smaller national units, which in turn subdivide into religious or linguistic groups. At the bottom of the hierarchy, we think of small social units such as certain groups of people defending unique lifestyles or ideologies.

Such a hierarchical view, however, is problematic in the sense that it gives the impression of definite units adding together to form broader units[1]. As with dialects, languages, and linguistic groups, the overlap between the units is large but not always systematic, or even logical. Historical events, geographical conditions, trade routes, and so on, play some role in such overlap, but they also interact and produce different effects in different places. Therefore, one could possibly better conceive of cultunits in terms of overlapping circles (or ellipses), sending and receiving impulses to other cultunits that are more or less permeable to this kind of impulse. An alternative solution is to allow for different hierarchies, for example, one according to linguistic relations, one according to historical background, and one according to economic or political systems.

As pointed out by Berry et al. (1992), in many studies, the term *culture,* on a conceptual level, coincides with *country* on the empirical level. In this study, we mostly chose to speak about cross-national differences. We did so in order to indicate that our samples all pertain to one cultural tradition on the macrolevel (i.e., the Western culture). However, in line with the previous discussion, we consider the populations from which our samples were drawn as different culture bearing units. Hence, when we speak of cultural influences or differences, we refer to these specific cultunits. More specifically, we mean that our cultunits differ at least along the following dimensions: language, historical

---

[1]The discussion on the hierarchical structure of the self (Harter, 1983; Shavelson & Marsh, 1986) is actually a good parallel to this discussion.

and geographical context, political system, welfare system, school system, housing, finances, family setting, and nutritional habits.

Kohn (1987) proposed four types of cross-national studies. The first category is a type of study in which the nation is the object of study, that is, the researcher is primarily interested in understanding the uniqueness of the countries. In the hermeneutic circle proposed earlier, it would correspond to obtaining knowledge about cultures. The second category includes studies in which the nations are conceived as different contexts; the aim of the comparative research is primarily to test the generality of findings and interpretations in different contexts. This corresponds with our obtaining more knowledge about adolescence in different contexts. In the third category, the nation is the unit of analysis, statistically speaking. Here, researchers seek to establish relations among characteristics of nations. An issue on this level is to examine the relation between national income and health (on an aggregated level). In the fourth category, we find studies examining how nations are systematically interrelated and form larger entities (corresponding to a hierarchical nested model of culture). These two latter issues are not directly addressed in this volume.[2]

WHY DO WE NEED CROSS-NATIONAL EUROPEAN STUDIES OF ADOLESCENT DEVELOPMENT?

In line with the arguments presented earlier, we can conceive of Europe as offering a large number of cultunits. This rich cultural resource has not been utilized so far to any substantial extent in psychology. Especially when it comes to adolescent psychology, the mainstream research was conducted on the North American population. Although there has been a rapid development of adolescent research in Europe, very often there are not enough studies on the same topic within Europe to allow European cross-national comparisons; hence, results are primarily compared with North American studies. Moreover, the opening of the borders to the Eastern part of Europe has brought a new opportunity to examine the heterogeneity in European cultural backgrounds and the effects of different political systems on personality and social development.

The dominance of North American research on adolescence masked some true differences in patterns of social relations or social behavior in different Western countries. A typical example lies in the case of dating. It is extremely difficult for Europeans to understand what dating in the United States really means (e.g., the related formalities or rituals of dating). Adams, Gullotta, and Markstrom-Adams (1994) wrote: "When a boy and a girl plan to meet alone or in a group at some place at some time, a date

---

[2]Nevertheless, the cluster analysis presented in chapter 4 could be considered as falling into this category.

has been arranged" (p. 324). When does a lunch with somebody become a date? What do adolescents do when they date? Do they hold hands? Do they kiss? Is dating the same as going steady? Does dating imply that one is in love with another? How does sexuality fit in? In Europe, there is a girlfriend-boyfriend culture and girls and boys go out together without being one another's girlfriend or boyfriend. They are simply good friends. Very often they go out in mixed groups without any specific pairwise pattern. Nevertheless, European researchers describing cross-gender relationships feel compelled to use the term *dating* when they publish in English, even in the absence of a comparable dating culture in Europe.

The Presumed Role of Culture

Theoretical models, such as Bronfenbrenner's ecological perspective (e.g., 1979), clearly include culture as one of the factors influencing an individual's development. This influence is typically mediated through specific systems such as the legal, political, value, norm, and religious ones that regulate the daily lives of people living in the same cultunit. All these systems together form what we call the *cultural background* and are highly intertwined. Furthermore, the influence of the cultural background is always mediated through lower level interactions between people. Therefore, we conceive of the direct social context as a culture bearing factor.

When it comes to variables that may be receptive to cultural factors, the list seems to grow parallel to the field of research. For example, recent research shows that health and illness are not only the consequences of biological phenomena, but are also culturally mediated (Kessel, 1992). For example, starting with individuals' relationships to their own body, we find large variations across cultural groups as to the number of anatomical terms in use and the importance attached to them; also, it seems that the way people relate to or conceive of their bodies is seen as a cultural trait (Fabrega, 1972). This variance is furthermore reflected in definitions of illness that vary to a great extent from one cultunit to another. In fact, the same clinical manifestations may be ignored in one context, treated as tiredness, as part of a developmental process, or as illness in others.

We want to illustrate this point with a short depiction of the French liver crisis—la crise de foie. As indicated by the name, we are talking about a state implying a belief that one's liver suffered some attack. It usually includes pain concentrated to the upper right side of the abdomen and is accompanied by nausea (and vomiting) and a general unpleasant feeling in the body. This syndrome is usually considered the direct result of stressful events or the result of eating certain types of food; for example, chocolate, among other things, is considered by most French people to be responsible for liver crises. Who would dare say such a thing to Swiss people? The problem with this liver syndrome is that it has no clear somatic basis and it seems to exist only in France. So, while French people take great care of their often-stressed liver, other Europeans do not even know where their liver is. Alsaker vividly remembers the liver crises of her childhood and adolescent period in France, symptoms that totally disappeared after some years in Germany and Norway.

We chose these medical examples to demonstrate that even phenomena linked to biology may be highly influenced by the beliefs people share in a cultunit. Let us now go back to psychological variables, such as personality development, and consider the case of the self-concept. Within the same cultunit, *self-concept* is considered a highly individual trait that is defined as an organization of mostly evaluative representations and beliefs about oneself as a person in terms of characteristics, behaviors, feelings, and thoughts (Alsaker & Olweus, 1992). However, as Markus and Kitayama (1991) pointed out, the construals of the self are tied to normative tasks that various cultures hold for what people should do. These authors drew our attention toward a major cultural differentiation on the basis of the construction of the self—an independent view of the self versus an interdependent view. The independent view of the self corresponds to the typical North American and European view of the individual, whereas the interdependent view is best exemplified in Asian cultures[3]. Furthermore, we find different guidelines to the construction of the self within the same cultural orientation. For example, whereas Americans are typically encouraged to take the initiative and are brought up to believe that they are special and in control of most things, Norwegian children have to learn very early that it is better not to "stick one's head out," because it could get "cut off,"[4] and that nobody should believe that she or he is special. This kind of attitude is so deeply rooted in this culture that it has been given a name: *Jante-law* (Storm, 1989).

Such differences in basic attitudes to the self in different cultures might be expected to be reflected in the kinds of self-concepts we find in these various cultures. However, given that the self-concept is a multidimensional concept under the influence of many factors, some individual differences within cultures are larger than differences across cultures.

We should also keep in mind that culture can only be one of many factors impinging on psychological (or somatic) functioning in general and that cultural factors may interact with one another and with individual factors. Therefore, cultural differences are not necessarily reflected in obvious differences across cultures (where we would expect them to show up). Moreover, given that the influence of cultural factors is primarily mediated by other factors, we may think of more indirect effects. For example, a

---

[3]However, as noted by the authors, the interdependent view of the self may also be characteristic of the African, the Latin American, and many southern European cultures.

[4]This in fact corresponds well to a Japanese proverb, "The nail that stands out gets pounded down" (Markus & Kitayama, 1991, p. 224).

certain combination of values and social structures may produce a specific school system. The school system, in turn, produces specific developmental environments that regulate the lives of the students and offer them different opportunities to structure their daily lives and different self-relevant experiences. Therefore, cultural values may first show up in terms of differences in performed activities or in lifestyles that, in turn, play an important role in the development of the individual.

Search for Similarities or for Differences?

According to Kohn (1987), many discussions of cross-national research contrast two research strategies—looking for regularities and looking for differences. In our view, researchers in the field of cross-national (or cross-cultural) research do not necessarily decide on the use of one of these strategies before they start a project. Cross-cultural psychology is still a very young science; the main body of research in this area seems to be exploratory and must look, simultaneously, for similarities and differences. This situation is not an ideal one and this exploratory character may explain why, as noted by Kohn (1987), the critical issue still remains to interpret these similarities and differences.

There are, however, studies with the purpose of testing the universality of specific hypotheses (see, e.g., chap. 7). As noted by Berry et al. (1992), this kind of research often tests the transportability of hypotheses from one culture to others. Studies aiming at a test of the possible influence of cultural settings are, on the other hand, primarily looking for differences in results. Studies with the main goal of exploration of variation can also be considered to pertain to this same category.

Kohn (1987) claimed that differences are much more difficult to interpret than are similarities. In his view, when similar results are found, the interpretation ignores whatever differences there were between the countries and looks for common factors. This, however, seems to be a premature conclusion. Actually, finding similarities in results between countries offering very different contexts of development should lead to a discussion of why such differences in the context do not influence the results. In doing so, we should nevertheless be aware of the danger of overinterpreting similarities because they usually are confounded with the null hypothesis.

Different Approaches to the Analysis
of Cross-National Data

We want to distinguish some principal approaches to the analysis of cross-national data. They are highly related to the levels of comparisons just described, but they do not overlap completely. First, the main interest is in distributions and mean scores. This is the type of results we are most used to, reporting how one national sample differs from others, for example, in terms of the mean importance of certain beliefs in each cultunit. Second, comparisons consist of testing whether certain operationalizations of concepts mean the same thing to people in different countries—whether they yield the same loading patterns in principal component analses, whether they produce the same reliability coefficients, and so on. The aim of these two approaches to the data corresponds, to a great extent, to the exploratory intention described earlier. For example, we may, as is the case here, be interested in exploring whether there is any variation in daily life schedules and activities in adolescents living in different countries.

Third, we may be concerned by relationships between variables. One may also ask whether there is variation between countries in the relation of certain reported problems to psychological variables such as a subjective feeling of well-being. In doing so, we still describe our samples in terms of differences and similarities, but at the same time, we introduce a notion of interaction of cultural background with some other variable.

Actually, cultural influences are of greatest interest when the cultural context can be shown to interact with specific variables in predicting other variables. An interaction between, for example, gender (or age) and culture in predicting adolescents' life goals tells us that gender differences or developmental trends in the choice of life goals are not universal, but dependent on certain sociocultural contexts.

The interaction approach is not only applicable to background variables such as gender or age. On the contrary, we can ask if existing relations between variables in certain cultural samples are replicable in other cultural contexts. As in the example previously used, we may examine whether stressful events can interact with culture in predicting subjective well-being.

When no interaction is found, we cannot conclude that the results are universal until we include samples representative of all possible cultural contexts, but we can conclude that they are independent of cultural differences in a given sample of cultural units. On the other hand, when we find that culture interacts with some other variable, we continue comparing the countries in terms of distributions. That is, all approaches to the data are closely related to one another. In the following chapters, all approaches are used. That is, we look at possible differences between countries in certain variables and relations between variables, and interactions between the cultural contexts and some other independent variables are examined.

EURONET ON ADOLESCENCE

The Euronet (European Network) on adolescence study was born in 1991 in the context of an international postdoctoral course, where 10 researchers from different European countries met 10 researchers from the United States. As this was shortly after the fall of the iron curtain, the European researchers were eager to engage in new forms of collaboration. They decided not to wait long until a serious study was launched, but to start a pilot study very soon. So, it came about that those Europeans who were at Penn State University, together with an American colleague, undertook the present Euronet study. A few interested researchers joined, one from Norway, one from Romania, and some of the Bernese group, who coordinated the whole study and had an interest in including both French Switzerland and German Switzerland. The selection of participating countries, then, was arbitrary (depending on attendance at the Penn State University meetings). As often happens in cross-national studies, there was no scientific reason for inclusion or noninclusion of a given European country.

The Euronet project comprises 13 different samples, 6 stemming from Central European and Eastern European countries (Bulgaria, Czechoslovakian Federal Republic—at that time, Hungary, Poland, Russia, and Romania), 6 from Western European countries (Finland, France, Germany, Norway, French Switzerland and German Switzerland) and one from the United States.

The title of this project, Euronet on Adolescence, was chosen to indicate the major cultural focus of the study—possible similarities and differences in adolescents' daily lives in European countries. The North American sample was included as an important comparison sample.

Issues To Be Addressed

General Issues

Throughout this volume, three general issues are addressed that can be conceived of as general questions about the role of culture. The first two are based on the descriptive approach, the third corresponds to the interaction approach just presented.

East-West Differences: Fiction and Reality. How much reality is there in expectations about differences between countries from the former Eastern block and Western European countries? What we know for sure is that the Western and Eastern countries form two distinct clusters in terms of language and in their political history and context. Given their recent political history, they also differ in terms of economics. The question is whether these differences, possibly combined with differences in national traditions and beliefs, can be reflected in differences between the two clusters of adolescents in time-use schedules, preferred activities, values, feelings of well-being, and so on, and whether we find more similarity within each cluster than between them.

Language and Political Borders. Another issue that can be addressed throughout the specific topics that are examined is the issue of the importance of language borders versus national or political borders. This issue is typically one of overlapping features between cultunits. For example, Switzerland is a country including several language groups. These language groups have something in common—the political system, laws, and the organization of institutional life. Yet, they may form cultsubunits because the contact between the groups may be reduced due to the use of different languages and also because they may turn to the neighboring countries using the same language. For example, the influence of France is clearly greater in the French-speaking population of Switzerland than it is in the German- or Italian-speaking groups. How much cross-border permeability there is depends, however, on many factors. One of these factors is the degree of political and administrative centralization. In the case of Switzerland, for example, where the federal states have a high degree of autonomy, one expects more permeability across the borders than in countries with a high degree of centralization.

The question is whether we can find these language borders in our analyses. Are the French adolescents and the French-Swiss adolescents more similar to one another than the French-Swiss adolescents to the German-Swiss adolescents?

Gender and Age Differences. This third general issue, discussed earlier, can be formulated as follows: Are there interactions between age and/or gender and culture? Put in other words, are the gender or age differences that can be expected on the basis of earlier research replicable in all cultunits included in our study? Given a presumed high degree of variation between countries as to gender roles and gender stereotypes, it sounds reasonable to expect an interaction of gender with culture in many variables.

Specific Issues and Outline of the Volume

In line with the two main approaches previously presented, the aim of this volume is twofold. First, it provides specific information on the lifestyles and attitudes of adolescents in the countries included (descriptive, exploratory approach). Second, it provides answers to specific questions as to the relation between variables across the different national units (interaction approach).

Although most of the following chapters use both approaches, some focus, to a greater extent, on the information purpose (e.g., chap. 3 and chap. 4 on time use, and chap. 5 on future orientation) whereas others focus on specific issues (e.g., chap. 8 on minorities).

Before considering results on lifestyles, attitudes, or any specific questions, the reader finds a detailed description of samples and procedures in chapter 2. Because cross-national research is typically confronted with a wide range of problems, chapter 2 also addresses some of the main methodological problems that were encountered. In particular, the issue of sampling is addressed and illustrated using data from the present Euronet study.

When it comes to understanding the life conditions of adolescents in different countries, it seems crucial to study what they actually do in everyday life and how much time they spend on what types of activities. In our view, this provides essential information about individual and societal priorities and values (Alsaker & Flammer, in press). This does not mean that reported activities only reflect deliberate choices. In fact, some activities are definitely dictated by society, for example how much time is allocated to school. Two chapters are dedicated to time use (chaps. 3 and 4). In chapter 3, we report data on leisure activities, that is, activities usually performed after all duties and commitments are accomplished. In chapter 4, we focus on what we call *necessary activities,* including variables such as going to school, sleeping, or eating. Given that total leisure time depends on the time left by the necessary activities, these two chapters are tightly connected to one another. In all, chapters 3 and 4 give detailed information on what a typical day looked like for adolescents from European countries and the United States in the early 1990s.

With this new knowledge about what adolescents actually did on the day before they participated in the study (a yesterday questionnaire was used, see chap. 3), we turn to their thoughts about the future, their attitudes toward specific values, and their perception of the timing of certain future commitments in chapter 5. Whereas the chapters on time use are expected to give us much information on the actual priorities of individuals and societies, and consequently, on implicit values, chapter 5 is expected to provide us information on the perceived values in the different cultunits.

In chapter 6, the focus is on adolescents' beliefs about how much influence they think they have in different areas of their lives and how important it is to them to feel in control in these domains. The three domains chosen here were individual personality development, future work, and subject matters to be treated in school.

In chapter 7, we turn to subjective well-being and a model is tested, including variables such as age, gender, country, and daily problems encountered by the adolescents as well as control beliefs and different reactions to stress as predictors of well-being. The main focus is on the test of the model across all countries and the possible interaction of some of the predictors with the adolescents' cultural background.

At this point in this volume, we should have gained some more knowledge about the adolescents as individuals in the specific cultunits included in the study. That is, we should know more than we did before about how they use their time, how they feel and perceive their possibilities to influence their own lives, how they think about the future, and which values are important to them. In addition, we should know more about differences and similarities among the 13 cultunits. The adolescents who participated in the study, however, did not have this opportunity to compare their answers with those of adolescents from the other countries. They were asked to participate in an *international* study, but they were questioned in their *national* contexts;

they never met across these national borders. The question is: What do they think about adolescents in other countries? In chapter 8, we, therefore, turn to the question of adolescents' preferences in regard to peers from other countries. With whom would adolescents from the different countries like to have more contact? Is there a typical East—West trend? Is the United States especially attractive to adolescents? These issues are of particular interest today—at the end of the 1990s—knowing how alive nationalistic values are and how much damage they still engender.

Similarly, a special case is examined in chapter 9—the case of Hungarian adolescents who live as a minority in Romania, (Transylvania). This sample is compared with a Hungarian sample living in Hungary and a Romanian sample. Issues are discussed about the role of sharing a common language, a common political system, and of being a minority.

In chapter 10, we try to integrate the findings presented in the chapters just described and come to some conclusions. We also take the opportunity to make some suggestions about ways to go in the near future.

REFERENCES

Adams, G.R., Gullotta, T.P., & Markstrom-Adams, C. (1994). *Adolescent life experiences*. Pacific Grove, CA: Brooks/Cole.

Alsaker, F.D. (1992). Pubertal timing, overweight, and psychological adjustment. *Journal of Early Adolescence, 12,* 396–419.

Alsaker, F.D. (1995). Timing of puberty and reactions to pubertal changes. In M.Rutter (Ed.), *Psychosocial disturbances in young people: Challenges for prevention* (pp. 39–82). New York: Cambridge University Press.

Alsaker, F.D., & Flammer, A. (in press). Time use in children and adolescents. In A.N. Perret-Clermont, J.M.Barrelet, A.Flammer, D.Miéville, J.F.Perret, & W.Perrig (Eds.), *Mind and time*. Göttingen, Germany: Hogrefe & Huber Publishers.

Alsaker, F.D., & Olweus, D. (1992). Stability of self-evaluations in early adolescence. A cohort longitudinal study. *Journal of Research on Adolescence, 2,* 123–145.

Berry, J.W., Poortinga, Y.H., Segall, M.H., & Dasen, P.R. (1992). *Cross-cultural psychology:. Research and applications*. New York: Cambridge University Press.

Bronfenbrenner, U. (1979). *The ecology of human development*. Cambridge, MA: Harvard University Press.

Fabrega, H. (1972). The study of disease in relation to culture. *Behavioral Science, 17,* 183–203.

Grossmann, K., Grossmann, K.E., Spangler, G., Suess, G., & Unzner, L. (1985). Maternal sensitivity and newborns' orientation responses as related to quality of attachment in Northern Germany. In I.Bretherton & E.Waters (Eds.), *Growing points of attachment. Theory and research. Monographs of the Society for Research in Child Development, 50 (Volumes 1–2, Serial No. 209,* pp. 233–256). Chicago: University of Chicago Press.

Harter, S. (1983). Developmental perspectives on the self-system. In P.H.Mussen (Ed.), *Handbook of child psychology: Vol. 4. Socialization, personality and social development* (pp. 275–385). New York: Wiley.

Kessel, F. (1992). On culture, health, and human development. *Items, 46,* 65–72.

Kohn, M.L. (1987). Cross-national research as an analytic strategy. *American Sociological Review, 52,*713–731.

Kroeber, A.L., & Kluckhohn, C. (1952). *Culture: A critical review of concepts and definitions (Vol. 47).* Cambridge, MA: Peabody Museum.

LeVine, R.A., & Norman, K. (1995). Culture and attachment: The case of German infant care. *Newsletter of the International Society for the Study of Behavioural Development, Serial No. 27,* 4–6.

Markus, H.R., & Kitayama, S. (1991). Culture and the self: Implications for cognition, emotion, and motivation. *Psychological Review, 98,* 224–253.

Naroll, R. (1970). The culture bearing unit in cross-cultural surveys. In R.Naroll & R.Cohen (Eds.), *Handbook of method in cultural anthropology* (pp. 721–765). New York: Natural History Press.

Petersen, A.C., & Crockett, L. (1985). Pubertal timing and grade effects on adjustment. *Journal of Youth and Adolescence, 14,* 191–206.

Seltzer, W.J., & Seltzer, M.R. (1988). Culture, leave-taking rituals and the psychotherapist. In O.Van der Hart (Ed.), *Coping with loss* (pp. 171–200). New York: Irvington Press.

Shavelson, R.J., & Marsh, H.W. (1986). On the structure of self-concept. In R.Schwarzer (Ed.), *Anxiety and cognition* (pp. 305–330). Hillsdale, NJ: Lawrence Erlbaum Associates.

Silbereisen, R.K., Petersen, A.C., Albrecht, H.T., & Kracke, B. (1989). Maturational timing and the development of problem behavior: Longitudinal studies in adolescence. *Journal of Early Adolescence, 9,* 247–268.

Simmons, R.G., & Blyth, D.A. (1987). *Moving into adolescence: The impact of pubertal change and school context.* New York: Aldine de Gruyter.

Storm, O. (1989). *Janteloven: Aksel Sandemose.* Copenhag, Denmark: Gyldendal

2

Methodological Challenges in Cross-National Research: Countries, Participants, and General Procedures

Françoise D.Alsaker
University of Bergen, Norway
University of Berne, Switzerland

Connie Flanagan
Pennsylvania State University

Benö Csapó
Attila Jozsef University, Szeged, Hungary

As pointed out in chapter 1, cross-national research is confronted with a wide range of problems (Berry, Poortinga, Segall, & Dasen, 1992). Some methodological problems result in differences between groups that should not be taken as indicators of cultural or national differences without closer examination. In this chapter, we argue that many of these problems are inherent in cross-national research and are better conceived of in terms of challenges. We also examine methodological issues in the cross-national project in great detail in order to illustrate some of these challenges.

One of the typical problems in cross-national research is that it is hard to determine if a measure that works well in one cultural setting will be valid in another. This is partly due to translation problems, but it is also a consequence of different representational systems in different countries. Concepts from one culture might have another meaning, be rather uncommon, or even meaningless in another culture (Lonner, 1990). Thus, measurement equivalence is a concern and issues of cross-cultural measurement receive a good deal of attention.

Less attention is paid to the issue of sampling procedures, potential sampling differences, and/or biases. Given, for example, that different countries have different educational systems, trying to control sampling differences by including the same types of schools in different countries may, in fact, lead to problems as to how representative the samples are for the student populations in different countries. That is, sample similarities across countries may be obtained at the expense of representativeness within each country. On the other hand, representative samples in each country could produce heterogeneity between the samples as to school contexts.

The two issues raised here are, actually, tightly connected to one another. For example, the appropriateness of an instrument and the meaning of certain concepts may depend more on characteristics of the sample than on characteristics of a society or culture. Factors such as the educational climate or curriculum in certain types of schools, the family background, or socioeconomic status of participants, may vary within a country as well as between countries. Given that a particular background variable is likely to vary in each of the countries involved, selecting samples on different levels of this variable in different countries would necessarily lead to a confounding of sample particularities with culture.

In this chapter, we introduce the Euronet samples and the general procedures in detail; we also discuss some of the challenges that seem to be inherent in cross-national research. The samples are presented and compared in terms of: typical background variables, such as age, gender, and family settings, and additional information received from the researchers who participated in the study.

GENERAL PROCEDURE

From the beginning, the Euronet study was designed as a cross-national study. Well aware of the many pitfalls of such studies, the researchers attempted to bring under control some of the factors that usually interfere with cultural explanations. The general procedure in organizing the study was of great importance in order to ensure as much standardization as possible without becoming coercive. Actually, too much rigidity could have been detrimental and might have produced artificial differences between the countries.

The topics of interest were decided on at an initial meeting of the participants in the research project. The researchers agreed that coordination would be ensured by a team of researchers at the University of Berne, Switzerland. The procedures for data collection, data coding, punching, processing, and analysis were developed by the coordinating team. Furthermore, two meetings were organized after the data collection, providing all researchers with an opportunity to discuss problems that occurred as well as strategies of data analysis. In order to obtain a detailed description of all samples, especially with respect to their representativeness, about 3 months after the data was collected, the researchers were interviewed and asked to give detailed, written information on issues such as the school system in their country, the accessibility of the subjects, the familiarity of the subjects with surveys, or problems that occurred with the instruments or some specific concepts.

The answers to these questions serve as rough approximations of differences in the life settings of the adolescents in the various countries. Although they cannot be used as reliable independent variables in the analyses, they help with the interpretation of the results of the study. In addition, they provide some guidelines for future cross-cultural and national studies of the same type.

The methodological conditions agreed to by the Euronet project were as follows:

1. The translation of the instruments were checked using back translations.
2. In each country, the researchers selected at least 200 subjects.[1]
3. The samples included about 50% girls and 50% boys.
4. The samples included about equal parts of younger (around 14 years of age) and older (around 16 years of age) adolescents.
5. Subjects were recruited in public schools and the samples were representative of adolescents in schools in the respective countries (no further specification was given as to types of schools or tracks).

However, sampling was not always that consistent across countries. For example, although all students were to be selected from public schools, there was easy access to a private school in Russia that seemed to be comparable to public schools. Therefore, the Russian data were collected in this school.

The timing of data collection is another example. The surveys were administered on a day after a normal full day of school. This procedure was crucial in order to ensure comparability on questions of students' time use because a yesterday questionnaire was used. However, according to the data on time spent in school on the day before the survey was conducted (see chap. 3), it appears that this procedure was not always followed. In fact, in some countries, conditions set by the schools forced the researchers to compromise, accepting classes on a day not following a full school day. These subjects were excluded from the time-use analyses.

Such problems do not necessarily influence the results in any significant way and can possibly be ignored. However, we think that they are typical of cross-national research and should therefore be reported. In fact, the cultural differences of interest in cross-national studies are also characteristics of the researchers who engage in the project and who are themselves bearers of cultural traditions. This necessarily produces differences in the research

---

[1]The reason for the rather small sample size required was that no special research funds were available at this time. The research started on the sheer enthusiasm of colleagues from East and West, shortly after the fall of the iron curtain (see chap. 1).

procedures and has to be addressed in the research process. In line with this argument, we think that differences in procedures and sample composition, for example, can themselves be considered findings, indicating possible cultural differences.

COUNTRIES AND PARTICIPANTS: THE ISSUE OF SAMPLING

The study is comprised of 13 samples representing either different countries (political units) or language groups within one country (French and German speaking adolescents in Switzerland; see also chap. 9). The origin of the samples is indicated in Table 2.1. The data were collected during the spring of 1992 (the Norwegian data were collected in May, 1993). The whole data set includes 3,250 subjects. The Eastern (defined here as Central and Eastern European) and Western countries contributed about one half of the subjects each (51% from Eastern countries and 49% from Western countries).

An additional sample was added (May, 1993) that included adolescents from a Hungarian minority living in Romania (Transylvania). Because of its uniqueness, this last sample was not treated as a Euronet sample in most analyses presented in this volume. Data from the Transylvanian sample is used in chapter 9 to examine the minority issue specifically.

TABLE 2.1
Sample Description (n) According to Country of Origin, Age, and Gender

Country	Girls: n (%)	Boys: n	Up to 14 yrs: n	Over 14 yrs: n (%)	Missing Age or Gender	Total
Bulgaria	127 (54.0)	108	135	100 (42.6)	1	236
CSFR[1]	106 (42.7)	142	91	157 (63.3)	0	248
Finland	100 (48.3)	107	58	149 (72.0)	1	208
France	106 (58.9)	74	66	114 (63.3)	0	180
Germany	164 (61.7)	102	125	141 (53.0)	1	267
Hungary	238 (41.6)	334	259	313 (54.7)	0	572
Norway	150 (49.2)	152	147	155 (51.3)	3	305
Poland	110 (54.7)	91	91	110 (54.7)	0	201
Romania	119 (55.6)	95	111	103 (48.1)	1	215
Russia	98 (51.9)	91	58	131 (69.3)	2	191
G-Switzerland[2]	128 (54.9)	105	112	121 (51.9)	1	234
F-Switerland[3]	114 (61.0)	73	94	93 (49.7)	0	187
USA	118 (58.1)	85	71	132 (65.0)	3	206
Total	678 (51.8)	1,559	1,418	1,819 (56.2)	13	3,250

[1]CSFR=Czechoslovakian Federal Republic.
[2]G-Switzerland=German-speaking Swiss sample.
[3]F-Switzerland=French-speaking Swiss sample.

Note that the CSFR sample was comprised only of Czech adolescents. However, because they were still citizens of the CSFR at the time of the study, we chose to use the CSFR abbreviation throughout the volume. Also, even if the correct designation of the two Swiss samples would have been "French-speaking Swiss adolescents" and "German-speaking Swiss adolescents," as a matter of convenience, the terms French-Swiss and German-Swiss are more often used in the text and in tables and figures.

Size of Samples, Age, and Gender

As is seen in Table 2.1, most samples were of approximately the same size—*n* around 200. However, some samples departed from the norm and the sample sizes varied from a low of 180 to a high of 572. Such differences are important if one wishes to pool the data over countries in some analyses. This should not be done unless one has tested whether the larger samples would bias the results in one way or another. Furthermore, whereas Eastern and Western countries contributed about one half of the students each (1,663 students, or 51%, from Eastern countries and 1,587 students, or 49%, from Western countries), it should be noted that Hungary contributed 34.4% of the subjects in the Eastern sample. When we take into consideration that Hungary actually belongs to the Central European tradition, as CSFR also does, data from the Eastern part of the study should not be pooled together without considering this bias. Furthermore, effect sizes (not only significance level) should be taken into consideration when differences are found between some samples and not between others, given that the larger samples are involved.

In addition, whereas the distribution of gender is acceptable on the level of the entire sample (51.8% girls and 48.2% boys, computed on the basis of valid answers only), this becomes more complicated when analyzing age. Given that students repeat some classes in some countries and not in others, and given that children may start 1 year earlier or later than what is the norm in their country, the samples included subjects aged 13 to 17 (0.7% were younger than 13 and 3.6% were older than 17). The 15-year-olds were as frequent (22%) as the 14- and 16-year-olds (26% and 25%, respectively). We decided to set the cutpoint for the two age groups of adolescents at 14 years. That is, the older group of adolescents is composed of subjects older than 14 and is slightly overrepresented (43.8% up to and including 14 years of age and 56.2% over 14 years). A closer look at Table 2.1 also shows that gender, as well as age is not equally distributed in all samples. This again may be of great importance when the results from the different countries are compared if age and sex are correlated with the dependent variables.

Cross-tabulations were conducted for each sample ($2_{gender} \times 2_{age}$ groups) and Chi-squares were computed in order to examine possible additional problems of distribution. Significant values were obtained in four samples: Germany ($X^2=4.01$, $p<.05$; younger boys were underrepresented), Hungary ($X^2=9.66$, $p<.01$; older boys were overrepresented), Romania ($c^2=6.52$, $p=.01$; younger girls were overrepresented), and French-Switzerland ($X^2=6.19$, $p<.05$; older girls were overrepresented and older boys were underrepresented).

These findings make it necessary to control for these two variables when gender or age effects are found with respect to some dimensions. For example, it is well-established in Western studies that girls score lower than boys on self-esteem instruments (see Alsaker & Olweus, 1993). Therefore, gender should always be used as a covariate in cross-national analyses if the outcomes of interest are, in some way, related to self-esteem. Similar recommendations apply for variables that may be sensitive to age effects (e.g., future orientations; see chap. 5).

To illustrate this point, comparison between countries of self-esteem scores were conducted, first for girls and boys pooled together, followed next by separate analyses for each gender group. The results showed that French adolescents were significantly lower on self-esteem than were American, German, Norwegian, and German-Swiss adolescents. However, this was only true for the French girls; French boys did not significantly differ from other adolescents in terms of self-esteem scores. However, it should also be noted that the North American and German samples included more girls than boys and were among those with the highest self-esteem scores. In addition, the two samples including more boys than girls (Hungary and CSFR) were among the low self-esteem samples. Therefore, it does not seem that the gender bias affected the results in any dramatic way. Nonetheless, all results were carefully examined for artifacts due to sample biases in age and gender.

In all countries, the researchers sampled their subjects according to the expected age of students in different grades. Because there are differences between countries as to the modal ages of students at given grade levels, there was some variation among the samples as to the grade level from which the students were recruited. Younger students came from the 7th through 9th grades, and older students from the 9th through 11th grades in the different countries (see Table 2.3 later). That is, our standardization as to chronological age worked well, but it produced heterogeneity in terms of social age (grade level).

Procedure of Data Collection

In all countries, data were collected in the adolescents' ordinary classrooms and questionnaires were used. The study was presented as a cross-national project on adolescence, with the aim of getting information about adolescents' daily activities, feelings, and thoughts in different countries.

No instruction was given as to who should administer the questionnaires. In general, data were collected by the researchers themselves or by research assistants. However, there were exceptions to this rule. In some countries, the questionnaires were given to the teachers who administered them to the students (Hungary and France). Also, in one sample (France), some of the students were allowed to fill out the questionnaires at home. Typically, teachers were absent from the classroom during survey administration, but this was not always the case. In Poland, they helped the researcher to administer the questionnaires. Because the questions were not of any intimate character, the presence of the teacher was not expected to influence the answers. However, the activity of the teacher may have introduced some achievement aspect to the situation and possibly jeopardized (in the mind of the students) the credibility of the researchers' statements on confidentiality. But again, in some countries, the presence of the teacher may have seemed normal to the students; thus, his or her absence could have also been a signal that something special was going on. An overview of differences in the procedures used is presented in Table 2.2.

Permission to conduct the study was obtained from the head of the school in all countries. Permission from teachers, parents, and students was only necessary in some countries. Answers from the students were anonymous in all countries, and assurance of confidentiality was given. As is seen in Table 2.2,

TABLE 2.2

Procedures: Sample Description According to Country of Origin, Who Administered the Questionnaire, and Familiarity With Surveys

Country	Role of the Teacher During Data Collection	Who Administered the Questionnaires?	Permission Had to Be Obtained From[1]	Familiarity With Surveys
Bulgaria	Not present	Researcher and colleague	HS	Urban: High Rural: None
CSFR	Not present	Psychology students	HS	None
Finland	Not present	Research assistant	HS	Low
France	Some classes: Active	Psychology student/Teachers Some classes: Home	HS	Used to
Germany	Present, not active	Psychology students	HS, P, and S	Some degree
Hungary	Active	Teachers	HS	Used to
Norway	Not present	Research assistant, two all the time	ECA, HS, T, P, S, and data protection committee.	High
Poland	Present, helped	Researcher	HS, S	Low
Romania	Not present	Researcher	HS, T	Very low
Russia	Not present	Researcher	HS	High
German Switzerland	In general, not present	Research assistant	HS, S	Used to
French Switzerland	In general, not present	Research assistant	HS, S (difficult to obtain)	Used to
USA	Present	Research assistants	ECA, HS, T, P, S, and human subjects review committee.	Used to

[1] From whom the research team needed permission to collect data. ECA=Educational central administration in town or district; HS=Head of school; T=Teachers; P=Parents; S=Students themselves, i.e., the students had to be told clearly that they were free to participate or not.

the U.S. and Norwegian studies had to go through many administrative units before the students were allowed to participate. Because the questionnaires did not pose any ethical problems, these administrative steps did not play any role as to the data finally collected. However, such differences in administrative procedures produce differences when the issues are more personal or considered intimate. Also, the fact that parents had to give their permission in some countries but not in others can produce differences. The need for parental consent may vary depending on the issues studied, but inevitably introduces some selection bias, the most common being the systematic exclusion of lower Socioeconomic status (SES) groups (Klepp, 1995). Given the restrictions applied in some countries, the samples in these countries cannot always be characterized as representative of the general population they are drawn from. In fact, they can only be considered representative of the population of parents who were willing to let their children participate.

Representativeness

Beside gender and age, the students were asked to indicate whether they frequented a high school (i.e., gymnasium or academic type school) or a vocational school. In Czechoslovakia and Hungary, additional types of schools (i.e., technical training) were added to the list. Also, researchers were asked to answer questions focusing on the kinds of schools used in the study, the SES of the students attending these schools, and the percentage of students attending different types of schools. As to SES, all but the Russian sample can be considered as reasonably mixed samples. Also, when ethnicity was mixed in the population, it was also mixed in the sample (U.S. and German samples especially). An overview over the types of schools used is given in Table 2.3.

As noted earlier, researchers were asked to select schools that would provide representative samples of the adolescent population in their country or area. As shown in Table 2.3, the instruction was not always followed. The Russian sample, as noted earlier, can only represent a small fraction of the Russian population. In addition, students attending high school (general theoretical orientation) were often overrepresented when compared to the approximate distribution in the populations. This, however, was not true for all samples. In Finland, students frequenting vocational schools were included in accordance with the distribution in the general population[2]. Thus, this sample, probably highly representative of the population of adolescents in Finland, differs from others in the study because it includes a higher percentage of students from vocational schools than do the other samples. It should also be noted, that in some countries, adolescents aged 14 to 16 years do not have any choice as to the type of school they attend (e.g., Norway) or

---

[2]In Finland, there are about 10% of adolescents who drop out of the system and do not enter any school the year after comprehensive school. Those adolescents, however, often enter some vocational school later on. Therefore, the distribution of adolescents in the sample is to be considered representative of the population of adolescents that age.

TABLE 2.3
*Sample Characteristics: Country of Origin, Grade in School, Type of School
(Approximate Percentage of Adolescents in These Schools in Parentheses), and
Familiarity of Students With Surveys*

		Younger Students		Older Students	
Country	Grade	Type of School[1] Used in the Study (Estimated Percentage of Students Attending These Schools in the Population)	Grade	Type of School[1] Used in the Study (Estimated Percentage of Students Attending These Schools in the Population)	Percentage of Students in the Present Study
Bulgaria	8	Elementary (100)	11	SH (40)	72
				Technical (40)	28
CSFR	8	Elementary (95)	10	SH (Gymnasium, 25)	75
				Vocational (50)	19
				Special Secondary (25)	6
Finland	8	Junior High (100)	11	SH (48)	43
				Vocational (33)	57
France	8	College / JH (90)	11	SH (60)	100
Germany	8	SH (Gymnasium, 20)	10	SH (Gymnasium, 20)	66
		Realschule[2] (30)		Realschule[2] (30)	34
Hungary	8	Elementary (100)	10	SH (Gymnasium, 18)	38
				Technical (25)	39
				Vocational (43)	20[3]
Norway	7	Junior High (100)	9	Junior High (100)	100
Poland	7	Elementary (100)	9	SH (30)	89
				Vocational HS (40)	11
Romania	8	HS (20)	10	SH (20)	80
				Industrial HS (20)	20
Russia	9	SH, special sample[4]	11	SH, special sample[4]	100
German Switzerland	7–8	Elementary (30)	9–10	Elementary track (30)	30
		JH (70)		Secondary track (50)	40
				Gymnasium/SH (20)	30
French Switzerland	7–8	JH (100)	9–10	SH (90)	85
				Vocational School (10)	15
USA	8	JH (100) or Middle HS	10	SH (x)	100

Note. X=missing information.
[1]Elementary=All elementary, primary schools; JH=Junior high school; HS=High school; SH=Senior high school, gymnasium, i.e., general theoretical curriculum.
[2]Realschule is the middle track in an institutionalized tracking system providing three major tracks.
[3]In Hungary, 3% of the older adolescents still went to elementary school.
[4]The sample consisted of students from families of artists, scientists, and intellectuals. It was not possible to find out what percentage of the adolescent population attends these schools.

they have a choice between different types of high school only (e.g., German Switzerland). In other words, achieving the goal of obtaining representative samples of adolescents in so many different countries may inevitably result in other systematic differences between the samples. Therefore, in planning such a broad study, one should definitely decide on what is most important—to have samples that are representative of a certain age category in all respective countries or comparable samples in terms of specific educational tracks. If the level of schooling were to be chosen as a selection criterion, one should be aware of the fact that this might introduce a biased gender distribution in some countries when certain tracks or types of schools are included.

With respect to this study, we are confident that the samples are at least fairly representative of adolescents enrolled in some type of high school education, and this population, for the most part, is equivalent to the general population of adolescents in the 14- to 16-year-old's age range.

Background Variables

The students were asked questions about the type of area they lived in (urban, suburban, or rural) and who lived with them (same apartment). The persons listed were their mothers (or stepmothers), fathers (or stepfathers), siblings, grandparents, and other relatives.

Except for two countries, the adolescents came from urban and suburban areas. In most samples, the percentage of adolescents living in a rural area varied between 4% (United States) and 23% (Germany). The two exceptions were the French (57%) and the French-Swiss samples (42%), which included more adolescents from rural areas.

The samples varied in terms of one-parent versus two-parent families, from a low of 75% of the adolescents living with two parents (U.S. sample) to a high of 93% (Poland). The U.S. sample had significantly fewer two-parent families than did the Polish sample as well as the Bulgarian sample (91%; the results are based on an overall one-way analysis of variance, followed by a Scheffé's test of pairwise differences). The data were also analyzed for differences in living with one's mother (or stepmother) or one's father (or stepfather). There were no significant differences between the samples when it came to mothers (92% was the lowest rate, French Switzerland, and 99% the highest, German Switzerland and Russia). As for fathers, the differences paralleled the one-parent—two-parent comparison (77% was the lowest rate, United States, 92% and 94% the two highest rates, Bulgaria and Poland). These results and the following results on other family members are presented in Fig.2.1.

Another interesting difference was found between the Romanian and Russian samples in contrast to all other samples. The adolescents from these two samples had significantly fewer siblings. Thirty-nine percent of the Romanian subjects and 46% of the Moscow adolescents said they had siblings. In all other samples, the percentages varied from a low of 72% (Bulgaria) to a high of 85% (CSFR).

As for grandparents, the pattern was very clear. The Russian (31%), Bulgarian, and Polish adolescents (both 21%) reported significantly more often than did most other adolescents that their grandparents lived with them. This family setting was also relatively usual in Romania (16%). The difference between Romania and the three Eastern countries mentioned earlier was not significant. Finland was at the other end of the distribution with .01%. Interestingly, other

Family Settings

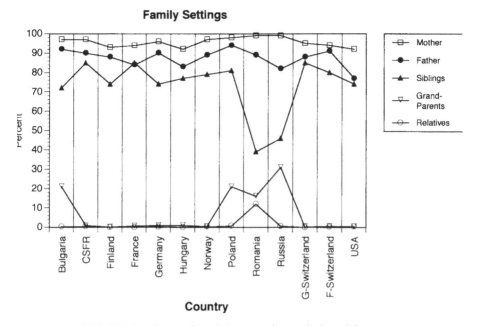

FIG. 2.1. Family members living together with the adolescents
in the different countries.

relatives were mentioned only in Romania (12%). In the other countries, they
were never mentioned by more than .07% of the adolescents.

We can speculate that the lower percentage of Russian adolescents who
live with siblings might be due to the special population from which they were
drawn (higher educational level), whereas it is rather unexpected in Romania,
because the explicit policy of the government had been to augment birthrates.
These differences create a clear picture of the living settings of adolescents
and of different traditions in these countries. The clear gap between the four
Eastern countries (not Central European) and all other countries is of particular
interest in this context. In terms of their daily life, the presence of grandparents
and other relatives restrict the space allocated to each person in the family
and consequently, the adolescents' possibilities to have a private space. On the
other hand, living near the older generation may increase the responsibility one
feels for taking care of older parents at a certain stage in life. This is reflected in
the adolescents' expectations about their future (see chap. 5).

OTHER FACTORS THAT MAY PRODUCE
DIFFERENCES BETWEEN THE SAMPLES

Instruments and Issues

Especially in surveys with children or adolescents, the wording of questions
and the choice of topics are crucial. Actually, the often-used back translation

technique cannot guarantee equivalent meaning of the instruments. In order to be relevant to subjects, questions have to be worded in ways that are directly understandable to them (i.e., according to the cultural or subcultural unit they belong to). This, in turn, often implies a wording that departs from the original formulation. Therefore, in order to be useful, back translations should take such cultural differences into account. As an illustration, we mention surveys on adolescents' nutritional habits; what is considered a healthy habit in one country may in fact not be relevant in another country just because of totally different eating traditions. For example, Norwegian students only eat sandwiches in their regular classroom during the school day, whereas Swiss or French students are accustomed to a warm meal and often go home around noon. Therefore, a question about meals can only be formulated either in general terms (see chap. 4) or in minute detail, respecting all possible cultural habits.

Most instruments used had already been utilized in national projects. These were instruments tapping daily hassles, future orientation, the way adolescents react to stressful events, their control beliefs, and their general subjective psychological well-being. In addition, a method for assessing the adolescents' daily activities was designed for the study, in order to get information about the concrete differences in adolescents' daily lives in the different countries.

A subgroup of researchers representing different countries jointly decided on the topics to study and instruments to use. This step was intended to ensure that the issues to be examined were of relevance to the participants in the respective countries. This was typically true. However, the researchers from France, Romania, and Russia reported that the adolescents had difficulties in answering some questions on control beliefs about school. In those settings, having an influence on topics to be taught was not part of student's representation of what one can control. The Czechoslovakian, Finnish, German, Hungarian, and Polish researchers also reported some problems with the control beliefs questions. These latter difficulties seemed to be related to the format of the instrument, but were not apparent in the other samples. Also, some researchers (American, Hungarian, Norwegian, and Romanian) reported difficulties with the format of the time-use instrument. Another interesting issue is that some students in Bulgaria reported difficulties in using the response formats as they were formulated: "very true," "somewhat true," "somewhat false," and "totally false." For these students, "true" could only be "true" and not "somewhat" or "very" true. Thus, not only the wording of the questions is important, but also the choice and wording of the categories for responding.

Beside the control beliefs about school, these different types of difficulties encountered by students did not show any clear between-country pattern. Therefore, it would have been difficult to prevent them on a general basis. However, they can serve as an illustration of the issue previously addressed, that is, a good translation alone does not suffice. Concepts may be more or less relevant and equivalent words may have slightly different meanings even within European cultures. Such difficulties typically resulted in missing data rather than in specific patterns of results.

Familiarity With the Procedure

The procedure (and the setting) used to collect the data may in itself be familiar or unfamiliar to the subjects. Whereas many Western European students living in larger cities with a university are likely to have participated in surveys earlier and to be familiar with answering questionnaires, this may not be the case everywhere. Checking small boxes to express one's meaning may be rather alienating to children who have never done it before.

As shown in Table 2.2 (Column 5), the students' familiarity with surveys varied to a great extent from sample to sample. Also, one sample (Bulgaria) was composed of some adolescents who were not used to surveys at all and some who were highly familiar with this kind of research.

The School Context

Because school classrooms were the setting for sample recruitment and the data were collected in this environment, we felt it was necessary to understand the role played by the school and the relationship between teachers and students in the different countries. The role of the school, the teacher, and the relationship between students and teachers may actually be good markers of cultural differences. We therefore asked all researchers to give us a general idea of the school climate, the status of school in the general population in their country, and so on.

As is seen in Table 2.4, according to the researchers, there are differences among countries regarding the role of teachers. Whereas most researchers answered that the primary role of the teacher is to communicate knowledge (teacher as instructor), in Norway, Switzerland, and the United States, the teacher also plays an important role as a counselor or is at least expected to help the students and to listen to their personal problems. Also, whereas the relationship between teachers and students is characterized as "relaxed" in Norway, it is described as "distant" in CSFR, and the teacher is clearly not expected to be a friend in Bulgaria, where he or she is no more than an educational authority.

On the basis of these data, Bulgaria, CSFR, France, and Romania can be grouped together as countries, where the school atmosphere is characterized by instrumentality and authority. French Switzerland, to a certain extent, can also be included in this tradition. Norway, the United States, and German-Switzerland would be labeled as countries with a school system focusing more on emotional and social variables as well as using a cooperative, democratic educational style. The remaining countries are less extreme and can be placed somewhere in between.

Interestingly, parents seem to have very little influence on what is going on in school, except for Finland and possibly Switzerland. This in itself may

TABLE 2.4
*Status of the School, Teacher-Student Relationships,
and Teacher-Parent Relationships According to Researchers*

Country	Status of School in the General Population	Teacher–Student Relationship/Primary Role of Teachers (RT)	Teacher–Parent Contact/ Parents' Influence
Bulgaria	Very important	Teachers are authorities, not friends. School is not a friendly place. RT = Teaching	Parent committees do exist, but they have no real influence
CSFR	Respected, important	Distant relationship	Monthly meetings
Finland	High	Teacher-oriented, nonauthoritarian to permissive climate	Parent councils and cooperation with teachers
France	Very important	Authoritarian, RT = Teaching	Active parental organizations exist, but one-way communication: Teachers inform parents
Germany	Very important but ambivalent attitudes	Democratic, neutral atmosphere	Information meetings, low parent participation. Parents have the last word in the choice of school track.
Hungary	Basic value	Friendly atmosphere RT = Teaching	Information meetings, once or twice a year, but parents have no important role
Norway	Ambivalent attitudes	Friendly, relaxed climate RT = Instructor and Counselor, Socialization	Meetings twice a year, individual meetings once a year, but parents have no important role
Poland	Very important	Collaborative climate RT=Teaching	x
Romania	x	Neutral climate RT = Transmission of knowledge	No regular meetings
Russia	Important	Varies with teacher	Meetings twice a year, parents do not have any influence
German-Switzer-land	Very important	Friendly atmosphere RT = Instructor & Counselor	Regular meetings, parents have more and more influence
French-Switzer-land	Very important	Traditional / authoritarian to some extent RT = Instructor and counselor	Less influence than in German-Switzerland
USA	Relatively low	Friendly atmosphere, social place RT = Instructor and Counselor	No formal regular contact at high school level

Note, x=missing information.

not be of crucial importance to all variables. However, when it comes to adolescents' beliefs about their possibility to influence their school life, such differences are important in order to understand differences on the country level. Noting that parents have some influence conveys a sense of indirect control at least. Living in an authoritarian school system, where not even parents have any influence, represents a situation of extremely low control.

CONCLUSION

One may pose the question whether the finding that some samples did not correspond exactly to the prescriptions given by the coordination team is worth discussing. Actually, in a typical national study including a few samples, unequal distribution of gender or age, for example, would be treated as a flaw of the study and may also be an indication of a laissez-faire attitude on the part of the researcher. However, in the case of large cross-national studies, we proposed that this is part of the researchers' reality and that it might be an indicator of genuine differences among the countries included.

For example, there may be differences in gender distribution in different schools in different countries. Therefore, if some specific types of schools are to be included where the gender distribution is skewed, the sample will necessarily be skewed toward an overrepresentation of one gender or the other. In other words, sample differences and unequal distributions are an inherent element of cross-cultural research. They should be taken seriously, but it should not be a reason to dismiss a study. Sample differences may reflect errors, but they should not merely be conceived of as such. On the contrary, they may carry interesting information as to the cultural context for development that should not be thrown away.

In this study, girls were overrepresented to a certain extent in France, Germany, the French-speaking part of Switzerland, and the United States. If we look at Table 2.3, we find that there are no evident reasons to expect the higher representation of girls in these samples, except possibly their willingness to participate. Nonetheless, one may wonder if there are more dropouts among boys in high schools and if there would be more boys in vocational schools in these countries. Actually, we found that especially older girls were overrepresented in French Switzerland, whereas older boys were clearly underrepresented; only 15% of the older sample came from vocational schools (corresponding to the distribution in the population). In France and in Germany, the types of schools used in the study (all general theoretical high schools) only represent one half of the adolescent population. There may actually be an unequal distribution of gender across different types of schools, which is reflected in this sample. In conclusion, the unequal representation of gender may be due to sampling fluctuations, reflect a general, real skewed distribution in the school population of the countries included, and be confounded with the types of schools involved.

When it comes to age groups, the same questions may be raised. The two rough age groups were chosen on expectations of age distribution in different grades in the different countries. In a country like Norway, where all students start school at the same age, and follow the normal progression for 9 years (almost without any exception), it is no wonder that the two age groups are very homogeneous. This, however, cannot necessarily be true in countries with highly differentiated school systems. In most other countries, one must expect a much larger age variation at each grade level.

How Should One Choose Samples?

Sample differences may be inherent in cross-national research, but it does not mean that we should stop trying to standardize the sampling procedure. Therefore, the first question one should ask is about the aim of the comparative study. What is going to be compared? Is it likely to be affected by cultural traditions? In this case, samples should be chosen to represent the different cultural traditions one wants to compare and must be allowed to differ on some other variables. Let us take an example: Assume that one wants to compare the effect of living in settings, in which gender roles are more or less conservative or in which women's rights are more or less taken seriously, on the development of girls at puberty. As a first step, we may find countries in which equality of genders is highly developed and other more traditional countries. However, we have to take into account that these attitudes and practices may be changing even in the traditional countries. Accordingly, there may be great variations between subgroups (e.g., social class or level of education). The most progressive subgroups in traditional countries may indeed have much more progressive attitudes than the majority of people living in a less traditional country. This, in turn, means that we have to be careful in the selection of the samples and may even have to choose different social or educational subgroups in different countries. In such a case, we do not compare countries per se, we compare attitudinal settings that are best represented through subgroups in different countries. The attitudinal background varies between countries and is confounded with the country background. The countries are primarily bearers of different attitudes.

On the other hand, if one wants to compare the living conditions of a given age group in different countries more generally, as we did in the Euronet study, the most appropriate sampling method is the one of representative samples of adolescents at a certain age. All variables that vary between the countries are of interest and serve to describe the settings and cultural backgrounds in which adolescents live. They may also serve as explanations as to differences in dependent variables (e.g., psychological states, attitudes, etc.) and in relations between variables.

However, we may also restrict the comparison concerning only particular subgroups in order to avoid systematic differences between samples. For example, we could have chosen high school students from the beginning. The school type would have been constant and we would have compared high school adolescents in different cultural settings. The danger of such a procedure is that existing differences between countries may be minimized. This is actually one of the questions we have to ask regarding our samples because high school students were generally overrepresented. On the other hand, the overrepresentation of high school students perfectly corresponds to the population in some countries but not in others. Therefore, one may also look for maximized differences that typically depend more on differences between adolescents on various school tracks than on differences due to some specific cultural background.

In conclusion, it is clear that the sampling procedure, like all methodological steps in a research project, depends on the issues of interest, and clear criteria should be worked out on this basis. However, to be sure that samples fit with the criteria we set up, a very high degree of coordination seemed to be necessary. Researchers in different contexts are accustomed to different procedures and misunderstanding may easily arise. Concretely, this means that a group of researchers should collectively assure the coordination of the different projects and actively take part in the sample selection in all countries involved, discussing the pros and cons of different solutions regarding the issues to be studied.

Meaning of Representativeness

Until now, the issue of representativeness seems to be a relatively easy one. We have discussed it only in relation to the school system. However, one may ask what is a representative North American sample, what is a representative European sample, or what is a typical 14-year-old German boy. As discussed earlier, there may be great variations between subgroups within one country. Therefore, when the sample comes from a certain living area, one may ask whether this area is representative of most other areas in the country. Choosing adolescents from rural areas in the North of Finland or of Norway would definitely not produce a representative sample for these countries. On the other hand, the urban samples in the southern part of these countries might represent far more adolescents but clearly not all.

Therefore, representativeness has to be qualified. Even if we speak of the U.S. sample, the Russian sample, and so forth, we have to keep in mind that these samples are representative of certain adolescent populations in their countries of origin. This implies that one should be careful in generalizing differences between samples to differences between countries. However, when findings are replicated in several samples that are connected to one another in some way (e.g., the two Swiss samples, the two Scandinavian samples, or the Central European samples), they may be seen, with more confidence, as indications of possible cultural effects and interpreted in this way.

What Is Culture? What Is Sample?

In this study, we found differences in the researchers' reports on the role of school and the educational climate in their countries. These differences are not linked to the samples. They represent differences at the level of society. Nevertheless, we all know that schools vary and that the educational and social climate of schools vary with headmasters, teachers, and the population of students frequenting the schools (i.e., low versus high SES, high-risk area, etc.). Therefore, we can expect the samples to reflect the educational system of the country, but we must be aware of possible sample pecularities.

What is true for the educational system is also true for other variables collected on an aggregate level. Therefore, ideally, when a variable is to be used as an independent cultural variable, it should be measured along with the other variables, to make sure that the sample is representative of the cultunit to be studied.

The use of the same instruments in a wide range of samples at the same time makes it possible to compare the results much more directly than has often been the case in cross-cultural comparisons. Thereby, it strengthens the reliability of conclusions as to what may be called *universal* and as to the influence of cultunits. However, as shown throughout this chapter, sampling problems occur and are partly inherent in cross-cultural research. Therefore, in order to ensure a test of cultural effects, comprehensive efforts should be made to enhance the comparability of the samples involved and the measurement of the cultural background variables. Otherwise, confounding sampling errors with cultural differences or uncertainty regarding what can be considered an independent cultural variable would most probably attenuate any conclusions about cultural effects.

REFERENCES

Alsaker, F.D., & Olweus, D. (1993). Global self-evaluations and perceived instability of self in early adolescence: A cohort longitudinal study. *Scandinavian Journal of Psychology, 34*, 47–63.

Berry, J.W., Poortinga, Y.H., Segall, M.H., & Dasen, P.R. (1992). *Cross-cultural psychology: Research and applications*. New York: Cambridge University Press.

Klepp, K.I. (1995). Nonresponse bias due to consent procedures in school-based, health-related research. *Scandinavian Journal of Social Medicine, 23*, 53–59.

Lonner, W.J. (1990). An overview of cross-cultural testing and assessment. In R.W.Brislin (Ed.), *Applied cross-cultural psychology* (pp.56–76). Newbury Park, CA: Sage.

3

Time Use by Adolescents in an International Perspective. I: The Case of Leisure Activities

August Flammer
University of Berne, Switzerland

Françoise D.Alsaker
University of Bergen, Norway
University of Berne, Switzerland

Peter Noack
University of Jena

If the life conditions of adolescents in different countries and different cultures are to be understood, it is important to study what adolescents actually do in everyday life, how much time they spend on what types of activities, and at what time during the day they typically perform them. In addition, getting information about the way people organize their everyday life provides essential information about individual and societal priorities and values (Alsaker & Flammer, in press). This does not mean that reported activities only reflect deliberate choices. Some are deliberate choices, but some are dictated by society (e.g., how much time children and adolescents spend in school). Furthermore, society's influence on adolescents' time use may also be indirect through the allocation of certain duties to certain roles, especially to gender roles.

If we ask adolescents about the importance of certain values (as is the case in chap. 5, this volume), we get information that largely represents the agreed-on norms in the society people live in, but this may not necessarily tell us what impact these perceived values have on the adolescents' lives. For example, most people in industrialized societies affirm that school is important or that artistic education is important. However, the actual place occupied by school or by musical education in the everyday life of different societies varies to a large extent, which, in turn, affects the (remaining) importance attributed to certain other activities. That is, cross-national research on time use can provide valuable information on actual values.

We are not the first to study everyday activities. Sociologists, marketing researchers, broadcasting companies, and government officials started early in this century collecting data on the duration, frequency, and time of beginning and ending different classes of activities (for an early large-scale study, see Szalai, 1972). Many of these studies concentrated on specific activities such as leisure or work (e.g., DeGrazia, 1962; Katz & Gurevitch, 1976). With regard to adolescence, early descriptions of daily time use were undertaken by Barker and Wright (1951), Csikszentmihalyi and Larson (1984), Csikszentmihalyi, Larson, and Prescott (1977).

This chapter and chapter 4 are on adolescents' time use, that is, how they allocate a specific range of activities across a 24-hour school day. In this chapter, we concentrate on leisure-time activities. In chapter 4, we turn to so-called necessary activities. This distinction is, admittedly, somewhat arbitrary. Definitions of *leisure time* often refer to the individuals' degrees of freedom; *leisure* is typically characterized by more degrees of freedom than work, for example. For convenience, we define *leisure time* (or free time) as the time left after all commitments and duties are accomplished. The duties might be formal (e.g., schooling) or informal (e.g., body care). The latter still are optional for some people. On the other hand, leisure-time activities themselves may end up in rather inflexible commitments and tight schedules (e.g., Herzberg, Hössl, & Lipski, 1995).

Many of the earlier studies found clear age differences . For example, according to Timmer, Eccles, and O'Brien (1985), American adolescents aged 12 through 17 years spend more time conversing, watching television, listening to music, and participating in active sports than do children aged 3 through 11 years. Children, however, spend more time eating, sleeping, and playing than do adolescents.

Across Grades 5 through 9, American adolescents increased the proportion of time they spent with peers, at the cost of time spent with family members (Richards & Larson, 1989). Interestingly, those adolescents who spent a decreasing amount of time with their family increased the amount of time spent listening to music. In turn, listening to music was associated with less time spent watching television (Larson, Kubey, & Colletti, 1989). Girls spent more time talking than did boys, and this was evident more in ninth grade than in fifth grade (Raffaeli & Duckett, 1989).

As for gender differences, American boys in Grades 5 through 9 watched more television (Larson et al., 1989) and participated more in active sports than did girls (Timmer et al., 1985). Girls, on the other hand, spent more time listening to music (Larson et al., 1989) and conversing with peers (Raffaeli & Duckett, 1989).

There are also geographic differences in time use. For example, adolescents (aged 15–24 years) in rural areas spent more time performing active sports than did adolescents living in the city, both in Australia (Garton & Pratt, 1987, 1991) and in India (Verma & Saraswathi, 1992). Within Western Australia, Asian immigrants were less engaged in active sports as well as in social/leisure activities (Garton & Pratt, 1991).

Leisure time, previously defined as what is left when duties are done, might imply that leisure-time activities are less valued than nonleisure-time activities. In societies in which adolescents do not have clear roles or duties, other than being a student, and in which leisure time has generally become increasingly important for most citizens, this connotation has to be revised. Typically, and also in this chapter, leisure activities include playing and listening to music, reading, sports, watching television or listening to the radio, hanging around with friends, dating, and working for money. A closer look at each of these activities leads to the conclusion that they can be considered as important for the personality and social development of adolescents. Also, a study on self-definition through activities (Ryser, 1997) clearly showed that adolescents and young adults (16–28 years old) primarily mentioned leisure activities as activities that they considered central to their self-definition.

Actually, time-use studies on leisure activities also provide valuable information on the daily life of adolescents with particular problems. For example, it is wellknown that depression is associated with impaired interpersonal relationships (Harrington, 1993) and with passivity. However, we are not told how this influences depressed adolescents' daily lives. Also, we may ask whether depressed adolescents structure their days in ways that make it more difficult to get a positive perspective on the world. Results from a comparative Swiss-Norwegian study on adolescence showed that depressed adolescents spent much more time alone and seemed to avoid social situations involving many peers. Among other things, they reported spending more time on day-dreaming, watching television on Sundays, and just hanging around. When they engaged in sports, they preferred to do it alone. These results from their time-use reports fit well with the fact that they reported good friendship quality, but they felt alienated in peer groups (Alsaker & Flammer, 1996).

In sum, we expect the results on leisure activities to provide valuable information on differences and similarities among the 13 samples (exploratory approach described in chap. 1, this volume) and also on the universality or specificity of clusters of activities. For example, do adolescents who report doing a lot of sports on a specific day usually do it at the expense of other specific activities in most or only in certain countries (interaction approach)?

Although this chapter focuses on leisure activities, necessary activities are considered in correlational analyses because the time allocated to leisure time, in general, necessarily depends on the time occupied by activities that are required. Furthermore, reports on activities are correlated with indexes of well-being and of experienced strain in terms of daily hassles.

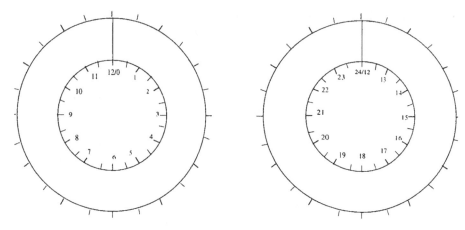

FIG. 3.1. Clock-faces, as used to indicate yesterday's activities.

METHOD

The selection of participants is described in detail by Alsaker, Flanagan, and Csapó (chap. 2, this volume). For these analyses, participants were excluded if their data met one of the following criteria: (a) sum of time per day was indicated as less than 24 hours, (b) time spent in class was less than 4 hours (a full school day was an a priori requirement for being included in the sample), and (c) sleeping time was less than 4 hours. Following these criteria, 2,315 out of the 3,250 adolescents were included in the following analyses. Sample size within country varied between 112 (United States) and 335 (Hungary) participants. An analysis of the distribution of gender and age by country revealed slight differences in Germany and in Romania (boys' average age was higher than that of girls' in Germany and Romania, respectively; Chi-square=4.80; df=1; $p<.05$, and Chi-square=5.14; $df=1$; $p<.05$). In the French-speaking part of Switzerland, girls were slightly older than boys (Chi-square=9.63; $df=1$; $p<.01$).

The participants were asked to report in detail their activities on the previous day, using two 12-hour clock faces as depicted in Fig. 3.1. They were invited to draw lines at the beginning and at the end of each activity and not to leave any interval blank.

In order to simplify writing on the clock faces, we gave adolescents a list of activities, and assigned letters to those activities, which were used to fill out their clock faces:

A = sleeping
B = dressing/body care
C = mealtime
D = way to and from school

```
E  = staying in school
F  = school homework
G  = playing a musical instrument
H  = reading (not for school)
I  = shopping
J  = active sports & playing games
K  = work for family/household/mother
L  = dating girl-/boyfriend
M  = hanging around with friends
N  = working
O  = watching TV & listening to the radio (& doing nothing else besides)
P  = other (specify...)
Q  = other (specify...)
```

This method invited the participants to consider the entire range of activities in which we were interested in addition to other activities that they were allowed to add. There is no doubt that people often do more than one thing at a time (e.g., listening to the radio and dressing). We asked the participants in such cases to code only the most important activity. We coded all intervals in units of quarters of 1 hour. The data are presented either in decimals (e.g., 1 hour and 30 minutes as 1.50 hours, within tables), or in an hour-minute format (e.g., 1h30, within text).

Reports about the previous day's activities have clear advantages and disadvantages. They are single event samples and therefore not subjective averages of activity durations and timing. Therefore, reports about the previous day's activities therefore allow capturing the actual range and timing of the activities on a particular day. These reports rely on episodic memory over more than 24 hours and are therefore subject both to forgetting and to assimilation because of schematic knowledge about the typical day. However, such shortcomings are still estimated to be less consequential than the subjective averaging of typical individual time and so on. Clearly, because these estimates are not meant to be typical or to represent individual habits, their correlation with personality characteristics are attenuated.

Among the further measures included in the complete questionnaire, two are selected in this chapter. Eight items measured positive attitudes toward life, and five items measured self-esteem. The psychometric properties of these items are documented in Grob, Stetsenko, Sabatier, Botcheva, and Macek (chap. 7, this volume) and are satisfactory. Both scales correlate highly (Grob, Little, Wanner, Wearing, & Euronet, 1996; Grob et al., 1991) and are aggregated in one variable called well-being in the following analyses. Eleven items asked for the amount of strain the participants perceived in relation to 11 different life domains. Again, the psychometric properties of these items are documented in chapter 7 and are satisfactory.

RESULTS

We focus on three sets of results, namely means of time spent on each activity, differentiated according to country, age, and gender; correlations among activities; and correlations between time spent on specific activities and variables of strain and well-being. Because of space limitations, the correlational analyses are not conducted for each country by age by gender cell.

As for the comparisons of means among countries, we proceeded as follows. Given that the activities cannot be regarded as completely independent of one another, especially in terms of duration (see the following discussion on the correlations), we chose to conduct multivariate analyses of variance (MANOVAs) in which the activities (duration) were entered as the dependent variables. An omnibus test including all three factors of interest (i.e., country, gender, and age) was performed, followed by univariate post hoc analyses. We corrected the alpha levels to protect against Type I error, following the Dunn procedure described by Kirk (1982). When post hoc analyses were indicated, comparisons among the different countries were made using Scheffe tests for multiple pairwise comparisons.

The Complexity of the Correlation Coefficients

Because daytime is restricted to 24 hours, correlations between durations of different activities are negatively biased. Using a substantial part of time for one activity necessarily leaves less time for all the other activities. Therefore, the expected value of the correlations is below zero. However, the usual procedure for testing the statistical significance of correlation coefficients tests the null hypothesis—the correlation will be zero. Thus, this procedure underestimates the probability of negative correlations and overestimates the probability of positive correlations.

Are such correlations inadequate? Yes and no. Even if a technical boundary for the correlations exists, these correlations are real in the sense that they reflect the fact that doing one thing more extensively covaries with doing less of another. If one aims at simply testing this covariation, there is no problem using the raw correlation coefficient and the usual statistical testing procedure. Yet, this procedure is inadequate if one wants to take into account the fact that after having used time for one activity, there remains less time for the other activities, independently of how much they are liked. This is especially crucial in cases in which somebody typically spends much time on two specific activities, but might not be able to perform both on the same day.

---

[1]Given that the alpha level was originally set to .05, a design including three factors produces a "family alpha" of .05×(number of possible effects=7)=.35. The corrected alpha level is then calculated as follows: Family alpha/(sum of levels in the variables=13 countries+2 genders+2 age levels= 17). In this example the corrected alpha level is .35/17=.02. When the post hoc analyses involved a significant 2-way interaction including country, the corrected alpha for the simple main effects was .15/15=.01, etc.

There are three ways of resolving this dilemma: (a) One could calculate the expected correlation coefficient for each pair of activities; (b) an easy approximation would be to adjust a levels (e.g., choosing $a=.001$ for negative correlations and $a=.100$ for positive correlations), (c) the way we chose was to correlate the actual value for one variable with the proportion of remaining time for the other variable. Because one can choose which of the two variables to transform to a proportion value, one can also calculate two possible coefficients:

- If activity x is to be regressed on activity y, y can be transformed as follows: $y'=y/(24-x)$. y' thus indicates the proportion of activity y within the time remaining after removing the time for activity x. The correlation is then calculated between x and $(y/(24-x))$.
- If y were to be regressed on activity x, x is transformed as $x'=x/(24-y)$. The correlation is then calculated between y and $(x/(24-y))$.

Note that the correlation between x and y' is not equal to the correlation between y and x'. If clarification is needed in this text, we refer to x (or y) as the *source variable* and to y' (or x') as the *target variable*. We call these correlations, which do not express relations between absolute durations but between the duration of one activity and the other activity's proportion of the remaining time, *proportion of the remaining time correlations* (*PRT correlations* or *PRTCs*). On the interpretation level, they may simply be understood as expressing the correlation with the remaining priorities. However, because these remaining priorities are sometimes imposed (e.g., school), we prefer to use the more general term *proportion of remaining time*.

The following example illustrates the facets that become visible by this method. In the sample of American boys, the correlation between sleeping time and working time was negative ($r=-.52$). This means that those who slept longer spent less time working (and the reverse: those who spent more time working, slept less). This is an interesting result. One of the possible interpretations is that workers simply consume time at the expense of sleep. However, the PRTC working-sleep' was .38. This means that for those who spent more time working, the proportion of sleeping time within the remaining time increased. That is, although it is true that those who worked longer slept less ($r=-.52$), it is also true that they allocated a larger time proportion of the rest of the day for sleep when compared to the other activities. On the other hand, the PRTC sleep-work' was not significantly different from zero, which indicates that those who slept less did not increase the proportion of the remainder of their day for work.

Given this transformation, the mathematically expected value of PRTC under the null hypothesis is zero, and the statistical test is not biased. However, there is an additional problem to be taken into account. Our participants were probably less free to perform certain activities (e.g., attending school) than other activities (e.g., watching television). We may therefore expect PRTCs with target activities like school to be more positive than with targets like television. Therefore, the *asymmetry* between the ab' PRTC and the a'b PRTC allows us to approach more closely the direction of possible cause-effect relations than with noncorrected correlation coefficients (although correlations still remain standardized expressions of mere covariation).

Overall Statistics

Table 3.1 shows the average durations of each leisure activity per country. On the total average, there were 4h25 spent on leisure activities, 18h54 on necessary activities, and 0h41 on activities not included in our classification scheme. A content analysis showed that these other indications were very heterogeneous.

On the whole, the share of what we defined as leisure activities was around 18% of the total day (4h25) which seems reasonable. Yet, it varied enormously among countries. The highest value was found in Norway, the lowest in France. On the sample day, our French adolescents had barely one half the leisure time of their Norwegian peers. Other countries on the high end (more than 5 hours) are Bulgaria, Finland, Germany, and the United States. On the low end (less than 4 hours), are Hungary, Poland, Russia, and the French and German parts of Switzerland.

A large part of all leisure time is used for watching television (39%), especially high in Bulgaria, CSFR, and Romania. The second largest portion is spent hanging around with friends (17%) and engaging in sports activities (16%). Not surprisingly, correlations between each leisure activity in time and the total average leisure time per country was highly positive, except for playing music ($r=.12$; n.s.) and leisure reading ($r=-.04$; n.s.). These activities are unrelated to the overall free time available to adolescents (on average, within their country).

A multivariate analysis on all variables except other activities, with the factors country (13 levels), age (2 levels, that is, ≤14 vs. >14 years of age), and gender (2 levels), yielded a significant three-way country by age by gender interaction ($pwilks < .001$). Of the leisure activities, the following contributed to this interaction ($p ≤ .05$): music, leisure reading, sports, and working for money (a separate analysis including only leisure activities yielded consistent results)[2].

---

[2]Breaking the three-way interaction—for these five variables only—down by countries, multiple age by gender interactions remained for Bulgaria (music, school, and working), CSFR (school), Germany (sports), Hungary (school), Norway (music), Romania (school, and leisure reading), and the United States (music and working). Single main effects of age remained for Germany (school), Norway (working), Poland (school), the German-speaking part of Switzerland (school), and the French-speaking part of Switzerland (school and leisure reading) and single main effects of gender were found for Finland (school and leisure reading), France (school and leisure reading), Hungary (leisure reading), and Poland (working).

TABLE 3.1

Average Accumulated Duration of Each Leisure Activity per Country (in Hours)

Country	Playing Music	Leisure Reading	Doing Sports	Watching Television	Hanging Around With Friends	Dating	Working	Total Leisure Activities	Total Necessary Activities	Others	Grand Total
Bulgaria	0.10	0.55	0.35	2.37	1.23	0.39	0.04	5.03	18.44	0.53	24.00
CSFR	0.10	0.53	0.90	2.20	0.81	0.22	0.06	4.82	19.17	0.01	24.00
Finland	0.19	0.64	0.52	1.83	1.63	0.54	0.13	5.48	17.73	0.79	24.00
France	0.11	0.27	0.38	1.31	0.54	0.12	0.00	2.73	21.12	0.15	24.00
Germany	0.27	0.54	0.87	1.92	0.22	1.23	0.15	5.20	18.02	0.78	24.00
Hungary	0.10	0.51	0.82	1.46	0.64	0.35	0.02	3.90	19.55	0.55	24.00
Norway	0.25	0.44	1.43	1.60	1.47	0.18	0.22	5.59	17.71	0.70	24.00
Poland	0.11	0.44	0.66	1.46	0.77	0.41	0.14	3.99	19.02	0.99	24.00
Romania	0.03	0.86	0.38	2.13	0.40	0.22	0.05	4.07	19.51	0.42	24.00
Russia	0.17	0.83	0.32	1.49	0.70	0.44	0.01	3.96	19.00	1.04	24.00
F-CH	0.25	0.47	0.79	1.66	0.19	0.33	0.03	3.72	19.53	0.75	24.00
G-CH	0.34	0.68	0.62	1.46	0.33	0.33	0.06	3.82	19.14	1.04	24.00
United States	0.09	0.18	1.18	1.78	0.85	0.53	0.66	5.27	17.82	0.91	24.00
Average	0.16	0.53	0.71	1.74	0.75	0.41	0.12	4.42	18.90	0.68	24.00

Note. F-CH=French-speaking Switzerland; G-CH=German-speaking Switzerland.

Among the two-way interactions, two were significant, that is, the country by age interaction (p_{wilks}<.001) and the country by gender interaction (p_{wilks}<.001). Among the dependent variables not included in the three-way interaction, the country by age interaction involved the following leisure activities: watching television, dating, and hanging around with friends. As for the country by gender interaction, it involved—other than the activities included in the three-way interaction—only dating. All three factors also yielded significant multivariate main effects. However, no leisure activity was not already included in the interactions.

We now proceed to the analysis of each leisure activity, guided by the multivariate results just reported. This means that we disregard any univariate effect that was not included in the multivariate effects.

Playing a Musical Instrument

Time spent playing music contributed to the three-way interaction age by gender by country and the main effect of country. Age and gender interacted in three countries. In Bulgaria, the older boys reported playing music longer (average of 0h 18) than the younger Bulgarian boys and both age groups of Bulgarian girls (average between 0h01 and 0h06).[3] The interaction in Norway was due to the younger girls spending significantly longer time (0h32) playing music than the older girls and the younger and older boys (between 0h08 and 0h16). Among the U.S. participants, the younger girls (0h13) and the older boys (0h10) excelled over the younger boys (0h04) and the older girls (0h01).

The interaction occurring in Norway could be explained on the basis of a relatively well developed music educational system during the years in elementary school. This type of course may be more attractive to girls than boys of that age. However, girls' interest may decline when they enter puberty and become interested in other activities (e.g., dating). In Bulgaria and the United States, we have no explanation for the (similar) interaction.

These three interactions did not affect the differences among the countries for the two age groups and the two gender groups. Also, in older boys and in younger girls, no significant pairwise difference was found among the countries. Therefore, we proceeded to post hoc comparisons between countries over all genders and ages. It was mainly in the German-speaking part of Switzerland where the participants played musical instruments significantly longer than in most other countries. The average figures varied enormously, that is, from 0h02 in Romania through 0h20 in the German-speaking part of Switzerland.

Because in all countries, the majority of the participants did not play a musical instrument at all on the sample day, we present, in Fig. 3.2, the percentage of adolescents having actively played a musical instrument the very day before data collection instead of the average time over all participants.

---

[3]We exclusively report statistically significant results; for the sake of readabilty, however, values for F, df, and p are omitted most of the time.

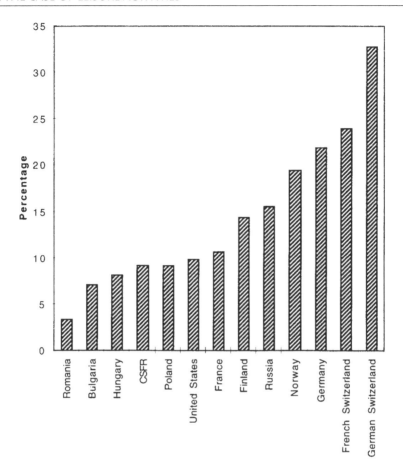

FIG. 3.2. Percentage of adolescents having played a
musical instuments on the sample day.

There were never more than 43% (i.e., older Swiss girls) of adolescents reporting musical activities in any gender by age subgroup; in certain groups the percentage was even zero (younger Romanian boys and older Romanian girls). Generally, the average time spent on a musical instrument per country corresponded well to the percentage of participants being involved in actively playing. However, there was a noticeable exception: In the United States there were rather many adolescents—mainly girls—playing only for short periods.

Playing music typically comes at the expense of other free-time activities. This is what the negative correlations between playing music and time spent watching television ($r=-.13$; $p<.01$; see Table 3.2) or doing active sports ($r=-.08$; $p< .01$) confirm.

TABLE 3.2

Correlations Between Activities: Complete Sample

	Sleeping	Body Care	Eating Meals	Way to and From School	Staying in School	Home-work	Playing Music	Leisure Reading	Sports	Television	Dating	Hanging Around With Friends	Chores	Shopping	Working for Money
Body care	-.15**														
Eating	.04	.02													
Way	-.13**	-.01	-.01												
School	-.08**	-.05*	-.02	.03											
Home	-.09**	.04	.01	.02	-.01										
Music	.00	-.06**	.04*	.07**	-.07**										
Read	-.05*	-.04	-.04	-.01	-.13**	-.10**									
Sports	-.00	.01	-.06**	-.10**	-.11**	-.15**	.05*								
Television	-.04*	-.15**	-.09**	-.06**	-.16**	-.20**	-.08**	-.11**							
Dating	-.16**	.04*	-.13**	-.06**	-.10**	-.15**	-.13**	-.08**	-.07**	-.11**					
Friends	-.16**	-.00	-.17**	-.10**	-.15**	-.20**	-.03	-.07**	-.08**	-.08**	-.05*				
Chores	-.07**	.01	-.12**	.03	-.12**	-.02	-.04*	-.05*	-.11**	-.05*	-.03	-.02			
Shopping	-.06**	.07**	-.04	-.07**	-.12**	-.04*	-.00	-.03	-.07**	-.01	-.01	-.02	.05*		
Working	-.13**	.02	-.05*	-.07**	-.08**	-.08**	.04*	-.04*	-.05*	-.02	.01	-.00	-.04	-.04	
Others	-.10**	-.03	.01	-.06**	-.14**	-.12**	-.01	-.04	-.13**	-.19**	-.07**	-.08**	-.07**	-.05*	-.03

*p≤.05. **p≤.01.

This competitive relation remained even when the correlations were calculated with the proportions of the remaining time (Table 3.3: PRTC music-television'= −.11; $p<.01$; PRTC music-sports'=−.07; $p<.01$, as well as PRTC TV-music'= −.12; $p<.01$ and PRTC sports-music'=−.07; $p<.01$).

There were also competitive relations between playing music and time spent in school and on homework (Table 3.2: r=−.07; $p<.01$, in both cases). However, corrected correlation analysis (Table 3.3) yielded a different picture. PRTC music–school' and PRTC music-homework' were nonsignificant. This means that spending more or less time playing music did not alter the proportion of the remaining times used in relation to school and to school homework. The explication seems easy: School is strictly obligatory and homework is too. Although it may be true that some adolescents neglect homework, spending less time on it than necessary, it is less likely that those who play musical instruments are also those students who would neglect school duties. Our data are at least at variance with such an interpretation.

The relations between time spent on musical instruments and time spent on school and homework demonstrate another finding: When playing music was the target activity, the PRTCs were significantly negative, although low (PRTC school-music'=−.05; $p<.05$; PRTC homework-music'=−.05; $p<.05$). This means that when it came to competition between music and school or between music and homework, music gave way.

Looking at the PRTCs only (Table 3.3) shows that some relations that were nonsignificant at the uncorrected correlation level become positive. This is true when music was the source variable and sleeping, eating meals, and leisure reading were the target activities. This means that after some time was spent on musical activities, these three activities were boosted in their remaining priority. Apparently, the musicians in the sample did not consequently reduce time for sleep, meals, or leisure reading. The reverse PRTCs were not significant except for the significantly positive PRTC reading-music' (=.06; $p<.05$). Apparently, music-oriented adolescents often like reading and vice versa.

It may be expected that playing music mostly makes people feel good. Indeed, across all countries, the correlation between time spent playing music and subjective well-being was (r=.08 ($p<01$). Single-strain items correlated negatively and significantly with playing music. This was true for strain related to school (r=−.07; $p<.01$), available money (r=−.04; $p<.05$), and girlfriend or boyfriend (r=−.05; $p<.05$). Those who played music experienced less strain in these areas. Playing music might have served as consolation in difficult situations.

Leisure Reading

Time spent on leisure reading contributed to the significant three-way interaction in the multivariate test. Separate analyses by country yielded

TABLE 3.3

Proportion of Remaining Time Correlations (PRTCs) Among Activities (Upper Margin: Source Activity; Left Margin: Target Activity; Complete Sample)

	Sleeping	Body Care	Eating	Way	School	Home-work	Music	Leisure Reading	Sports	Tele-vision	Dating	Hanging Around With Friends	Chores	Shopping	Working for Money	Other
Sleeping		-.03	.25**	.08**	.43**	.36**	.18**	.24**	.38**	.43**	.23**	.31**	.15**	.11**	.07**	.32*
Body Care	-.04*		.07**	.04	.06**	.14**	-.03	.01	.09**	-.05*	.14**	.10**	.06**	.12**	.07**	.06**
Eating	.14**	.05*		.04	.11**	.11**	.09*	.02	.02	.01	-.06**	-.09**	-.08**	-.00	-.01	.10*
Way	-.03	.02	.03		.14**	.11**	.03	.05*	-.04	.04	.00	-.02	.08**	-.04	-.05*	.02
School	.23**	.02	.11**	.16**		.26**	.03	.04*	.13**	.13**	.14**	.13**	.01	-.03	.05*	.12**
Homework	.00	.06**	.05*	.05*	.07**		-.05*	-.06**	-.10**	-.14**	-.11**	-.16**	.01	-.02	-.06**	-.07**
Music	.02	-.06**	.05*	.01	-.05*	-.07**		.06**	-.07**	-.12**	-.02	-.03	-.04	.01	.06**	.01
Read	-.01	-.03	.05*	.01	-.09**	-.07**	.06**		-.09**	-.05*	-.05*	-.02	-.01	-.01	-.04	-.01
Sports	.04	.02	-.04*	.09**	-.07**	-.13**	-.07**	-.09**		-.04	-.07**	-.09**	-.05*	-.04	-.02	-.11**
Television	.04*	-.13**	-.06**	.02	.09**	-.15**	-.11**	.04	.01		-.06**	-.02	-.02	.02	.01	-.14**
Dating	-.13**	.05*	-.12**	-.06**	-.08**	-.14**	-.02	-.06**	-.07**	-.08**		-.03	-.02	-.01	.02	-.05*
Friends	-.12**	.01	-.15**	-.09**	-.12**	-.18**	-.04	-.04	-.10**	-.05*	-.02		-.01	-.01	.01	-.06**
House	-.03	.02	-.11**	-.05*	-.08**	.00	-.03	-.01	-.05*	-.02	-.00	-.00		.06**	-.03	-.05*
Shop	-.03	.08**	-.03	-.06**	-.10**	-.02	.00	-.01	-.03	.01	.00	-.00	.06**		-.03	-.04
Working	-.11**	.02	-.05*	-.07**	-.06**	-.07**	.05*	-.04	-.02	-.01	.02	.01	-.04	-.03		-.02
Others	-.07**	.02	.02	-.05*	-.10**	-.10**	.01	-.02	-.11**	-.17**	-.05*	-.06**	-.06**	-.04*	-.02	

*p≤.05. **p≤.01.

one age by gender interaction for Romania, one age effect for French Switzerland, and gender effects for CSFR, Finland, France, and Hungary.

With respect to the age by gender interaction for Romania, the older Romanian girls spent far more time reading (1h36) than did the other Romanian adolescent groups (between 0h30 and 0h55). The younger French-Swiss adolescents spent twice as much time reading than their older peers (0h36 vs. 0h18). The gender effects favored girls: Girls read more than boys in four countries. The overall gender difference (0h37 for girls and 0h28 for boys) replicates Garton and Pratt's (1991) results.

Given these effects, we conducted comparisons between the countries for each gender by age cell. Although these analyses yielded overall significant differences between countries, only the analysis for older adolescent girls showed significant pairwise differences between countries. The Romanian girls read much more than did girls of the same age in most other countries.

When all gender and age subgroups were pooled together, Romania (due to the older girls), Russia, and the German-speaking part of Switzerland on the higher end differed significantly from the United States and France, which were on the lower end. The other countries lay in between. A comparison with the results from Csikszentmihalyi and Larson's (1984) study shows that our American data are markedly lower (0h11 as opposed to 0h32[4]). Yet, the Csikszentmihalyi and Larson results lie in the range of all other countries in our study. In general, our figures might be lowered by the fact that they were all generated on school days, thus excluding the reading that might occur on weekends.

The raw correlations between leisure reading and all other variables (except for music) were negative (Table 3.3), significantly so with school, homework, sports, watching television, hanging around with friends, and dating. It might be that leisure reading was a passion that did not leave enough time for other activities, but it might also be that leisure reading served as a time filler after required activities were done. PRTCs should provide some clarifications for this (Table 3.3). Indeed, leisure reading received a reduced remaining proportion of time for those adolescents who spent above average time in school (PRTC=−.09; $p<.01$), on homework (PRTC=−.07; $p<.05$), and on sports (PRTC=−.09; $p<.01$). Playing a musical instrument, however, did not reduce the remaining proportions of time allocated to reading (PRTC=.06; $p<.05$; see above). On the other hand, doing above average leisure reading (source activity) also reduced the remaining time proportion for homework (PRTC=−.06; $p<.05$), sports (PRTC=−.07; $p<.05$), and dating (PRTC =−.06; $p<.05$), but yielded an increased proportion of time devoted to sleep (PRTC =.24; $p<.01$). If calculated separately for girls and boys, basically the same pattern of PRTCs appeared.

----

[4]Csikszentmihalyi and Larson indicated 3.5% of waking time; 3.5% out of 15.5 hours=0.5425 hours (p. 63).

Unlike playing music, leisure reading was not correlated with well-being, but it was weakly related to strain ($r=-.04$; $p<.05$), specifically to strain related to school ($r=-.12$; $p<.01$) and to available money ($r=-.04$; $p<.05$). As to the first correlation, it could be that those who read more are more intellectual and perceive less strain related to school. The second correlation might indicate that the readers are relatively well off (i.e., come from relatively wealthy families).

Sports

The time spent on active sports varied according to all independent variables and their interactions. Post hoc analyses by country yielded one significant gender by age interaction (in Germany). This interaction was due to a much higher report of involvement in sports activities in younger adolescent boys compared to their female peers. Moreover, the younger German adolescents reported spending significantly more time on sports activities than did the older ones, and German boys spent significantly more time than did girls.

Furthermore, there were age effects in Hungary, Russia, and the French-speaking part of Switzerland and gender effects in France, Hungary, Norway, Poland, Russia, German Switzerland, and the United States. In all these countries, as in Germany, younger adolescents reported spending significantly more time in sports than older adolescents and boys more than girls.

Post hoc tests for differences among countries (comparing each age by gender cell) showed that Norwegian adolescents, with an average of 1h26, reported the most sports activity followed by American adolescents; the Russian adolescents, with an average of 0.32 hours, were at the low end. On the whole, the Norwegian adolescents reported significantly more time spent on sports activities than did most other adolescents (i.e., Russian, Bulgarian, French, Romanian, Finnish, both Swiss samples, Polish, French, Hungarian, and German). The American adolescents were significantly above the Russian, Bulgarian, French, Romanian, Finnish, and German-Swiss adolescents. Finally the Csechoslovakians, the Germans, and Hungarians beat the Russians and Bulgarians.

The results reflect the American school system's strong emphasis on sports. As for the Norwegian adolescents, the results correspond well with the cliché of the Norwegians born with skis on their feet. However, there is also an alternative interpretation. The Norwegian adolescents reported having very short school days. The French adolescents, on the other hand, reported being in school for a longer time than others and belong to the participants reporting low scores on time spent on sports. They simply might not have had enough time to spend on sports on typical school days. They may compensate on their school-free day in the middle of the week, but we do not have data on this.

Whether the essential differences in this respect are due to differences in the weekly schedule or on differences in preferences is a question that can only be examined using a different method for the measurement of time use. In fact, when comparing Norwegian and Swiss adolescents using the average time method (Tschanz, 1997), we found Swiss adolescents to report doing more sports than the Norwegian ones. Due to very different school schedules, the Norwegian adolescents may typically do sports on school days, whereas Swiss adolescents may use the half-school days or free days to do it. As for the American data, it is remarkable that Csikszentmihalyi and Larson (1984) found much lower times spent on sports (0h32 hours per day as opposed to 1h07 in our study; p. 63)[5].

Sports was very much in competition with other activities. Table 3.2 shows 11 significant negative correlations, with: eating meals (no significant correlation within a single country), way to and from school (significant negative correlations in CSFR, France, Hungary), staying at school (Finland, France, Germany, Hungary, Romania, and German Switzerland), homework (France, Hungary, Poland), music (Germany, Hungary, Norway, and German Switzerland), leisure reading (Germany, Hungary, and Norway), television (CSFR and USA), hanging around with friends (CSFR, Finland, Hungary, Norway, and United States), dating (Germany and French Switzerland), chores (no single country) and shopping (Poland). As for the PRTCs over the whole sample, most negative correlations remained negative and significant (Table 3.3). Only two were positive (i.e., PRTC sports-sleep'=.38, (p<.01) and PRTC sports-school'=.13, (p<.01). This means that except for the relation with sleep and school, active sports really was a choice at the expense of other possible choices. The correlations within the age by gender cells were very much the same, except for dating: Although the correlations between sports and dating were negative for the older boys and for almost all younger boys, they centered around zero for the girls in most countries. Is it that sports and dating are in an either-or relation for boys and not for girls or is it simply that most boys partake in sports on one day and date on another?

Spending time for active sports was related both to well-being (r=.08; p<.01) and to the sum of experienced strain (r=-.09; p<.01). Specifically, adolescents who spent less time in active sports reported experiencing more strain related to school, health, leisure opportunities, and sports (r's=-.06, -.08, -.11, -.10, respectively; all p<.01).

Television and Radio

Time spent exclusively watching television or exclusively listening to the radio was subject to an age by country two-way interaction as well as to gender and country main effects. The simple main effect of age was significant only in Hungary (the younger adolescents reported spending more time on these

---

[5]Csikszentmihalyi and Larson indicated 7.2% of waking time for watching TV and 1.4% for listening to music; 8.6% out of 15.5 hours=1.333 hours (p. 63).

activities than did the older ones). According to our findings, the increase in television and radio consumption from childhood to adolescence, as it was found in the American population by Timmer et al., (1985), does not seem to continue in the adolescent period. The possible increase of radio consumption at the expense of television consumption (Larson et al., 1989) cannot be tested with our data, because television and radio consumption were pooled within the same activity category. Indeed, when we mention television in this report, we always mean watching television and/or listening to the radio.

Over all countries, boys spent more time on television and radio than did the girls, (i.e., 1h56 and 1h31 per day, respectively, $p<0.01$), which matches previous results (Larson et al., 1989). The countries significantly differed for both age groups. Bulgaria showed the highest figures, followed by CSFR and Romania (Fig. 3.3). Our data roughly correspond to that of

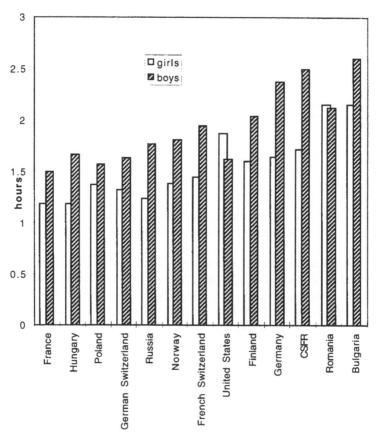

FIG. 3.3. Time (in hours) spent on exclusively watching television or exclusively listening to radio.

Csikszentmihalyi and Larson's (1984; that is, 1h20 per day[6]) and to the German viewing times for 14- to 29-year-olds (1h38; Lutz, 1991, p. 96).

Watching television was often in competition with both school-related activities as well as with other leisure activities. Specifically, there were significant negative correlations (Table 3.3) with sleep (significant also in the following countries: France, Norway, and French Switzerland), body care (CSFR, Finland, Germany, Hungary, Poland, Russia, and Romania), eating meals (Hungary), way to and from school (Russia), staying in school (France, Hungary, Poland, United States, Romania, and French Switzerland), homework (Bulgaria, CSFR, France, Germany, Hungary, Norway, Poland, Russia, Romania, and German Switzerland), music (Bulgaria, France, Germany, Hungary, and French Switzerland), leisure reading (CSFR, Germany, and Hungary), sports (CSFR and United States), hanging around with friends (Bulgaria, Germany, and Norway), dating (Bulgaria, Finland, Germany, Russia, and United States), and chores (CSFR, Hungary, Poland, and French Switzerland).

Again, correlations with the proportion of remaining time did not change the picture dramatically, except for sleep, which had a very high PRTC (television-sleep'=.42; $p<.01$) and school which was evidently inevitable (PRTC television-school'=.13; $p<.01$). As with sports, television did not change the signs of the correlations when it was the target in the PRTC, but did so with sleep and school when it was the source. This means that television did not affect sleeping and school times and had no specific priority among other activities. Television times were not correlated with well-being or with experienced strain.

Dating

As noted in chapter 1, *dating* does not necessarily correspond to the same behavior patterns in all countries. Also, the particular American dating culture does not exist in exactly the same form in Europe. The activity category was described as "time spent with one's boyfriend or girlfriend." However, for the sake of convenience, we refer to it here as dating.

Time for dating was characterized by two 2-way interactions—age by country and gender by country—as well as by two main effects—age and country. The interactions were ordinal, meaning that in all countries, older adolescents spent more time dating than did younger adolescents (significantly so in Germany and Hungary). Although girls generally spent more time dating than boys, this was significant within countries only for Finland and the French-speaking part of Switzerland (see Table 3.4).

Although one can assume that girls mostly date boys and boys mostly date girls, the average time spent dating differed, probably indicating that

---

[6]Csikszentmihalyi and Larson indicated 7.2% of waking time for watching television and 1.4% for listening to music; 8.6% out of 15.5 hours=1.333 hours (p. 63).

TABLE 3.4
Hours Spent on Dating by Age and by Gender for Each Country
(Significant Figues Only; p=<.01)

Countries	Age		Gender		Total Average
	≤ 14 yrs	> 14 yrs	Girls	Boys	
Bulgaria					.39
CSFR					.22
Finland			0.89	.18	.54
France					.12
Germany	0.93	1.49			1.23
Hungary	0.18	0.52			.35
Norway					.18
Poland					.41
Russia					.44
German Switzerland					.33
United States					.53
Romania					.22
French Switzerland			0.46	0.15	.33
Total Average	0.32	0.50	0.48	0.36	0.41

the girls tended to meet older boys, that is, of an age group not included in this survey. In fact, when the scores for the younger girls were compared with the scores for the older boys, the gender difference was only significant in Hungary, where it was reversed; older boys spent more time dating than did younger girls. However, it should be noted that the gender effect was only significant in a few countries.

The differences between the countries are enormous; they might be partly due to the time available during school days. Note that the French adolescents, having the longest average school day, indicated an average of only 0h07 as compared to the 1h14 of the German adolescents. In fact, German adolescents had significantly higher scores than all other adolescents.

In terms of uncorrected correlations, dating was in competition with several other activities (negative correlations), but not with body care, with which the correlation was positive ($r=.04$; $p<.05$; significantly positive in no single country). Correlations were significantly negative with sleeping (significantly so in Bulgaria, Germany, Hungary, Russia, and Romania), eating meals (Germany, German Switzerland, and United States) way to and from school (Hungary), staying at school (France, Germany, Norway, Poland, Russia, Romania, French Switzerland, German Switzerland), homework (Finland, Germany, Hungary, Norway, Romania, and German Switzerland), leisure reading (Germany and Russia), sports (Germany and French Switzerland), television (Bulgaria, Finland, Germany, Russia, and United States), and hanging around with friends (Finland and Romania).

PRTCs basically repeated the pattern we had with sports and television (i.e., consistent negative coefficients where dating was target, except for body care!) and emerging positive coefficients with sleeping and school when dating was the source, (again positive PRTC with body care). We understand that dating, like sports and television, yielded higher remaining time proportions for sleeping and school (but not for homework), but was itself pushed down in remaining priority when most other free activities were chosen. The specific exception here is body care, evidently more important at times of dating.

Correlations between time spent dating and well-being were nonsignificant. Among the hassles, there were three that were significantly correlated with time spent dating, namely related to girlfriend or boyfriend ($r=-.10$, $p<.01$), family life ($r=.09$; $p<.01$), and leisure opportunities ($r=-.05$; $p<.05$). Note the signs: Dating obviously went together with having fewer problems with girlfriend or boyfriend and with leisure opportunities, but more problems with parents and siblings.

Hanging Around With Friends

Time spent with friends was not related to gender, neither in any interaction nor as a main effect. This is surprising. However, because we did not ask whether these activities were in groups or with single peers, the typical gender difference in social behavior (boys more in groups, girls more in same-sex pairs) could not be captured here. It is noticeable, however, that Garton and Pratt (1991) did not find gender differences in participation in gregarious leisure activities either.

Age and country were significant, both as main effects and in interaction. Older adolescents spent more time hanging around with friends than did younger adolescents. This general age difference fits well with previous results (Garton & Pratt, 1991; Richards & Larson, 1989), and it was significant in several single countries, namely Bulgaria, France, and the German-speaking part of Switzerland, favoring the older participants in each case. The overall figures were 0h50 for the older and 0h35 for the younger adolescents. On the other hand, there were substantial differences between the different countries, the Western countries (except for the United States) being the leaders (Fig. 3.4).

All significant correlations between this variable and other activities were negative (Table 3.2), that is, with sleeping (Bulgaria, Finland, Hungary, Romania, Russia, and United States), eating meals (Bulgaria, Germany, Hungary, Norway, and Russia), going to and from school (Poland), staying at school (Bulgaria, CSFR, Finland, France, Poland, Romania, and Russia), homework (Bulgaria, Finland, France, Hungary, Norway, Poland, Romania, Russia, and German Switzerland), listening to music (no single country), doing some leisure reading (France, Hungary, and Norway), participating in sports (CSFR, Finland, Hungary, Norway, and United States), television (Bulgaria, Germany, and Norway), and dating (Finland and Romania).

PRTC analyses (Table 3.3) again yielded the typical pattern for free activities: If hanging around was the source, the PRTC was significantly

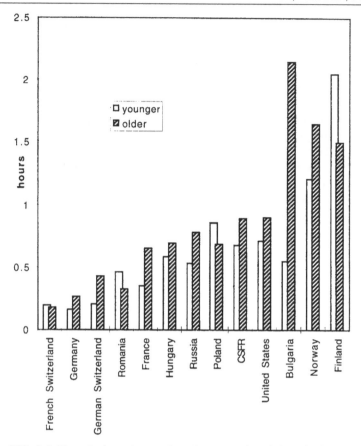

FIG. 3.4. Time (in hours) spent hanging around with friends, by age.

positive with sleep and school (unavoidable), but not with homework (compromises are possible). It was also positive with body care (as in the case of dating). If hanging around was the target, then all significant PRTCs were negative, which is interpreted as hanging around with friends having low overall priority; adolescents do that if there is time left.

Time spent hanging around with friends was negatively correlated with subjective well-being ($r=-.06$; $p<01$), but positively correlated with the sum of experienced daily hassles, although the correlation was low ($r=.05$; $p<.05$). Specifically, hanging around with friends was positively and significantly correlated with problems related to available money, sports, and family life, but negatively correlated with problems related to peers and to leisure opportunities. It seems that hanging around with friends is given priority under some favorable conditions (e.g., having friends and having no specific aspirations as to other leisure activities) and some unfavorable conditions (problems with family, money, and sports).

Working for Money

Time spent on working for money was included in the three-way interaction. Separate analyses by country yielded an age by gender interaction for Bulgaria and the United States. In Bulgaria, the interaction was due to the fact that only the older boys reported having worked for money the day before the data collection (an average of 0h12). In the United States, the younger girls spent no time earning money (0h00) and thus worked significantly less than older girls (1h06) and boys their age (0h34). Furthermore, there was an age effect in Germany and in Norway. In both countries older adolescents worked more than younger adolescents.

Given that the interactions were primarily due to the fact that younger adolescents of one or the other gender, or both, did not report having worked for money at all, we conducted separate comparisons between the countries only for the two age groups.

There were no pairwise differences among countries for younger adolescents. Among the older ones, American adolescents (0h49) topped the list, working significantly more than all other adolescents (Fig. 3.5). Csikszentmihalyi and Larson (1984) found an average of 7.4 hours per week across the complete high school sample (p. 65). Distributed over 6 days, this would make 1h14 as compared to 0h40 in our study. This is probably due to the fact that we sampled only school days and not the full week.

These impressive differences between countries led to the question of how many adolescents were indeed involved in working for money, both over all countries and in the United States—the leader in this respect. As Table 3.5 shows, in all but two countries, 10% or less of the older adolescents were working at all on the sample day. The exceptions are the United States (22.5%) and Norway (18.3%).

These results, together with the results on sports, may indicate some structural differences in the organization of the different societies. Older Norwegian and German adolescents were in second and third position as to time spent working. Even although the latter were not significantly different from the other countries, they are interesting because all three countries were among the ones with the shortest school days.

Most correlations with other activities were negative (significantly so with sleeping time in Romania and the United States), eating meals (significant in no single country), going to and from school (Romania), staying at school (CSFR, Romania, and United States), doing homework (Bulgaria and Norway), and doing some leisure reading (significant in no single country). The only significant positive correlation was with playing music (Finland and Norway). This could mean that many adolescents working for money do so in order to be able to buy musical equipment.

The PRTC analysis confirms this result. If working was the target, all significant correlations were negative, probably meaning that working had a low remaining priority, except with playing music as target. Continuing

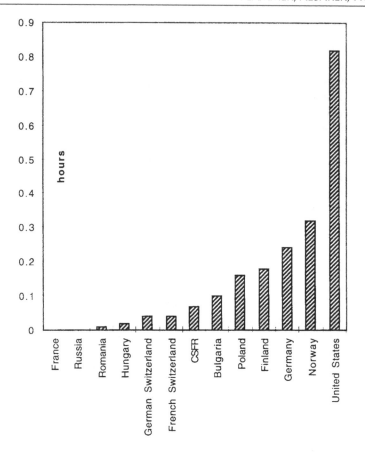

FIG. 3.5. Time (in hours) spent working for money on the sample day
by the older adolescents (older than 14 years of age).

with our tentative interpretation, this could mean that indeed many of those
playing music had to work for money in order to buy their equipment. If
working was the source, then the PRTC pattern was very much the same
as with other leisure activities: Working increased the remaining proportion
of time used for sleep, school, and bodycare, but lowered it for homework.
Again, the relation to playing music was positive.

The correlations between time spent working for money and the well-
being scale as well as the total hassle scale were not significant. The only
single significant correlation was found with experienced problems with
one's own room ($r=.05$; $p<.05$): Adolescents working for money had more
problems related to their room. They could possibly come from less well-off
families.

TABLE 3.5
*Time Spent Working for Money. Frequency Distribution
in Percentages for Adolescents Older Than 14*

Country	Hours Spent on Working for Money						Total
	.00	≤ .50	≤1.00	≤1.50	≤2.00	≥2.00	
Bulgaria	96.2	.0	.0	.0	1.2	2.6	100%
CSFR	93.9	1.0	3.1	2.0	.0	.0	100%
Finland	95.6	.0	1.1	.0	.0	3.3	100%
France	100.0	.0	.0	.0	.0	.0	100%
Germany	90.7	.0	3.1	1.5	.8	3.9	100%
Hungary	96.3	3.1	.6	.0	.0	.0	100%
Norway	82.5	2.0	8.7	2.9	.0	3.9	100%
Poland	91.6	.0	.9	2.8	1.9	2.8	100%
Romania	98.6	.0	1.4	.0	.0	.0	100%
Russia	100.0	.0	.0	.0	.0	.0	100%
F–CH	98.5	.0	.0	.0	.0	1.5	100%
G–CH	95.9	.0	3.1	1.0	.0	.0	100%
US	82.7	.0	1.3	1.3	2.7	12	100%

DISCUSSION AND CONCLUSION

When the results from the 13 cross-national samples are compared, there seems to be more similarities than differences in gender and age differences. Even where there were many interactions between age and country and between gender and country, these interactions were mostly ordinal. Given the relatively small country samples and given our conservative criteria for significance, some of the nonsignificant differences might mirror true differences and could have turned out to be significant in larger samples.

One of our general issues had to do with similarities and differences between East and West. Were there some common leisure-time patterns in Eastern and Central European countries? The pairwise comparisons between countries and a bird's eye look at Table 3.1 showed that some countries seem to have a rather specific profile on leisure activity distribution. Bulgaria, for example, was especially high on watching television and hanging around with friends, but rather low on partaking in sports and working for money. CSFR was comparable to Bulgaria in time spent watching television and working, but average in hanging around with friends and in sports. Romania too was comparable to Bulgaria in terms of high television, low sports, and low working, but Romanian adolescents were also low in music. The two other Central Eastern European countries, Hungary and Poland, were very near to the general average, except that the Hungarians were very little engaged in working for money. The Russian participants departed somewhat from the overall average; they were higher in leisure reading, lower in sports, and extremely low in working for money. That is, there was no typical Central

Eastern European pattern, even if the three biggest consumers of television and radio were found in this part of Europe.

Looking at other European subareas, we expected the two Scandinavian countries to form a rather distinguished cluster. Both are very high in total leisure-time availability and both countries yielded extended time spent hanging around with friends. However, whereas Norway is also especially high in time spent with sports, Finland is especially low in sports. The reverse is true for dating: Finland is high and Norway is low. That is, those are two countries providing adolescents with much leisure time, probably because of similarity in the school systems. The fact that the adolescents in these two countries reported by far the highest proportion of time spent hanging around with friends may mirror a Scandinavian educational tradition allowing children a great deal of unstructured activity.

The remaining European countries do not show much similarity. Whereas Germany is high in total leisure-time availability, France is definitely at the bottom of the distribution and Switzerland is in between. Germany and Switzerland excel in playing music and are both low in time spent with friends. The Swiss do rather little work for money. The Germans use three times as much time for dating as the overall average. The American sample had clearly more than average free time. They used it more than average on leisure reading, sports, and working for money. The only activity where they were clearly below average was playing music.

We also defined the leisure activity profile per country by taking the average durations per activity in each country (from Table 3.1). In addition, an average profile over all countries was defined (also taken from Table 3.1). The correlation between these profiles served as a measure of similarity. Naturally, these coefficients are very high due to the fact that some activities occupy a lot of time in all countries (e.g., television) and that other activities have a minor place in all countries (e.g., working and playing music). Of interest is the relative size of the correlation coefficients, not the absolute size. Germany showed the lowest similarity coefficient with the average profile ($r=.974$; $p<.05$), followed by Norway and Romania ($r=.976$, $.979$, respectively). The most prototypical countries—that is, the most similar to the average—were Poland, Hungary, CSFR, and France ($r=.999$, $.998$, $.996$, respectively).

The Proportion of the Remaining Time correlations proved to be an effective way to cope with restricted degrees of freedom. The fact that they are asymmetric, according to which activity is taken to be the source or the target activity, allowed some additional insight into the relations. Most leisure activities apparently are in a mutually competitive relation. One either does one thing and not the other or the other way around. Thus, the raw correlations were mostly negative, even with necessary activities. The PRTCs changed the pattern when the given leisure activity was the source: PRTCs were still negative with other leisure activities, but not with clearly required activities like sleeping and staying in school. That is, if one given leisure activity was to win more space, this happened at the expense of other leisure activities, not at the expense of school or sleep, for example. Interestingly, this was mostly not the case with homework as target. Homework may be required just as is staying in school, but individuals can reduce this activity because there is no immediate structure to control it.

Overall, our results on leisure activities in an international perspective seem to indicate that both structural factors (e.g., school) and traditions are central to the way adolescents organize their leisure time. There is still room, however, for individual differences and there are more similarities than differences among our 13 samples, at least in terms of age trends and gender differences.

REFERENCES

Alsaker, F.D., & Flammer, A. (1996, March). *Social relationships and depression in adolescents: Social causation and social selection*. Paper presented at the Biennial Meetings of the Society for Research on Adolescence, Boston.

Alsaker, F.D., & Flammer, A. (in press). Time-use in children and adolescents. In A.N. Perret-Clermont, J.M.Barrelet, A.Flammer, D.Miéville, J.F.Perret, & W.Perrig (Eds.), *Mind and time*. Göttingen, Germany: Hogrefe & Huber Publishers.

Barker, R.G., & Wright, H.F. (1951). *One boy's day*. New York: Harper & Row.

Csikszentmihalyi, M., & Larson, R. (1984). *Being adolescent: Conflict and growth in the teenage years*. New York: Basic Books.

Csikszentmihalyi, M., Larson, R., & Prescott, S. (1977). The ecology of adolescent activity and experience. *Journal of Youth and Adolescence, 6*, 281–294.

DeGrazia, S. (1962). *Of time, work and leisure*. New York: The Twentieth Century Fund.

Garton, A.F., & Pratt, C. (1987). Participation and interest in leisure activities by adolescent schoolchildren. *Journal of Adolescence, 10*, 341–351.

Garton, A.F., & Pratt, C. (1991). Leisure activities of adolescent school students: predictors of participation and interest. *Journal of Adolescence, 14*, 305–321.

Grob, A., Little, T.D., Wanner, B., Wearing, A.J., & Euronet (1996). Adolescents' well-being and perceived control across fourteen sociocultural contexts. *Journal of Personality and Social Psychology, 71*, 785–795.

Grob, A., Lüthi, R., Kaiser, F.G., Flammer, A., Mackinnon, A., & Wearing, A.J., (1991) Berner Fragebogen zum Wohlbefinden Jugendlicher (BFW). [Bernese Questionnaire on the Weil-Being of Adolescents.] *Diagnostica, 37*, 66–75.

Harrington, R. (1993). *Depressive Disorder in Childhood and Adolescence*. Chichester, England: Wiley.

Herzberg, I., Hössl, A., & Lipski, J. (1995). *Freizeiträume für Schulkinder in den neuen Bundeslandern*. Ergebnisse einer Regionalstudie 1992–1995 [Leisure time places for school-children in the new federal states. Results from a regional study 1992–1995]. München, Germany: Verlag Deutsches Jugendinstitut.

Katz, E., & Gurevitch, M. (1976). *The secularisation of leisure. Culture and communication in Israel*. London: Faber & Faber.

Kirk, R.E. (1982). *Experimental design: Procedures for the behavior sciences* (2nd ed.). Belmont, CA: Brooks-Cole.

Larson, R., Kubey, R., & Colletti, J. (1989). Changing channels: Early adolescent media choices and shifting investments in family and friends. *Journal of Youth and Adolescence, 18,*583–599.

Lutz, B. (1991). Die telemetrische Messung der Fernsehnutzung von Kindern— Methode, Ergebnisse, Probleme [The telemetric data collection of TV use among children—method, results, problems]. In W.Tietze & H.G.Rossbach (Eds.), *Mediennutzung und Zeitbudget* (pp. 86–107). Wiesbaden, Germany: Deutscher Universitätsverlag.

Raffaeli, M., & Duckett, E. (1989). "We were just talking…" Conversations in early adolescence. *Journal of Youth and Adolescence, 18,* 567–582.

Richards, M.H., & Larson, R. (1989). The life space and socialization of the self: Sex differences in the young adolescent. *Journal of Youth and Adolescence, 18,* 617–626.

Ryser, A. (1997) *Erkenntnisprinzip und Regulationsprinzip im zentralen Selbstbild* [The central self: Self-definition and regulation]. Master's Thesis, University of Berne, Switzerland.

Szalai, A. (Ed). (1972). *The use of time. Daily activities of urban and suburban populations in twelve countries.* Paris: Mouton.

Timmer, S.G., Eccles, J., & O'Brien, K. (1985). How children use time. In F.T.Juster, & F.P. Stafford (Eds.), *Time, goods, and well-being* (pp. 351–381). Ann Arbor: University of Michigan.

Tschanz, U. (1997). Was tun Jugendliche in ihrer Freizeit? [What do adolescents do in their free time?] In A.Grob (Ed.), *Kinder und Jugendliche heute: Belastet— überlastet?* (pp. 69–90). Zürich: Rüegger.

Verma, S., & Saraswathi, T.S. (1992). *At the crossroads. Time use by university students.* Chandigarh, India: Department of Child Development, Panjab University.

4

Time Use by Adolescents in an International Perspective. II: The Case of Necessary Activities

Françoise D.Alsaker
University of Bergen, Norway
University of Berne, Switzerland

August Flammer
University of Berne, Switzerland

An adolescent's regular day is filled with activities that he or she is rarely free to choose from, mainly related to school and personal maintenance. The activities we explicitly included in this study were sleeping; body care; eating; going to, being in, and coming back from school; homework; household chores; and shopping. According to our informal observations, many adolescents feel that these necessary activities take too much time in their lives, and they enjoy more their holidays and vacation times. In this respect, their situation is not very different from adults. In both cases, an overload of obligations is considered as an indicator of possible strain and subjective stress. Timmer, Eccles, and O'Brien (1985) reported that children aged 3 through 17 years old use 60% of their day time on what they called *nondiscretionary activities* (p. 365). A closer look at their findings showed that boys aged 12 through 17 years old used 70% of their time for such activities and that girls in the same age group used as much as 74% of their time for what we call *necessary activities*. This chapter is intended to give a description of these daily obligations in the 12 countries represented in Euronet.

This chapter also aims to find out what activities compete with what other activities. We expect little competition among the required or necessary activities, but much competition between required activities and leisure activities, at the expense of the latter.

In addition, this chapter pools the data from the present and preceeding chapters (on leisure activities) and determines whether the 12 countries cluster in any meaningful way, yielding (or confirming) some kind of broader cultural European regions.

The literature on adolescents' daily activities shows that there are substantial age and gender differences in adolescents' time use as for necessary activities. Across Grades 5 through 9, American girls spent more time doing homework than did their male peers according to one study (Timmer et al., 1985). Leone and Richards (1989), however, found that girls in Grades 5 through 8 spent more time on homework than did boys, but not in Grade 9; girls' involvment in homework, unlike boys', decreased over the years. Moreover, Timmer et al. (1985) found that girls of this age used more time than did boys for eating their meals, caring for their bodies, and performing household chores.

It is not clear a priori what to expect in the different countries. In earlier times, one could have expected that adolescents in the Central and Eastern European countries would spend more time on compulsory activities than would Western adolescents (e.g., for household chores and shopping), because most parents were working outside their homes and shopping was very time-consuming due to long lines. These conditions drastically changed by 1992 when our data were collected.

There is also some reason to expect time-use patterns not to differ among European countries and the United States because all Western societies share comparable concepts and values, for example, as to the importance of education (see chap. 5, this volume). However, there might be practical reasons for expecting certain specific differences, for example, as a result of national differences in the organization of the schoolday. In many countries, students stay in school until early or mid-afternoon, Monday through Friday, eating a sandwich during breaks. In other countries, such as France and Switzerland, children and adolescents go to school twice a day (morning and afternoon), having a fairly extensive lunch at home (or at school in France). In France, there is no school on Wednesday, but there is on Saturday, at least in the morning (Tillard, 1991). Moreover, in Switzerland, students in most *cantons* (counties) attend school on Saturday morning, and during the week, they have one or two free afternoons.

In Switzerland, lunch is still the main meal in many families. In most other countries (e.g., CSFR, Germany, Hungary, Poland, Russia, and Romania), according to our investigations, lunch is still regarded as the main meal although it is eaten at school. In other countries (e.g., Finland, Norway, and the United States), however, dinner is the main meal of the day. We should not forget that the French are known for celebrating their meals. Not only is the French cuisine the most prestigious of all, but French people also invest a high proportion of their resources in everyday meals.

Northern countries have longer nights in wintertime and longer days in summertime than the more southern European countries, which could have some impact on sleeping times and the general organization of the day. In Norway, for example, work days are shorter during summer than during winter. In light of all these considerations, we expect to find evidence of differences and similarities among the countries, in addition to gender and age differences.

METHOD

This study is based on the same 2,315 participants as chapter 3 on leisure time use by Flammer, Alsaker, and Noack. The same instruments were used as described in chapter 3. As for correlations between specific activities and reported strain, a general index of strain was used in a first step. When this overall correlation was significant, correlations between this activity and the specific-strain variables were conducted. Also, correlations between an activity and a specific-strain item were calculated when there was a reason to expect some relation. This would be the case, for example, for the relation between school time and strain related to school.

RESULTS

There are four sets of results. The first three sets concern means of time spent on each activity (differentiated according to country, age, and gender, if the interactions were statistically significant), correlations among activities—both necessary and leisure—and correlations between time spent on specific activities and reports of strain and well-being. The fourth set focuses on similarities among countries based on both the necessary and the leisure activities.

Overall Statistics

Table 4.1 shows the average accumulated durations of each of the required activities by country. On the average, 18h54 were spent on what we defined as *necessary activities*, 4h25 on leisure activities, and 0h41 on other activities.

We conducted a multivariate analysis of variance (MANOVA) in which the durations of all activities—leisure and necessary—were entered as the dependent variables. An omnibus test including all three factors of interest—that is, country, gender, and age—was performed, followed by univariate post hoc analyses (see Flammer, Alsaker, & Noack, chap. 3, this volume).

There was a significant three-way country by age by gender interaction (p_{wilks} <.001). Of the necessary activities, only time spent in school was influenced by this interaction. Breaking the interaction down by country

TABLE 4.1
Average Accumulated Duration of Each Necessary Activity per Country (in Hours)

Country	Sleep	Body Care	Eating	Going to School	School	Home-work	Chores	Shopping	Total Necessary Activities	Total Leisure Activities	Other
Bulgaria	8.40	0.53	0.98	0.86	5.12	1.94	0.41	0.20	18.44	5.03	0.53
CSFR	8.61	0.61	0.79	1.12	6.02	1.20	0.59	0.23	19.17	4.82	0.00
Finland	8.29	0.64	0.93	0.58	6.10	0.82	0.23	0.14	17.73	5.48	0.79
France	8.82	0.55	1.88	0.70	7.04	1.87	0.16	0.10	21.12	2.73	0.13
Germany	8.40	0.66	1.00	0.86	5.32	1.30	0.19	0.29	18.02	5.20	0.78
Hungary	8.53	0.75	0.86	0.98	5.98	1.90	0.40	0.15	19.55	3.90	0.55
Norway	8.48	0.55	0.94	0.77	5.45	1.05	0.33	0.14	17.71	5.59	0.69
Poland	7.64	0.76	1.08	0.99	5.16	2.35	0.67	0.37	19.02	3.99	0.98
Romania	8.80	0.53	0.98	1.05	5.21	2.41	0.33	0.20	19.51	4.07	0.42
Russia	7.91	0.52	1.19	1.18	5.82	1.85	0.40	0.13	19.00	3.96	1.06
French Switzerland	8.82	0.50	1.47	0.92	5.93	1.45	0.21	0.23	19.53	3.72	0.76
German Switzerland	8.69	0.54	1.39	1.09	5.75	1.21	0.33	0.14	19.14	3.82	1.06
United States	7.69	0.80	0.91	0.50	6.06	1.38	0.33	0.15	17.82	5.27	0.90
Average	8.39	0.61	1.11	0.89	5.77	1.59	0.35	0.19	18.90	4.42	0.67

yielded simple age by gender interactions for Bulgaria, CSFR, Hungary, and Romania, and simple main effects of age for Germany, Poland, Russia, and both parts of Switzerland, as well as simple main effects of gender for Finland and Germany.

Among the remaining necessary activities, sleeping, eating, way to and from school, homework, chores, and shopping were influences by the country by age multivariate two-way interaction ($p_{wilks} < .001$). Breaking the interaction down by country yielded age effects for Bulgaria (sleeping, eating, and homework), CSFR (sleeping, eating, and way to and from school), Finland (way to and from school and homework), France (sleeping and eating), Germany (sleeping), Hungary (sleeping, eating, way to and from school, homework, chores, and shopping), Norway (sleeping, way to and from school, homework, and chores), Poland (sleeping, way to and from school, homework, and chores), Romania (way to and from school and homework), and German Switzerland (way to and from school). None of these activities was characterized by a country by gender multivariate interaction; the gender by age multivariate interaction was not significant.

The only remaining necessary activity was time used for body care which was characterized by all three main effects (age, gender, and country).

Results Related to Personal Maintenance

Personal maintenance included the three following variables: sleep, body care, and meals.

Sleeping. As noted, time spent sleeping was characterized by an age by country interaction. The interaction was ordinal. That is, in all countries where there was a significant age difference, the younger adolescents slept longer than did the older adolescents. The difference was significant in seven countries (Table 4.2). On average, the younger adolescents slept 8h41 and the older ones 8h11. This corresponds roughly to the results of other surveys (Schweizerisches Bundesamt für Statistik, 1981; Williams, Karacan, & Hursch, 1974). Flammer and Tschanz (1997) reported 8h44 and 8h37, respectively, for Swiss and Norwegian adolescents aged 13 to 15 years. According to their data, the average difference between 13- and 14-year-olds and between 14- and 15-year olds was 0h28, which again makes the present figures comparable to theirs. These durations seem relatively short in comparison with what Verma and Saraswathi (1992) found for Indian college students (i.e., 8h28), given that sleeping times generally decrease with age.

As for differences among countries, the short sleepers live in Poland, the United States, and Russia, all sleeping less than 8 hours. The shorter sleeping times in the United States correspond well to the findings of Timmer et al. (1985). The long sleepers live in France, Romania, and the French-speaking part of Switzerland, averaging close to 9 hours.

TABLE 4.2
Sleeping Times by Age and Country
(Significant Figures Only; p≤.01; Higher Values Bold)

Sleeping	≤14 yrs	> 14 yrs	Total Average
Bulgaria	**8.77**	7.91	8.40
CSFR	**9.12**	8.33	8.61
Finland			8.29
France	**9.23**	8.58	8.82
Germany	**8.65**	8.22	8.40
Hungary	**8.96**	8.07	8.53
Norway	**8.82**	8.22	8.48
Poland	**7.86**	7.47	7.64
Romania			8.80
Russia			7.91
French Switzerland			8.82
German Switzerland			8.69
United States			7.69
Total average	**8.69**	8.18	8.39

Because all data were collected in between January and March 1992—except for Norway, where they were collected in May 1993—one could expect longer sleeping durations for Finland and shorter sleeping times for Norway, given the drastic differences in daylight in the North. However, our results did not confirm this expectation. A recent study comparing Norwegian and Swiss students in Grades 4 to 6 and 7 to 9 showed that the Norwegians slept less than the Swiss, both in May 1994 (9h36 vs. 9h48 for the younger Norwegian and Swiss adolescents, respectively, and 8h37 vs. 8h44 for the older Norwegian and Swiss adolescents, respectively) and in November 1994 (9h26 vs. 9h40 and 8h27 vs. 8h36). Because sleeping time decreases over this age range and because the same participants were tested in May and November, there is a decrease in sleeping time despite seasonal influences (Flammer & Tschanz, 1997). On the whole, it does not seem that Scandinavian adolescents sleep longer than continental European or American adolescents.

Given that the average sleeping time corresponds with medical recommendations, but individual differences are natural, shorter sleeping times do not automatically indicate an unhealthy lifestyle. Therefore, negative (uncorrected) correlations with time spent on other activities may or may not indicate a lack of needed sleep. Nevertheless, there are some correlations that should not be dismissed.

Correlations between sleeping time and school time, as well as between sleeping time and homework, time were negative in all countries, although they were not highly negative (however, an exception was found in older Russian boys: $r=-.50$; $p<.01$). PRTC sleep-school' was .23 for the complete sample (see Table 3.4 in chap. 3, Flammer et al., this volume). The negative uncorrected correlation coefficient between sleep and school time seems to indicate that the adolescents tend to sleep longer if school time allows; on the other hand and according to the positive PRTC sleep-school', priority for school seems to be, inevitable and this occurs indepedently of sleeping time. School time is fixed and not under the control of adolescents, and therefore takes an increased proportion of time available. That is, those who slept longer had to take their additional sleep from activities other than school.

Pooling all countries, time for school was correlated negatively with reported total strain ($r=-.09$), but not significantly with strain related to school or with well-being. In 11 out of the 13 samples, the correlation with reported total strain was negative, although not always significant; for strain related to school, there were 8 negative correlations out of 13. It seems that length of daily schooling increases the perception of strain in this area.

Body Care. There were only main effects for body care. Older participants invested more time in body care than did the younger participants (an average of 0h38 vs. 0h35), girls more than boys (0h41 vs. 0h33), and Hungarians, Poles, and Americans more than the Swiss, Russians, Romanians, Bulgarians, French, and Norwegians. These findings are in line with those from Timmer et al. (1985), who reported even higher figures (adolescent girls: 1h11, adolescent boys: 0h48, younger adolescents: 0h56, older adolescents: 1h00).

Gender differences in favor of the girls are plausible, given the emphasis on physical attractiveness among girls. They were also found by Timmer et al. (1985) and in different Swiss data by Nirkko (1994), but not by Roniger (1994).

Correlations with other activities were generally small, mostly negative with sleeping and watching television, possibly meaning that those who spent much time watching television/listening to the radio or sleeping did not find enough time for or did not care much for body care. For younger girls, there was a rather consistent pattern of positive (uncorrected) correlations with dating and hanging around with friends. We do not discuss PRTCs for body care because body care did not occupy much time of the day.

Evidently, extended body care may be the result of bodily or social satisfaction, but it also may indicate certain problems. The correlation of body care with the general well-being measure was near to zero, but the correlation with the sum of perceived hassles was significantly positive in the total sample ($r=.05$, $p<.05$), specifically with items related to problems with respect to money, sports, and own room. Probably, causal relations go in several directions. Having problems in sports may require more body care; extensive body care could require more money. Having a problem with one's own room could be related to the fact that the room has to be shared, which in turn, might induce participants to spend more time in the bathroom. Yet, these are speculations that we cannot test.

Time Spent on Meals. Considering time spent on meals, there was a two-way age by country interaction as well as country and age main effects. The

TABLE 4.3
Meal Times in Hours by Age and Country (Significant Figures Only; p≤.01)

Meal Time	≤ 14 yrs	> 14 yrs	Total Average
Bulgaria	1.09	.82	.98
CSFR	.63	.88	.79
Finland			.93
France	1.64	2.03	1.88
Germany			1.00
Hungary	.79	.95	.86
Norway			.94
Poland			1.08
Romania			.98
Russia			1.19
French Switzerland			1.47
German Switzerland			1.39
United States			.91
Total average	1.05	1.12	1.11

interaction proved to be disordinal, with older adolescents investing more time in eating meals than younger adolescents in CSFR, France, and Hungary, compared to Bulgaria, where the younger adolescents reported more time eating meals than did the older adolescents (Table 4.3). On the whole (and, even if not significantly, over most of the countries), the older participants took more time eating meals than did the younger participants.

Although the interaction between age and country is disordinal, the countries cluster the same way for the younger as for the older adolescents; that is, the French and both Swiss samples reported significantly longer times spent on meals than did most others. For the French, this corresponds to their gastronomic reputation; in addition, like the Swiss, many of them go home for lunch (as do many adults). Indeed, family lunchtime may take longer than school lunchtime. The American participants' time spent eating roughly corresponds with the figures reported by Csikszentmihalyi and Larson (1984, p. 65)—about 6 hours a week[1], which is slightly less than the figures reported by Timmer et al. (1985). American adolescents seem to spend less time eating than do most other adolescents. On the other hand, our Russian figures are somewhat higher than what Zuzanek (1980, p. 370) reported: 0h50 as compared to 1h11 in our study. Only the French and the French-speaking part of Switzerland are comparable with the long times reported in Japan—1h30 (Japanese Finance Ministry, 1980, cited in Csikszentmihalyi & Larson, 1984, p. 66).

Time spent eating competed with most leisure activities, like sports, watching television, dating, hanging around with friends, and doing chores. The uncorrected correlations were highly negative, both for the entire

---

[1]Our data found 7×0.91=6.37 hours.

younger sample and the entire older sample. In addition, they were either significantly negative or not significantly different from zero in each single country, both for the younger and for the older adolescents. There were, however, two exceptions: There was a positive correlation with watching television in younger Polish participants and a positive correlation with sports in older Norwegian participants. On the other hand, using more time for meals was positively correlated with sleeping, body care, and musical activity, again significantly for the younger and for the older participants and in all countries either significantly positive or not different from zero both for the younger and for the older adolescents. The PRTCs confirmed this profile: The proportions of remaining time allocated to leisure activities were low (negative PRTCs), but not to necessary activities like sleeping, body care, school time, and homework (positive PRTCs).

The correlation between mealtimes and well-being was positive ($r=.06$; $p<.01$). We might speculate that taking time for meals makes one feel better and relaxed. On the other hand, adolescents who are not feeling satisfied with their lives may engage in a more hectic eating style, or may have less appetite (depressive symptom) and may not enjoy meals. The correlation between mealtimes and reporting hassles was not significant.

Results Related to School Activities

We distinguish three school-related activities—going to and from school, staying in school, and doing homework.

Going to and From School. Our participants spent nearly 1 hour each day on their way to and from school. Because older adolescents often go to schools that cover larger geographical areas, a main effect of age was expected. This effect was found, but it was qualified by an age by country interaction (significant simple age effects were found for CSFR, Hungary, Poland, and the German-speaking part of Switzerland, Table 4.4). The age by country interaction proved to be ordinal. In addition, the gender by country interaction, as well as the country main effect, were significant, but none of the simple gender effects met the Dunn criterion of significance (Kirk, 1982).

Comparisons between countries were done for both ages separately because of the age by country interaction. For the younger participants, there was no significant difference among countries, except for the Russia-Finland comparison (1h04 vs. 0h26). For the older participants there were clearly three country groups with two extremes significantly different from one another. The group of those who spent little time going to and from school consisted of the United States (the shortest), Finland, France, Norway, and Germany. The group of those who spent the most time going to and from school comprised CSFR (the longest), Russia, Poland, the German-speaking part of Switzerland, Romania, and Hungary. Bulgaria and the French-speaking part of Switzerland were between these two extreme groups.

TABLE 4.4
Going to and From School in Hours by Age and Country (Significant Figures Only; p≤.01)

Going to and From School	≤ 14 yrs	> 14 yrs	Total Average
Bulgaria			.86
CSFR	.65	1.38	1.12
Finland	.44	.63	.58
France			.70
Germany			.86
Hungary	.83	1.13	.98
Norway			.77
Poland	.69	1.23	.99
Romania	.88	1.22	1.05
Russia			1.18
French Switzerland			.92
German Switzerland	.92	1.23	1.09
United States			.50
Total average	.79	.99	0.89

In the United States, children's trips to school are significantly shorter than in all other countries except Finland, France, and Norway. What accounts for this difference? Could it be, for example, that American students have relatively long distances to travel to schools, but they are more often brought to school in their parents' car? Moreover, in countries with few private schools and no possibility of school choice, one could expect the way to school to be short, as most students would be assigned to schools in their neighborhood; this would certainly be the case in Norway and in Switzerland. Russian adolescents' trips to school were reported to be the longest, significantly longer than in six other countries. The Russian sample came from private schools (see chap. 2, this volume), and apparently, these schools attracted students from very different geographical areas. Another important factor in the explanation of these differences between countries is the partition of the schoolday. Swiss students have a longer break at noon; almost all of them go home for lunch, which has them going to or from school four times a day. Yet, this seems to have consequences only in the German-Swiss sample; our French-Swiss students must have lived near their school. French school students also have the possibility of going home for lunch, but many of them stay in school for lunch time.

Going to school negatively correlated with many leisure activities like sports, watching television, dating, hanging around with friends, shopping, and working, but also with sleep (Table 3.3). This remained true when correlations were calculated for each country by age cell (all correlations were either significantly negative or not significant at all). Again the corrected correlations (Table 3.4) did not markedly change this picture except for sleeping: Despite long ways to school, sleeping remains a high priority.

Time spent on the way going to and from school was significantly negatively related to reported well-being ($r=-.06$; $p<.01$) and significantly positively related to reported overall strain ($r=.06$; $p<.01$), specifically with strain related to school ($r=.07$; $p<.01$) and to leisure opportunities ($r=.06$; $p<.01$).

Time Spent in School. Time spent in school was influenced by the three-way interaction between age, gender, and country, characterized by an age by country two-way interaction and age and country main effects.

The age by gender interaction was significant for some of the countries (CSFR, Hungary, and Romania), but according to simple main effect analyses, none was significantly disordinal[2]. In CSFR and Romania, the older boys spent significantly more time in school than did both the younger boys and girls and the older girls. Interestingly, and this probably produced the three-way interaction, in Hungary, the older girls spent more time in school than did the older boys, but still, the older Hungarian boys and girls spent significantly more time in school than did their younger, same-gender peers (ordinal interaction).

As for the remaining countries, there was a significant age effect in Poland and the French-speaking part of Switzerland (older adolescents stayed in school longer than younger adolescents) and in Moscow's private school sample; the younger participants spent significantly more time in school than did the older ones on the day before data collection.

Across all countries, the older adolescents spent more time in school than did the younger adolescents (5h52 and 5h35, respectively).

Comparisons among the single countries in younger girls, younger boys, older girls, and older boys, showed one country with significantly longer school times—that is, France. This probably reflects the fact that the French school week covers 4.5 days—Monday, Tuesday, Thursday, Friday (full days), and Saturday (morning), with more required hours per school day. According to a comparative European study by Tillard (1991), France has the longest school days (about 6 hours of presence), the longest lunchbreak (mostly 2 hours), a class length above average (55 minutes), but the least number of school days (4.5), and the shortest school year.

Significantly shorter school times, than in most other countries, appeared for the younger Romanian and Polish adolescents. Considering the older adolescents, Bulgaria showed the shortest school times, significantly so in comparison with most other countries.

On the whole, the length of average school days substantially varied among the countries (Figure 4.1), in some cases by as much as 2 hours.

---

[2]By significant disordinality of the Gender x Age interaction we mean that the Gender effect is significant at both Age levels, but with reverse signs, or that the Age effect is significant for each Gender, but with reverse signs.

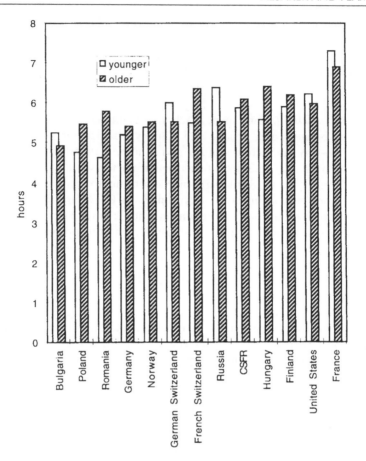

FIG.4.1. Time spent (hours) in school on a regular school day.

Csikszentmihalyi and Larson (1984) reported that 24.7% of waking time was spent on school or studying (p. 63). Taking an average of 15h30 waking time per day, this makes 26h30 of school and studying time a week. Distributed over 5 (normal or full school), this would come to 5h24 a day—the figure to compare with ours. Our average is 5h46, and only four countries lay below Csikszentmihalyi and Larson's figure—Bulgaria, Germany, Poland, and Romania. If we add school time and homework time, all our figures are higher (beginning with 6h51 in Norway and ending with 8h92 in France; see Table 4.5). On the other hand, our figures are lower than what is reported in Japan (59 hours per week=11h48 over 5 days or 9h48 over 6 days; Japanese Finance Ministry, 1980, cited in Csikszentmihalyi & Larson, 1984) and they are slightly lower than those reported in the Soviet Union (8h31 per weekday including Saturday, that is, 5h24 class work and 3h07 homework; Zuzanek, 1980).

TABLE 4.5
School Time and Homework Aggregated in Hours (in Ascending Order)

Country	Average (School Time + Homework)
Norway	6.51
Germany	6.62
Finland	6.92
German Switzerland	6.95
Bulgaria	7.05
CSFR	7.22
French Switzerland	7.38
United States	7.44
Poland	7.50
Romania	7.62
Russia	7.67
Hungary	7.88
France	8.92

School time was evidently in competition with many other activities, especially with leisure activities (i.e., music, reading, sports, watching television, dating, hanging around with friends, and shopping), but also with sleep, doing chores, and working (Table 3.3). Consistently, the correlations within each country by age by gender cell were mostly negative or nonsignificant. However, there were a few significant positive correlations, that might be attributable to error (1.92% of all coefficients). Interestingly, all these positive correlations were found in Bulgaria, Poland, Romania, and Germany, that is, in those countries with the shortest school days (Fig. 4.1); this may indicate that in countries with shorter school days, classes do not compete with leisure activities.

The corrected correlations (PRTCs) once more demonstrated the uncontested priority of sleeping (PRTC=.38), body care (PRTC=.11), eating (PRTC=.11), and doing homework (PRTC=.10). Although two of these variables had negative unconnected correlations with school time—sleeping ($r=-.08$; $p<.01$) and body care ($r=-.05$; $p<.05$)—the uncorrected correlations with eating and with homework were not significantly different from zero. This means that longer school days are, to some extent, in a competitive relation with sleeping and body care. However, given the remaining time after deduction of the school time, these activities have high priority (all PRTCs positively and statistically significant). Clearly, there was reduced priority after long school days for dating, hanging around with friends, working, and other activities (all PRTCs significantly negative).

Because France proved to have especially long school days, we were interested in the correlations between school time and other variables in the French sample alone. As Table 4.6 shows, most uncorrected correlations are negative; the salient exception is going to school. Doing homework also positively correlated with school time, but the correlation was not significant. Doing homework also retained a high relative priority (PRTC). Could it be

TABLE 4.6
Uncorrected and Corrected Correlations Between School Times
(Used As Source in PRTC) and the Remaining Activities in the French Sample

Target Activities	Uncorrected Correlations	Corrected Correlations (PRTCs: School as Source)
Sleeping	−.08	.56**
Body care	−.28**	−.12
Eating meals	−.25**	−.07
Going to and from school	.24**	.33**
Homework	.09	.21**
Music	−.02	.00
Reading	−.22**	−.16*
Sports	−.35**	−.30**
TV	−.17*	−.07
Dating	−.16*	−.13
Hanging around with friends	−.44**	−.39**
Chores	−.30**	−.24**
Shopping	−.25**	−.22**
Working	.02	.02
Else	−.17*	−.16*

*p<.05; **p<.01.

that in our French sample, in addition to the generally long school day, many participants took extra lessons at different locations, possibly in preparation of entrance exams?

All in all, the pattern of PRTCs shows that school interferes rather substantially with all leisure-time activities.

Time spent in school significantly correlated and positively with total degree of reported daily hassles ($r=.08$; $p<.01$), specifically with problems related to school ($r=.12$; $p<.01$), money ($r=.06$; $p<.01$), sports ($r=.05$; $p<.05$), and leisure opportunities ($r=.05$; $p<.05$).

Doing Homework. Time spent on homework was subject to one two-way interaction (age by country) and to two main effects (gender and country). The Age effect was significant in five countries: In Bulgaria, Norway, and Romania, the younger participants spent significantly more time doing homework than did the older participants; in Finland and Poland the reverse was true.

For the older Bulgarians, Norwegians, and Romanians, the variances proved to be very small. Inspection of the frequency distributions showed that in Bulgaria and in Norway, many older adolescents reported having not worked on homework at all, and at the same time in all three countries (Bulgaria, Norway, and Romania), there were fewer older adolescents working very long on their homework compared to the younger participants. Possibly, older adolescents take more liberties in these countries, spending their time on activities rather than homework.

The comparison among countries (see Fig. 4.2) for the younger adolescents showed that Romanians and Bulgarians did more homework than most others (2h53 and 2h17, respectively), whereas Finns did less than most others (0h25 hours). Among the older adolescents, Poland was significantly higher than did most others (2h35), whereas Norway and Finland showed significantly shorter times than did most others (0h45 and 0h58). The figures reported by adolescents in the United States in our study (1h38) were clearly higher than those reported by Timmer et al. (1985)—0h33.

A further interesting finding was that throughout countries and age groups, girls spent significantly more time on homework than did boys—1h44 versus 1h31 per school day.

Correlations with other variables were mostly negative, mainly with sleep, music, sports, shopping and working, and strongest with watching television, dating, and hanging around with friends (Table 3.3). A few significantly positive correlations appeared in the country by age by gender cells in countries with

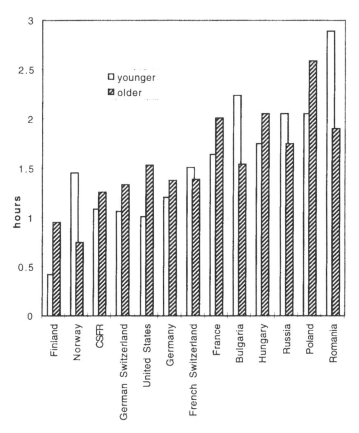

FIG. 4.2. Hours spent on homework in the 13 countries:
younger adolescents and older adolescents.

relatively little homework, that is, Finland, CSFR, Germany, and both Swiss samples (2.24% of all correlations). Possibly, in these countries, extended homework times were not so much a must, but rather an opportunity used by students with broader interests or more resources.

The corrected correlations (Table 3.4) are interesting for two reasons: (a) The correlation between homework and sleep was significantly negative ($r=-.08$; $p<.01$), whereas the corrected correlation (with sleep as target variable) was significantly positive (PRTC=.35; $p<.01$), meaning that long homework times interfered to some extent, with sleep, although sleep kept a very high remaining priority, (b) When homework was the source variable, it positively correlated with necessary activities and negatively with leisure activities—a typical pattern for a necessary source variable. However, when homework was the target variable, it was positively correlated with the necessary source variables, but not with the leisure source variables (Table 3.4). Homework seems to be a necessary activity that may be compressed in the case of extensive leisure activity, much unlike sleep or school.

The overall correlation of homework with well-being was $-.07$ ($p<.01$) and homework correlated at $-.08$ ($p<.01$) with hassles (total score), and was correlated significantly with difficulties related to school ($r=.08$; $p<.01$), peers ($r=.05$; $p<.05$), sports ($r=.10$; $p<.01$), health ($r=.10$; $p<.01$), and leisure opportunities ($r=.12$; $p<.01$). One might speculate that either the amount of homework produced daily hassles or that the daily hassles made students work longer on their homework. However, there is still the possibility that a third factor, such as fragile health, produced both. Homework time, indeed, correlated $r=.10$ with difficulties related to health. Flammer and Tschanz (1997), also, reported a slight positive correlation between homework time and health problems. A closer inspection of the data showed that this correlation was attributable to about 10% of adolescents who spent a great deal of time on homework and had markedly more health problems than average.

Results Related to Family and Home

Two activities related to family and home are examined in this study—chores and shopping.

Working in the Household (Chores). A big majority of adolescents (64%) did not report taking any household work the previous day. However, there were significant differences; the analyses revealed an age by country effect as well as two main effects—gender and country (no gender by country effect!).

Although in Norway, the older adolescents spent significantly more time on chores than did the younger adolescents, the reverse was the case in Hungary and in Poland (the overall age effect was not significant). Girls, in general, spent more time on chores than did boys (0h25 vs. 0h18) which corresponds to the findings reported by Timmer et al. (1985).

Because of the age by country effect, differences between countries were separately examined for each age group. Still, the same pattern emerged in both analyses. Polish adolescents clearly did more for the household than did adolescents in other countries. Among younger adolescents, Poland differed significantly from all Western European countries as well as from Russia, Bulgaria, and the United States. Interestingly, among the younger adolescents, the Eastern and Central European countries clustered together with high scores. Among older adolescents, Poland and CSFR lead with 0h31 and 0h33, respectively. These scores, however, were significantly different only from the lowest ones (both from the French with 0h08, and CSFR from the German with 0h09; see Fig. 4.3).

All significant correlations with chores were negative (Table 3.3: sleep, meals, school, and sports). However, as expected, the PRTCs, with chores

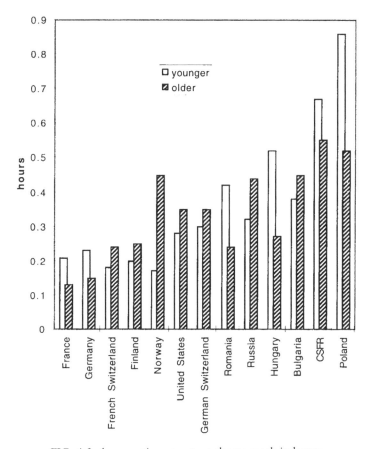

FIG. 4.3. Average time spent on chores work in hours.

as their source, were positive with the necessary activities (except for going to and from school) and around zero for the other activities. When doing chores was the target activity, most correlations were nonsignificant or negative (with meals and with school).

Time spent on chores was not correlated with well-being, but was slightly, positively correlated with hassles (r=.04; p<.05), specifically with problems related to money (r=.07; p<.01), health (r=.06; p<.01), and own room (r=.05; p<.05). Could this indicate that adolescents from poorer families had to do household chores?

Shopping. It is not clear from the outset whether this activity should be regarded as a leisure activity or as a type of household chore. The following results might give us some insight.

There was no three-way interaction as for time spent shopping. However, we found an age by country interaction and an overall gender effect. The interaction was due to age effects in Hungary, Norway, and Romania. Whereas younger adolescents spent more time shopping than did older adolescents in Hungary and Romania, the reverse was true in Norway. The overall significant gender effect was due to the girls' slightly higher scores (.23 in girls vs. .16 in boys).

Given the age by country interaction, pairwise comparisons between countries were separately conducted for each age group. Although the overall country effects were significant in both gender groups, there were no significant pairwise differences. Pooling both age groups, Poland had significantly longer shopping times than did France, Russia, German Switzerland, and Hungary. If shopping was a typical chore, one could have expected the Eastern countries to be higher on this variable, as we found for household chores. If it was a typical leisure activity, the adolescents in the Western countries could have been expected to spend more time on it. There were no such clear differences. Possibly, shopping was understood in both ways, thus balancing out the expected Eastern and Western bias.

The highest negative overall correlations with shopping were produced by time spent in school and by time spent on the way to and from school (Table 3.3). It might be that parents tend to ask their adolescent children to do shopping to the extent that they are free from school attendance. The same is probably true for shopping as a leisure activity: It might often be done after school, especially when classes finish early. A positive correlation with body care (caring for self-appearance as possible mediator) could indicate that shopping can be seen as a leisure activity and a positive correlation with chores may indicate that it could be regarded as a household-related activity. Specific correlational analyses per country were conducted to shed more light on this question. Positive correlations with chores were found only in Poland and Romania. A positive correlation with body care was found only in France.

The PRTCs with shopping as a source activity were positive with sleeping (like most other activities were when used as source activities with sleeping). However, the PRTCs with body care also showed positive relations, possibly stemming from leisure shopping, and with chores, possibly stemming from shopping as a chore (Table 3.4). The PRTCs with shopping as a target variable were significantly negative with the very necessary activities of school and going to and from school, but not with sleep. School-related activities possibly hindered shopping, but long sleeping time did not. However, the PRTCs with shopping as a target were significantly positive with body care and with chores, which again may indicate that shopping can be considered both a leisure-time activity and a chores.

Time used for shopping did not correlate with well-being, but negatively correlated with the subjective experience of hassles ($r=-.05$; $p<.05$). The only single hassle item that correlated significantly (negatively) with shopping time was hassle related to school ($r=-.05$; $p<.05$). This means that those who did much shopping tended to have a good time in school.

Similarities Among Countries

One of the general questions we wanted to examine in this volume was whether there were clear patterns on the country level. As for the daily activities, a few patterns have emerged. For example, in accordance with traditional eating habits, France and Switzerland yielded the longest time spent on meals.

In order to identify some more general clusters of countries, cluster analyses were performed using aggregated means of all activities described in chapters 3 and 4. Given that the gender by country and age by country interactions were mostly ordinal, the analysis was run for all age by gender groups pooled together. The results showed that both parts of Switzerland clustered together at the first step, Norway and Finland formed a cluster with the United States and France was included in the common cluster on the last step only. Also, Bulgaria, Romania, and Poland formed a relatively well-defined cluster. The dendrogram for the cluster pattern (using average linkage between groups; SPSS cluster procedure) is shown in Fig. 4.4.

The patterns are derived from the meaning of the variables included in the analysis. The fact that France did not form any cluster with other countries is mostly due to French adolescents' high scores in using school time, their short trips to school, and so on. Thus, the question arose as to whether the cluster pattern would remain the same when only subgroups of variables were used. One could, for instance, expect France not to be an outsider anymore if the school-related variables were excluded. In order to differentiate the cluster pattern, separate analyses were conducted on the basis of three maintenance variables (sleep, body care, and meals), three school-related variables (time in class, going to school, and doing

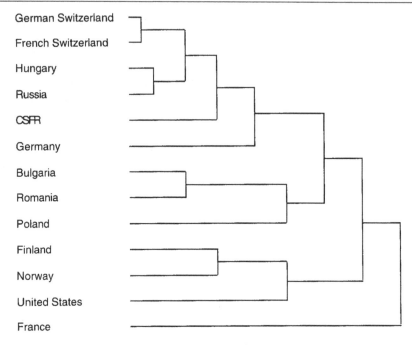

FIG. 4.4. Cluster pattern for the 13 samples using all daily activities.

homework), six leisure-time activities (music, reading, sports, watching television, dating, and hanging around with friends), and the remaining three variables (chores, working, and shopping).

As for maintenance, the French adolescents joined the Swiss ones very early in a clear cluster, possibly due to time spent on meals. The Scandinavian adolescents (Finland and Norway) were together in a broader cluster including also Bulgaria, CSFR, Germany, and Hungary.

As for school-related variables, the French were clearly left alone, thus indicating that the overall pattern was due primarily to these variables. The Swiss adolescents joined CSFR. Also, Bulgaria, Poland, and Romania formed a clear cluster.

In terms of leisure time, both Swiss samples clustered together again and joined a broader group of countries, including France.

As for the remaining variables, the American participants were the outsiders. The Scandinavian participants formed a cluster and joined a group of five countries (Bulgaria, Hungary, Romania, Russia, and the German-speaking part of Switzerland).

Apparently, there is no country cluster that is valid over all activities. We, therefore, try to sum up by pointing to some distinguished single-country patterns. Possibly, the most distinguished pattern was that of the French: longest school days, shortest trips to school, least time spent free reading, and—unexpectedly in terms of cultural clichés—least amount of dating. Finland scored lowest on going to school and doing homework. Poland was highest in household work and body care, but belonged to the lowest in school time and in sleeping time. Bulgaria excelled against all others in watching television and listening to the radio. Contrary to the stereotypes concerning the American lifestyle, it was not the American adolescents, but adolescents from three Eastern European countries, who had the highest scores on watching television and listening to the radio. Is it that Americans often watch television as a parallel activity to others, whereas Europeans tend to do this activity exclusively? The German-speaking part of Switzerland was the leader in time spent on meals, music, and leisure reading. The American adolescents spent much time on sports and body care, but little time on sleep, going to school, and reading. The German adolescents had the highest dating time scores. Both Scandinavian countries, Finland and Norway (for older adolescents only), yielded the lowest times for homework. This may reflect some Scandinavian educational policy. However, Finland and Norway did not form a cluster on the basis of the school-related variables.

DISCUSSION AND CONCLUSION

When the results from the 13 cross-national samples are compared, there seems to be more similarities than dissimilarities in gender and age differences. As noted earlier, there were many interactions between age and gender on one hand and country on the other hand. However, these interactions were mostly ordinal. Nevertheless, these interactions still indicate that significant age or gender differences were found in some samples and not in others. That is, further studies in the different countries would be needed to tell whether the pattern of significant versus nonsignificant differences in the various samples is replicable.

Replication studies would be even more interesting in cases where disordinal interactions were found, for example, in regard to homework in younger and older adolescents. It may be noted here, for instance, that the previous results from the United States (Leone & Richards, 1989) could not be replicated: Older American adolescents in our study did not do more homework than their younger peers.

Are There Universal Gender and Age Differences Over the Samples?

Trying to sum up the results, we found some striking similarities in age and gender effects across the countries. Some of the gender differences fit astonishingly well with gender stereotypes in Western societies. Girls used more time for body care, chores, and shopping, and boys reported doing more sports. These results are in line with Timmer et al.'s (1985) conclusions.

In other words, even if the 13 samples came from countries that possibly vary to a great extent as to their emphasis on the equality of status between men and women (e.g., in terms of occupational and political roles), some aspects of traditional gender roles still seem to be alive in most European countries.

Some additional differences deserve our attention. Girls spent more time on homework and unrequired reading, whereas boys spent more time watching television or listening to the radio. Is this an expression of an overall greater compliance with school requirements in girls than in boys? Or are girls more interested in academic activities than are boys?

As for age effects, most results could be expected. Some of the differences are clearly due to structural factors—e.g., older adolescents had somewhat longer school days and they also needed more time to get to school. Other results reflected general development, for instance, when the older adolescents reported more dating activities and also used more time for body care. In the same sense, younger adolescents slept longer than did their older peers. Another interesting result was that younger adolescents generally spent more time on sports activities than did older adolescents. Given that the older adolescents reported more school-related activities (time in class, going to school, doing homework), one could also consider their lower sports activities as a reflection of simply less time available for sports and not of less interest. Still, the corrected correlations indicate that the amount of time used for sports activities is the result of a clear choice; for example, boys who reported having done more sports, also reported lower priority for dating activities.

As for clusters of countries, a few clusters emerged that we regard as meaningful. The two Swiss samples (French and German) showed a great deal of similarity, and some of the Central and Eastern European countries clustered together on several dimensions.

In sum, our results primarily reflect the overall cultural similarities of the samples, but they also seem to reflect the diversity of lifestyles and traditions that can be observed when traveling through Europe. One may wonder about the differences that could be discovered if 13 samples from different United States states or 13 samples from different Russian areas would have been used.

REFERENCES

Csikszentmihalyi, M., & Larson, R. (1984). *Being adolescent: Conflict and growth in the teenage years*. New York: Basic Books.

Flammer, A., & Tschanz, U. (1997). Ein typischer Schülertag [A typical student's day]. In A. Grob (Ed.), *Kinder und Jugendliche heute: Belastet—überlastet?* [Children and adolescents today: Challenged or strained?] (pp. 53–68). Zürich: Rüegger.

Japanese Finance Ministry. (1980). *White paper on adolescence* (pp. 10–91). Tokyo: Printing Office.

Kirk, R.E. (1982). *Experimental design: Procedures for the behavioral sciences.* San Francisco: Brooks/Cole.

Leone, C.M., & Richards, M.H. (1989). Classwork and homework in early adolescence: The ecology of achievement. *Journal of Youth and Adolescence, 18,* 531–547.

Nirkko, S. (1994). Zeitbudgets von Schülern und Schülerinnen. Eine Studie zum Zeitgebrauch an einem durchschnittlichen Vollschultag [Students' time budgets. A study on time-use on a regular school day]. Master's thesis. University of Berne, Switzerland.

Roniger, C. (1994). Der Zeitgebrauch von Schülern und Schülerinnen. Die Methode des "Yesterday"-Interviews [Students' time-use. The yesterday interview method]. Master's thesis. University of Beme, Switzerland.

Schweizerisches Bundesamt für Statistik [Swiss Office of Statistics]. (1981). *Zeitverwendung in der Schweiz* [Time use in Switzerland]. Berne: Swiss Federal Printing Office.

Tillard, J. (1991). *Le développement personnel et l'intégration sociale des jeunes par les loisirs* [Personal development and social integration of youth through leisure activities]. Rapport numéro 4171 du 14/15 mai 1991 du Conseil économique et social [Report number 4171 (May 14–15, 1991) of the Economic and Social Council]. Paris: Direction des Journaux Officiels.

Timmer, S.G., Eccles, J., & O'Brien, K. (1985). How children use time. In F.T.Juster & F.P. Stafford (Eds.), *Time, goods, and well-being* (pp. 351–381). Ann Arbor: University of Michigan.

Verma, S., & Saraswathi, T.S. (1992). *At the crossroads. Time use by university students.* Chandigarh, India: Department of Child Development, Panjab University.

Williams, R.L., Karacan, I., & Hursch, C.J. (1974). *Electroencephalography (EEG) of human sleep: Clinical applications.* New York: Wiley.

Zuzanek, J. (1980). *Work and leisure in the Soviet Union: A time-budget analysis.* New York: Praeger.

5

Future-Oriented Interests

Jari-Erik Nurmi
University of Jyväskylä, Finland

Aurora Liiceanu
Institute of Psychology, Bucarest, Romania

Hanna Liberska
Adam Mickiewicz University, Poznan, Poland

Adolescent development can be associated with thinking about and preparing for the future (Nurmi, 1991; Poole & Cooney, 1987; Seginer, 1988). It has been suggested that, by becoming interested in their future life and related adult roles, young people direct their own development in their social environment (Nurmi, 1993) and also construct their identity as members of a society (Erikson, 1959; Marcia, 1980). Such thoughts about the future is encouraged by significant others, such as parents, peers, teachers, and society in general.

Future orientation is defined as how people see their own future in terms of interests, hopes, expectations, and concerns (Nurmi, 1991; Nuttin, 1984; Trommsdorff, Burger & Fuchsle, 1982). Two major methodological approaches have been applied in this research area (see Nurmi, 1991). In the most frequent approach, future interests have been investigated by asking people in an open-ended manner what kind of goals, hopes, and concerns they have for the future. These responses are then typically analyzed according to the life domain they concern, such as education, occupation, family, and leisure activities (Mehta, Rohila, Sundberg & Tyler, 1972; Nurmi, 1987). Another approach is to ask people to rate how important certain life domains are for their future life. In this case, they are provided with a list of topics that they are asked to evaluate on a rating scale according to their importance. This approach was used in this research for two reasons. First, as earlier research has shown, it is possible to define the topics in which the majority of adolescents living in various contexts are interested (for a review see Nurmi, 1991). Second, a structured type of rating scale seems to be a much easier way of investigating future orientation in a large cross-cultural study.

It has been suggested that adolescents construct future-oriented interests by considering their individual motives (Nurmi, 1991; Nuttin, 1984) in the context of their view of what the future realistically may hold (Seginer, 1988) and their perceptions of future possibilities (Poole & Cooney, 1985). Consequently, the major age-related demands, norms, and opportunities of specific societal and cultural environments have been suggested as playing an important role in the construction of future-oriented interests because they provide a basis for anticipating what is truly possible, acceptable, and desirable at different ages (Nurmi, 1993). These age-graded demands and options have been described in various terms, such as developmental tasks (Havighurst, 1948, 1974), social constraints (Neugarten, Moore, & Lowe, 1965), and institutional careers (Mayer, 1986). Earlier studies have shown that a majority of adolescents' future-oriented interests and goals reflect the major developmental tasks and institutional transitions of their own age, such as those related to education, future career, family, and leisure activities (e.g., Nurmi, 1989; Seginer, 1992). Similar results have been found across several Western types of society (e.g., Nurmi, Poole & Seginer, 1995; for a review, see Nurmi, 1991).

Although acquiring a good education, becoming socialized into occupational life, and finding an intimate relationship are among the major normative tasks across various societies, it may be assumed that differences in other types of cultural and societal factors may also cause variation in adolescents' future interests. For example, religious beliefs, gender roles, standards of living, and career opportunities that vary across countries might be expected to produce differences in the ways young people see their future and how they direct their lives. Although a few cross-cultural studies have been carried out on adolescents' future interests, the majority of them involved Western-type countries (for a review, see Nurmi, 1991). For this reason, we decided to include adolescents' future-oriented interests in this study.

We assumed that an analysis of the interests of adolescents growing up in different parts of Europe would provide the possibility to examine the role of various cultural, societal, and institutional factors in the development of adolescents' future interests. In particular, we expected the former West-East political split to account for differences on several levels. This assumption was made for several reasons. First, although the former socialist countries have entered a new era of free markets and private economy, their former history and recent changes in their societies, institutions, and economies might be expected to create a different Zeitgeist, and also different opportunities, compared with the relatively stable developments in Western Europe. Second, the standard of living in the former socialist countries is still lower than that in most Western countries. Third, the rate of urbanization and related social development might be expected to be lower in the eastern parts of Europe. Therefore, the social values and cultural beliefs in Eastern European countries may be more traditional than in Western Europe. Some of the recent developments in these countries, such as the increasingly important role of the church and religion, may have even strengthened these differences during recent years (see also Nurmi, 1998).

There are also other cultural factors that vary across European countries. One major difference is based on religion. Europe is divided into the Protestant North, the Catholic South and the Catholic and Protestant Centre. Moreover, the Orthodox church has a strong influence in some of the countries of the former socialist block, such as Romania and Bulgaria. These differences can also be assumed to be reflected in adolescents' interests concerning the future (Nurmi, 1998).

Recent research on future orientation has shown that, in addition to culture and society, there are at least two major factors—gender and age—that seem to influence adolescents' thinking about the future (see Nurmi, 1991). For example, girls have been found to be more interested in future family- and marriage-related topics than have boys (Gillies, Elmwood, & Hawtin, 1985; Solantaus, 1987). However, the extent to which boys are more interested in education and career-related topics seems to vary across cultures. For example, Solantaus (1987) found that boys and girls in Finland did not differ in their hopes and worries concerning work and career, as did boys and girls in Austria and Great Britain. It has also been suggested that gender differences in adolescent future interests are larger in traditional types of society than in more urban ones (Sundberg, Poole, & Tyler, 1983). Consequently, we were interested in examining the extent to which there are gender differences in adolescents' future-oriented interests, and whether these vary across cultures. Earlier research also seems to suggest that adolescents become more interested in the developmental tasks of their own age, such as education, career, and family (see Nurmi, 1991) as they become older. To take account of these differences, age was also included in our analyses.

To investigate the role of these cultural and societal factors, we compared the future-oriented interests of the adolescents from all 11 European countries and the United States who participated in the Euronet study. Even though the United States basically has a similar type of society to that of Western Europe, there are some interesting differences, such as those related to their role as a super power and the relatively low level of social welfare. The adolescents' future interests were examined by asking them to rate the personal importance of several domains of future life, such as career, success (in terms of fame and money), family, social responsibility, and leisure activities.

METHOD

The participants filled in the Future Interests scale as the first part of the larger questionnaire. The instructions were as follows: "When you think about the future, what do you consider as being important to you? Please rate the following topics according to whether they are (4) very important,

(3) somewhat important, (2) not really important and (1) not important at all." Fourteen topics were included.

A first analysis showed that there were differences between countries in the extent to which adolescents rated the importance of all 14 items (sum total of the 14 items, $F(12,2939)=34.94$, $p<.001$). This difference in the general importance ratings may be due to cultural habits in responding to rating scales. In this study, however, our major aim was to examine the relative importance of an individual item compared with all the other items. Therefore, the following transformation was carried out for each item: First, the importance of each individual item was standardized within each of the 13 samples by taking into account the mean level of the importance ratings across all the 14 items. Second, the score for each individual item was subtracted from the mean score for all the 14 items within each cultural sample and then divided by the standard deviation of this score. In order to change this score back to a 4-point scale, it was multiplied by the standard deviation of the mean of all the 14 items for all 13 samples and added to the mean. All this resulted in standardized scores that measured the relative importance of a specific topic compared with the overall ratings of all the 14 topics. We expected that the use of these types of standardized scores would decrease the impact of cultural response patterns and differences in the exact meaning of the four response alternatives, which may differ across languages. Thus, in further analyses, the focus was on the relative importance of a specific future interest compared with all the topics rated by the participants. To decrease the number of variables in the subsequent analyses, and to increase their reliability, five indices were constructed:

The importance of career index included two items indicating how important education ("Getting a good education") and occupation ("Acquiring a good profession") in the future were for the participants. A high score was presumed to measure a realistic career orientation. The Cronbach alpha for this scale was .43 for the whole sample and ranged between .14 and .67 across the 13 samples (*Median alpha*= .39).

The importance of being successful was measured by 3 items indicating how important money ("Earning much money"), fame ("Becoming famous"), and professionalism ("Becoming important professionally") were. A high sum score was assumed to measure an unrealistic type of orientation toward future adult roles. The Cronbach alpha for this scale was. 59 for the whole sample, and ranged between .39 and .70 across the 13 samples (*Median alpha=.55*).

The importance of family was measured by two items including the importance of marriage ("Getting married/living permanently with a partner") and children ("Having children") in adolescents' thinking about the future. The Cronbach alpha for this scale was .68 for the whole sample and ranged between .50 and .84 across 13 the samples (*Median alpha=.69*).

The importance of social responsibility was measured by two items indicating the extent to which adolescents emphasized social responsibility related to their own country ("Being useful to my country") and their parents ("Taking responsibility for my parents") in the future. The Cronbach alpha for this scale was .45 for the whole sample, and ranged between .29 and .58 across the 13 samples (*Median alpha=.45*).

The importance of social pleasure was measured by three items, indicating the extent to which social leisure activities ("Having a good time with my friends"), peer relationships ("Being liked by other people"), and vacations ("Enjoying my vacations and leisure time") were important for the participants in the future. The Cronbach alpha for this scale was .38 for the whole sample, and ranged between .26 and .61 across the samples (*Median alpha=.51*).

The fact that the reliabilities for the importance of career and the importance of social responsibility scales were low for some individual samples in particular (e.g., interest in career among French-speaking Swiss adolescents, $\alpha=.14$; and social responsibility among German-speaking Swiss adolescents; $\alpha=.29$), is partly due to the number of items in the five scales. This should be taken into account in the interpretation of the results. Because there was only one item concerning the importance of health in the future, this was omitted from further analyses.

RESULTS

In addition to variations in future-oriented interests across the different countries, we were also interested in the extent to which boys and girls showed different interests and whether these gender differences varied across the countries. In order to control for the biased sampling with respect to age (see chap. 2, this volume), age was entered as a covariate. Thus, to test the country- and gender-related differences, two-way analyses of covariance—including country and gender as independent variables and age as a covariate—were carried out. This was done separately for the five indexes described earlier. There were also minor differences in the numbers of boys and girls in the different countries (see chap. 2, this volume). To take this into account, the treatment populations were expected to be equal in size, and the method of unweighted means was therefore applied in the analyses of covariance (Myers, 1979). Moreover, pairwise comparisons between the 13 samples were carried out using Tukey's HSD procedure.

Career

The results showed a statistically significant main effect for age ($F(1, 3207)=51.58$, $p<.001$) as a covariate: Surprisingly, the older adolescents rated career as less important for their future than did the younger ones ($\beta=-.13$). Moreover, there was a significant main effect for country ($F(12,$

3207)=13.15, $p<.001$). There were no effects for gender and no country by gender interaction.

The means, their rank-order, and the standard deviations for the adolescents' interest in a future career in the 13 samples are presented in Table 5.1. The results showed a clear pattern distinguishing the countries. Adolescents from the Western European countries (French Switzerland, Germany, Norway, German Switzerland, and Finland), and from the United States, showed more interest in a future career than did young people from Eastern Europe (Poland, Hungary, and Rumania). The countries that did not differ statistically significantly from those just mentioned were Russia, the Czech Republic, Bulgaria, and France.

Becoming Successful

There was also a statistically significant main effect for age $(F(1, 3209)=14.68$, $p<.001$) on the importance of becoming successful: the older adolescents rated success as less important for their future life $((\beta=-.07)$ than did the younger ones. Moreover, there was a statistically significant main effect for

Table 5.1

*The Means (M), Standard Deviations (SD), and Tukey's Paired Comparisons
for the Importance of a Career and Being Successful in 13 Countries*

Country	Career				Being Successful			
	Order[1]	M	SD	Tukey's Comparison[2]	Order[1]	M	SD	Tukey's Comparison[2]
Western Europe								
Finland	5	3.80	.32	a	9	2.50	.66	b, c
France	9	3.74	.49	a, b	7	2.63	.59	b, c
Germany	2	3.84	.35	a	8	2.57	.69	b, c
Norway	3	3.82	.43	a	11	2.49	.64	b, c
French Switzerland	1	3.87	.37	a	11	2.49	.61	b, c
German Switzerland	4	3.81	.50	a	13	2.44	.66	c
Eastern Europe								
Bulgaria	10	3.72	.49	a, b	3	2.96	.66	a
CSFR	8	3.75	.55	a, b	6	2.66	.65	b
Hungary	12	3.59	.40	c	9	2.50	.68	b, c
Poland	13	3.57	.37	c	2	2.97	.59	a
Rumania	11	3.65	.45	b, c	1	3.07	.61	a
Russia	7	3.79	.51	a, b	5	2.88	.59	a
Non-Europeans								
United States	5	3.80	.45	a	4	2.95	.65	a

[1]Decreasing order according to the mean.
[2]Group means with a different letter showed statistically significant differences $(p<.05)$ when tested using Tukey's HSD procedure.

gender ($F(1, 3209)= 63.15, p<.001$): Boys ($M=2.76, SD=.67$) emphasized the importance of becoming successful more than did girls ($M=2.58, SD=.69$).

The main effect for country ($F(12, 3209)=32.02, p<.001$) was also statistically significant. A comparison of the 13 samples (Table 5.1) showed that there was, again, a clear distinction between them in how important the adolescents rated success in their future life. This time, however, those from Eastern Europe (Rumania, Poland, Bulgaria, and Russia) and the United States showed more interest in success, when indicated in terms of fame, money, and professionalism, than those from the Western European countries (German Switzerland, French Switzerland, Norway, Finland, Germany, and France). Adolescents from Hungary and the Czech Republic were similar in this respect to those from Western Europe.

Family

There was no main effect for age as to interest in a future family. However, the main effects for country ($F(12, 3202)=8.53, p<.001$) and gender ($F(1, 3202)= 24.70, p<.001$), as well as their interaction ($F(12, 3202)=3.49, p<.001$), were statistically significant. Separate one-way analyses of variance by country were carried out separately for boys and girls, in addition to paired comparisons using the Tukey HSD procedure. These results showed statistically significant main effects for country among both girls ($F(12, 1662)=8.62, p<.001$) and boys ($F(12, 1555)=3.61, p<.001$). Moreover, one-way analyses of variance were carried out separately for all 13 countries (samples), comparing boys' and girls' interest in a future family. All these results are presented in Table 5.2.

The results showed first that, in most countries, either girls rated a family as being more important than did boys or there was no gender difference. The only exception was that Romanian boys showed more interest in this domain than did Romanian girls. Another interesting pattern was that girls from Eastern Europe, in particular, showed greater interest in a future family than boys: Girls from Hungary, the Czechoslovakian Federal Republic, Russia, and Poland considered a family to be more important for their future life than did boys. In Western Europe, girls and boys differed only in Germany, where the girls showed more interest.

Social Responsibility

Furthermore, the results showed that there was a statistically significant main effect for age ($F(1, 3201)=58.31, p<.001$) on the importance of social responsibility: The older adolescents rated responsibility concerning their own country and parents as being less important for their future life ($\beta=-.13$) than did the younger ones. Moreover, there was a statistically significant main effect for country ($F(12, 3201 =19.16, p<.001$).

Table 5.2

The Means (M), Standard Deviations (SD) and Tukey's Paired Comparisons for the Importance of a Family for Boys and Girls in 13 Countries

Country	Boys				Girls					
	Order	M	SD	Tukey's Comparison[1]	Order	M	SD	Tukey's Comparison[1]	F^2	p
Western Europe										
Finland	6	3.16	.64	a, b, c	5	3.31	.75	a, b, c	2.37	ns
France	4	3.24	.79	a, b, c	3	3.39	.67	a, b	1.89	ns
Germany	10	2.97	.76	b, c	7	3.27	.88	a, b, c	8.17	.005
Norway	2	3.25	.73	a, b	8	3.26	.81	a, b, c	.01	ns
French Switzerland	3	3.23	.73	a, b, c	5	3.31	.76	a, b, c	.55	ns
German Switzerland	13	2.90	.84	c	12	3.05	.84	c, d	1.86	ns
Eastern Europe										
Bulgaria	5	3.18	.70	a, b, c	10	3.12	.68	b, c, d	.35	ns
CSFR	8	3.75	.55	a, b	6	2.66	.65	b	1.78	ns
Hungary	1	3.28	.82	a	2	3.51	.66	a	2.43	.001
Poland	10	2.97	.85	b, c	9	3.18	.74	b, c, d	3.51	.060
Rumania	7	3.15	.67	a, b, c	13	2.88	.72	e	8.14	.005
Russia	12	2.94	.81	b, c	4	3.35	.59	a, b, c	5.42	.001
Non-Europeans										
United States	9	3.04	.85	b, c	11	3.10	.86	b, c, d	.28	ns

Note. ns=not significant at .05 level.

[1]Group means with a different letter showed statistically significant differences (p<.05) when tested using Tukey's HSD procedure.

[2]F for one-way analysis of variance comparing boys and girls within each country.

Comparison among the 13 samples (Table 5.3) showed that there was a clear distinction between Eastern and Western European adolescents: Youths from Eastern Europe (Poland, Hungary, Bulgaria, and Romania), and the United States emphasized the importance of social responsibility more than those from Western European countries (French Switzerland, France, Germany, and German Switzerland). This time, Finland, Norway, the Czech Republic, and Russia were situated between these two extreme groups.

Social Pleasure

The main effect for age ($F(1,3208)=9.54$, $p<.01$) on the importance of social pleasure was statistically significant: The older adolescents rated this domain as being more important than did the younger ones (($\beta=.06$). Moreover, the main effect for gender was also statistically significant ($F(1,3208)=44.02$, $p<.001$): Overall, girls seemed to value social pleasure more than boys.

TABLE 5.3

The Means (M), Standard Deviations (SD) and Tukey's Paired Comparisons or the Importance of Social Responsibility and Social Pleasure in 13 Countries

Country	Social Responsibility				Social Pleasure			
	Order[1]	M	SD	Tukey's Comparison[2]	Order[1]	M	SD	Tukey's Comparison[2]
Western Europe								
Finland	8	2.95	.63	c, d	6	3.31	.52	a, b, c
France	12	2.69	.75	f	3	3.38	.53	a, b, c
Germany	11	2.81	.72	e, f	5	3.32	.55	a, b, c
Norway	6	3.09	.66	a, b, c	4	3.34	.58	a, b, c
French Switzerland	13	2.64	.63	f	1	3.49	.59	a
German Switzerland	10	2.91	.67	d, e	2	3.44	.55	a, b
Eastern Europe								
Bulgaria	3	3.14	.61	a, b	10	3.08	.59	d, e
CSFR	7	3.06	.66	b, c, d	9	3.23	.52	c, d
Hungary	2	3.19	.71	a, b	8	3.28	.58	c
Poland	1	3.28	.52	a	11	3.10	.57	d, e
Rumania	5	3.13	.70	a, b	12	3.11	.56	d, e
Russia	9	2.94	.70	c, d	7	3.29	.56	b, c
Non-Europeans								
United States	3	3.14	.69	a, b	13	3.03	.58	e

[1]Decreasing order according to the mean.
[2]Group means with a different letter showed statistically significant differences ($p<.05$) when tested using Tukey's HSD procedure.

The results further showed that the main effects for country ($F(12,3208)=$ 14.39, $p<.001$) were statistically significant. There was a clear distinction between Western and Eastern European adolescents: Youths from Western European countries (French and German Switzerland, France, Norway, Germany, and Finland) emphasized the importance of social pleasure more than those from Eastern Europe (Romania, Poland, and Bulgaria) and the United States.

However, the results showed that the country by gender interaction was also statistically significant ($F(12,3202)=3.12$, $p<.001$). This interaction was mainly due to the fact that although the results for boys were similar to those reported for the whole sample, there were two exceptions for the girls: Hungarian and Russian girls valued social pleasure relatively highly and yielded the third and fourth highest means on this variable, just behind German-Swiss and French-Swiss girls.

DISCUSSION AND CONCLUSION

The aim of this chapter was to examine the extent to which adolescents' future-oriented interests differ in 11 European countries and the United States. Consequently, we were interested in finding out what types of cultural and societal features might provide explanations for the cross-cultural differences in adolescent thinking. Overall, the results showed a clear distinction between the future interests of Western and Eastern European adolescents. Interestingly, in most cases, North American youths were more similar to those from Eastern rather than Western Europe.

First, youths from the Western European countries, and in this case, also from the United States, showed more interest in their future education and career than did young people from Eastern Europe. Moreover, Western European adolescents emphasized the importance of social pleasure types of activity and vacation more than youths from Eastern Europe and the United States. This pattern was clearer among boys than girls. In contrast, adolescents from Eastern Europe, and also from the United States, showed more interest in becoming successful in the future in terms of fame, money, and professionalism, than did youths from the Western European countries. Similarly, youths from Eastern Europe, and again from the United States, emphasized the importance of taking responsibility for their parents and being useful for their country, more so than those from the Western European countries. In all cases, adolescents from the Czech Republic were somewhere between the Western and Eastern Europeans.

These results suggest that even though the adolescents in Western Europe emphasized the importance of leisure-time and social activities, it seems that this does not decrease their interest in a future education and occupation. Thus, they seemed to be able to orient themselves simultaneously toward leisure activities, education, and career as being important aspects of their socialization into adult life. The finding that adolescents from Western Europe perceived education and a career to be important for their future, but did not emphasize the importance of becoming rich, famous, and professional, as did *Eastern European youths,* suggests that they have a relatively more realistic attitude toward their future. This type of future orientation also seems to fit well with the normative expectations of parents, and society in general, who usually emphasize the importance of education as the way to a future occupation and major adult roles.

In turn, youths living in Eastern Europe seem to emphasize earning a lot of money, becoming famous, and becoming an important professional as a part of their future. One explanation for this might be that the rapid change to a free-market and capitalist economy has created a new type of Eastern European dream, which is then reflected in unrealistic types of attitudes toward future adulthood. Interestingly, American adolescents seemed to emphasize the importance of similar types of interest in their future life. Another explanation may be that the current situation in Eastern Europe provides more models of people who have been able to create fame and wealth within a relatively short period of time, and this may be reflected in adolescents' thoughts about their own future. Finally, it is possible that in Eastern Europe, which is going through a process of rapid change into a capitalist and free-market economy, this type of attitude is interpreted as part of the new society, modeling the American dream, which does not apply in Western Europe.

Adolescents from Eastern Europe and the United States also seemed to emphasize the importance of taking responsibility for their parents and being useful to their country more than did their Western age mates. Again, several explanations are possible. First, the high level of interest in social responsibility among Eastern European youths is based on more traditional types of values that are no longer current in Western Europe. A second explanation is that in Eastern European countries, the socioeconomic situation emphasizes the importance of these types of future goals. Third, growing nationalism in the Eastern European countries, and possibly also the instability of the geopolitical situation, may strengthen the importance of the issues related to being useful to one's own country.

In fact, similar types of features in the United States may explain some of the similarities between American adolescents and those living in Eastern Europe. The level of social welfare is lower in the United States than in Western Europe. Moreover, a certain kind of patriotism may arise from the fact that the United States has been one of the two super powers for the last 50 years.

However, there are a few reasons for not ending with too simple interpretations of the results. First, one must keep in mind that, despite the differences, in all countries, the adolescents rated career-related issues as being most important for their future; this was followed by issues related to a future family. These results, suggesting that adolescents' future-oriented interests reflect the major age-graded developmental tasks of their own age, are also similar to earlier research findings (Nurmi, 1991). In other domains of life, the cultural differences in future interests were larger.

Second, although some of the results showed a clear distinction between Eastern and Western Europe, there were also exceptions. In nearly all of the comparisons, adolescents from the Czech Republic were situated somewhere between those from Western and Eastern Europe. This is understandable from the historical point of view, because before the period of socialism Czechoslovakia was among the most industrialized and urbanized countries in Europe. This may explain some of the similarities with Western Europe. In a number of the cases, the Russian adolescents did not differ from the Western Europeans either. One possible explanation for this may be that the Russian sample represented youths from the Moscow metropolitan area rather than from rural Russia. Also interesting is that French adolescents showed less interest in a future career and more so in becoming successful when compared with adolescents in other Western European countries. This may be due to the special features of the French educational system and how it influences entrance into the social hierarchy. The system is based on relatively complex tracking on the basis of mathematical competence from early school years, quite unlike the Scandinavian system, for example (Motola, Guichard, & Sinisalo, 1998). Because pupils' competence in early school years is emphasized, this decreases their possibilities for independent choice later on, which may decrease their interest in thinking about a future career.

There were also evident gender differences, even though some of these seemed to vary across the countries. For example, boys emphasized the importance of becoming successful in terms of wealth and fame more than girls. These results are similar to those found earlier, suggesting that boys seem to be more interested in material aspects of life than do girls (Gillispie & Allport, 1955; Solantaus, 1987). On the other hand, in most of the countries investigated, girls seemed to value social pleasure and vacations more than did boys. Earlier research findings have shown cross-cultural variation in these gender differences. For example, Nurmi et al. (1995) found that Australian boys were more interested in leisure activities than girls, whereas the reverse was true in Israel.

Another interesting pattern was that girls from Eastern Europe showed more interest in a future family than did boys, whereas there were no gender differences in Western countries, including the United States. The only exceptions were Germany, where the girls were also more interested in the family than were boys, and Romania, where boys showed more interest than did girls. The lack of gender differences in Western Europe and the United States may reflect the more egalitarian pattern of gender roles developed in these countries in recent decades. On the other hand, the results for Eastern European countries may reflect more traditional roles, which have been suggested to have strengthened recently due to changes to more traditional cultural and religious values.

In this chapter, adolescents' future-oriented interests were compared across 11 European countries and the United States. The results showed both similarities and differences in young people's thinking about the future. First, in all countries, they seemed to emphasize the importance of future education, career, and family to a great extent. This suggests that their future-oriented interests reflect the anticipation of major adult roles in society, which do not vary much across the societies included in this study. The results also fit well with earlier findings on adolescents' future orientation (Nurmi, 1991), as well as theories of identity formation (Erikson, 1959) and self-definition (Nurmi, 1993). In turn, they also suggest that Western and Eastern European adolescents seem to differ in future-oriented interests in several ways. Western Europeans seemed to emphasize the importance of education, career, leisure activities, and traveling. In contrast, the Eastern Europeans seemed to stress becoming rich, famous, and professional, and the importance of taking responsibility for their parents and being useful to their country.

Overall, the fact that there were major differences between Western and Eastern European adolescents' thoughts about the future suggests that the sociocultural environments related to the current economic and political situation play an important role in young people's lives (see also Nurmi, 1998). It also suggests that more emphasis should be given to the examination of the role of the sociocultural environment in adolescent development.

REFERENCES

Erikson, E.H. (1959). *Identity and the life cycle*. New York: International Universities Press.

Gillies, P., Elmwood, J.M., & Hawtin, P. (1985). Anxieties in adolescents about employment and war. *British Medical Journal, 291*, 383.

Gillispie, J.M., & Allport, G.W. (1955). *Youth's outlook on the future (a cross-national study)*, New York: Doubleday.

Havighurst, R.J. (1974). *Developmental tasks and education* (3rd ed.). New York: McKay (Original work published 1948).

Marcia, J.E. (1980). Identity in adolescence. In J.Adelson (Ed.), *Handbook of adolescent psychology* (pp. 159–187). New York: Wiley.

Mayer, K.U. (1986). Structural constraints on the life course. *Human Development, 29*,163–170.

Mehta, P.H., Rohila, P.K., Sundberg, N.D., & Tyler, L.E. (1972). Future time perspective of adolescents in India and the United States. *Journal of Cross-Cultural Psychology, 3*,293–302.

Motola, M., Guichard, J., & Sinisalo, P. (1998). Social habits and future plans. A comparison of adolescent future projects in Finland and France. In J.E.Nurmi (Ed.), *Adolescents, cultures, and conflicts. Growing up in contemporary Europe*, (pp. 43–74). New York: Garland.

Myers, J.L. (1979). *Fundamentals of experimental design*. Boston: Allyn & Bacon.

Neugarten, B.L., Moore, J.W., & Lowe, J.C. (1965). Age norms, age constraints, and adult socialization. *American Journal of Sociology, 70*, 710–717.

Nurmi, J.-E. (1987). Age, sex, social class, and quality of family interaction as determinants of adolescents' future orientation: A developmental task interpretation. *Adolescence, 22*, 977–991.

Nurmi, J.-E. (1989). Development of orientation to the future during early adolescence: A four-year longitudinal study and two cross-sectional comparisons. *International Journal of Psychology, 24*, 195–214.

Nurmi, J.-E. (1991). How do adolescents see their future? A review of the development of future orientation and planning. *Developmental Review, 11*, 1–59.

Nurmi, J.-E. (1993). Adolescent development in an age-graded context: The role of personel beliefs, goals, and strategies in the tackling of developmental tasks and standards. *International Journal of behavioral Development, 16*, 169–189.

Nurmi, J.E. (1998). Growing up in contemporary Europe: An overview. In J.E.Nurmi (Ed.), *Adolescents, cultures and conflicts. Growing up in contemporary Europe* (pp. 3–20). New York: Garland.

Nurmi, J.-E., Poole, M.E. & Seginer, R. (1995). Tracks and transitions—A comparison of adolescent future-oriented goals, explorations and commitments in Australia, Israel and Finland. *International Journal of Psychology, 30*, 355–375.

Nuttin, J.R. (1984). *Motivation, planning, and action. A relational theory of behavior dynamics.* Hillsdale, NJ: Lawrence Erlbaum Associates.

Poole, M.E., & Cooney, G.H. (1985). Cultural differences in the exploration of career and leisure possibilities by adolescents in Australia and Singapore. *Australian Journal of Education, 29*, 249–265.

Poole, M.E., & Cooney, G.H. (1987). Orientations to the future: A comparison of adolescents in Australia and Singapore. *Journal of Youth and Adolescence, 16*, 129–151.

Seginer, R. (1988). Adolescents facing the future. Cultural and sociopolitical perspectives. *Youth and Society, 79*,314–333.

Seginer, R. (1992). Future orientation: Age-related differences among adolescent females. *Journal of Youth and Adolescence, 21*, 421–437.

Solantaus, T. (1987). Hopes and worries of young people in three European countries. *Health Promotion, 2*, 19–27.

Sundberg, N.D., Poole, M.E., & Tyler, L.E.(1983). Adolescents' expectations of future events. A cross-cultural study of Australians, Americans, and Indians. *International Journal of Psychology, 18*,415–427.

Trommsdorff, G., Burger, C., & Fuchsle, T. (1982). Social and psychological aspects of future orientation. In M.Irle (Ed.), *Studies in decision making* (pp. 167–194). Berlin: de Gruyter.

6

Macrosocial Context and Adolescents' Perceived Control

Alexander Grob
August Flammer
University of Berne, Switzerland

In recent years, sociopolitical changes have affected and still affect many parts of the world. From a Western perspective, the most extensive and important changes at the end of the 20th century have been the transitions in the Eastern and Central European countries toward democracy and a free market. Living in different macrosocial contexts provides subjects more or less individual degrees of freedom. These degrees of freedom can be used for the control of one's life conditions and one's development in personal, professional, and social respects. It may be expected that the political and economic changes—we call them *macrosocial changes*—in the Eastern and Central European countries have influenced, possibly enlarged, the individual degrees of freedom. Furthermore, it is expected that young people are especially responsive to these changes and correspondingly perceive more personal control.

Perceived control, as it is measured in psychology, originates from a sequence of processes on three levels (Flammer, 1995). The first is the level of *actual control* (controlling). The second is the level of the *subjective representation* of control (perceived control). The third level is the *translation* of this representation to a *communicative form.*

The first level—actual control or controlling—means regulating certain processes, specifically the attainment, the maintenance, or the avoidance of certain states of affairs. There is no doubt that certain people have more control in some domains than do other people. As people are more or less aware of these individual differences, they should be reflected in communicated personal control beliefs. Being in control of certain states of affairs presupposes at least two things: real causal relations between specific means and specific goals and the availability of such means to the given actor (Bandura, 1977; Flammer, 1990; Skinner, 1995; Skinner, Chapman, & Baltes, 1988).

The second level—perceived control—is the subjective representation of control. In order to believe in one's own control or in one's own noncontrol, people must typically be aware of their own former successes or failures. Although most control beliefs are rooted in personal control experiences, some may also originate from other people's feedback. Still another (relatively rare) possibility stems from the observation of comparable others (Bandura, 1977; Flammer, & Grob, 1994; Wicki, Reber, Flammer & Grob, 1994). However, there is no doubt that perceived control does not always exactly represent actual control. Many studies have shown that people generally overestimate their control competencies (Alloy & Abramson, 1982; Langer, 1975; Taylor & Brown, 1988).

The third level—measuring control beliefs—means translating the mental representation of one's control (Level 2) into a public form. In most cases, control is not an all or none process; people may have more or less control. When such beliefs are to be indicated through a rating scale, it is not at all evident how much control is meant by labels such as "average" or "very much." Typically, people compare their control with what they wish or what they judge to be normal or average for their age, life situation, or macrosocial context.

If one compares perceived control of people in different macrosocial contexts, it is worthwhile to consider possible differences on all three levels. For instance, it can be that certain things like the attainment of a given degree of schooling or the availability of professional careers are very much left to the individual control of the adolescents in some social systems but not in others. It also could be that people in some countries have ample opportunity to acquire important competencies such as foreign languages or knowledge about different kinds of professional lives, whereas they barely have such opportunities in other countries. This corresponds to level 1.

Concerning Level 2, it could be that success and failure and their conditions are very much a public concern for socialization in one country but not in another (e.g., how to acquire and keep good friends; Skinner, 1990). Also, certain social contexts encourage personal beliefs in control even beyond actual acquired levels of control, whereas others keep children's or adolescents' control beliefs at as realistic a level as possible (Oettingen, 1995). As for Level 3, one can imagine that certain cultures encourage their members to indicate more positive characteristics about oneself, whereas in other countries it is a social norm to be modest and to present oneself in an understated manner (Flammer et al., 1995; Weisz, Rothbaum, & Blackburn, 1984).

The Euronet data were not planned a priori to test hypotheses related to these three levels, but descriptive data that were collected can be used to investigate these perspectives. Three life domains were investigated: perceived control over personality development, perceived control over future workplace, and perceived control over subject matter to be learned in school. As for Level 1, we know that before the fall of the Iron Curtain, actual individual control was relatively restricted in all three areas in the former socialist countries (Oettingen, 1995). One might expect that things would have changed after the political change, but it is not very likely that actual individual control would have drastically changed within such a short time. Several external conditions have to be restructured first, for example, curricula, school organizations, teachers' attitudes, the apprenticeship system, the opening of the economy to a real market, and so on. With reference to Level 1, therefore, we expected that adolescents from the Eastern countries would have lower levels of control than did adolescents in the Western countries in public domains, but not necessarily in the private domains.

However, one could also argue that the changing context of the adolescents living in former socialist countries might have prepared a shift in the direction of enhanced control. Even if little time had passed since the political changes—notably, our investigation was carried out in 1992—many of the Eastern and Central European countries found themselves in the middle of dramatic changes in their systems. Therefore, one might expect that adolescents were faced with new conditions that were very similar to those of their Western peers. If this assumption holds true, one would expect no differences in control with respect to the adolescents' social context (Level 1).

The speculations about Level 2 lead to another hypothesis with regard to the adolescents' perceived control. If we assume that individuals reliably compare their actual situation with their former living conditions, they might enthusiastically overestimate their recent increase in control and therefore attribute to themselves more control in public domains than their Western peers, while remaining comparable in their control of private affairs.

On Level 3, we did not expect large differences among the studied countries, at least not between the European countries, except that differences in Level 1 and Level 2 should be reflected in Level 3. However, it seemed worthwhile to relate individual scores on personal control to the size of the country of origin. The reason for this is that a possible historical consequence of nationalistic thinking in Europe would be that those people from larger countries felt stronger and more in control than those from smaller countries. This would be a kind of spill-over from identification with their own country.

DOMAINS AND DIMENSIONS OF PERCEIVED CONTROL

Domain-specific assessments of perceived control are better predictors of domainrelevant outcomes than are general measures of perceived control. The literature that addresses this question concludes that at the very least, the number of persons involved in the control behavior context is important; the type and possibility of effective control behavior varies as a function of this dimension (Flammer, Grob, & Lüthi, 1989; Schneewind, 1995). The Euronet study covers three different control situations—personality development, future workplace, and school subjects. We consider the first as covering a private domain, the third a public domain, and the second to be in between.

All three of these domains are considered from two perspectives—control expectancy and control appraisal (Grob, Flammer, & Wearing, 1995). *Control expectancy* refers to the degree to which an individual believes that she or he can personally affect an outcome, independent of the specific actions that may be required. *Control appraisal,* on the other hand, reflects the relevance or importance of the specific task for the person.

Moreover, we not only asked subjects to rate the degree of personal control in absolute terms, but also in relative terms (i.e., as compared to peers in the same social and national context). It was expected that even in cases where the Eastern and Central European adolescents believed they had less control than their Western peers, they might still attribute to themselves more control relative to their own peers.

METHOD

The items addressing adolescents' perceived control were selected from the *Berne Questionnaire on Adolescents' Perception of Control* (Flammer, Grob, & Lüthi, 1989, 1994). This questionnaire refers to 9 typical life domains of adolescents clustered in three areas. In each domain, questions about 11 control aspects were asked. In this chapter, we included 7 control aspects. Furthermore, in the Euronet questionnaire 3 of the original 9 life domains were included—future workplace, personality development, and school subjects. Each domain was introduced by a typical life situation to be vividly imagined (i.e., "From time to time you sit down and ponder why it is….that you are the way you are, that you behave the way you do, and that you are active the way you are"—personality development). For the future workplace, the adolescents had to imagine the future job market situation and their wish to get a specific job. As for the school subject situation, they had to imagine the fact that teachers expected them to learn a specific matter, although they were more interested in another matter.

To measure the perceived controllability, we first asked whether or not the adolescents believed they were in control of the respective situation—"Do you think that you can influence the way you are and how you behave?" (personality development). The answer was either "rather yes" (feeling of being in control) or "rather no" (helpless). If the adolescents believed they were not in control, they were then asked whether or not they believed that the situation was *controllable* at all—"Do you think that anybody can influence the way he or she is and how he or she behaves?" The answers ranged from "certainly not" to "certainly yes" (4-point Likert scale). Adolescents who believed that the situation was controllable, but personally did not expect control, were subsequently categorized as personally helpless, whereas those who believed that nobody could control the situation were subsequently categorized as *universally helpless*.

Control expectancy was measured with two questions. The first questions asked about how much control the subjects believed they have in the present ("Indicate to what extent you can influence the way you are and how you behave") and the second asked about how much control the subjects believed they have in the future ("Indicate to what extent you will be able to influence the way you are and how you behave in three and up to five years"). The possible answers for these control aspects ranged from "I can't influence it at all (1)" to "I can influence it completely (10)". These two items were averaged per situation to measure domain-specific control expectancy.

The comparative control aspect was measured with a single item per domain, that is, by asking the adolescents to compare their amount of control in the respective situation with those of their peers and to judge whether it differed from them. The wording of the comparative control belief referring to personality development was the following: "Your friends of your age are also concerned with the way they are and how they behave. Compare your influence with theirs." The responses to this aspect of control were "I have much less (1)/a little bit less (2)/ a little bit more (3)/much more (4) control than my colleagues."

To measure control appraisal, a first item asked for the subjective importance of the domain—"On the whole, how important do you find the way you are and how you behave?" The answers ranged from "not at all important" to "very important" (4-point Likert scale). The second question of control appraisal tapped control motivation—"Do you try to get more influence over the way you are and how you behave than you have right now?" The answer to this aspect of control ranged from "not at all" to "very much" (4-point Likert scale). These two items were averaged, per situation, to measure domain-specific control appraisal.

The reliabilities of each aspect in each domain were generally uniform and at levels acceptable for the analytic procedures. The median disattenuated reliability was .68 (details in Grob, Little, Wanner, Wearing, & Euronet, 1996). General validity information is available in Flammer et al. (1989) and in chapter 7, this volume. More details on the theoretical model that underlies the instrument are available in Flammer et al. (1994) or Grob et al. (1995).

RESULTS

Perceived Controllability: Feeling of Being in Control, Personal and Universal Helplessness

Table 6.1 presents the percentage of adolescents in Eastern and Western contexts who believed they were in control, were personally helpless, or were universally helpless (for the sake of brevity, "Eastern" or "East" are used as

TABLE 6.1

*Perceived Controllability: Feeling in Control, Personal Helplessness,
and Universal Helplessness by Domains and Macrosocial Context (Percentages)*

	Personality Development			Future Workplace			School Subjects		
	East	West	Both	East	West	Both	East	West	Both
Feeling in control	87.4	81.8	84.6	87.3	88.4	87.9	47.1	51.1	49.0
Universal helplessness	3.6	7.1	5.4	3.5	5.3	4.4	19.1	21.5	20.2
Personal helplessness	9.0	11.1	10.0	9.2	6.3	7.7	33.9	27.5	30.8
Total	100.0	100.0	100.0	100.0	100.0	100.0	100.0	100.0	100.0

synonyms for "Eastern and Central European;" by "Western" or "West" we mean "Western European and American"). In both macrosocial contexts, more than four fifths of the adolescents believed they were in control of their personality development as well as of their future workplace. As to what they have to learn in school, only about one half of the participants in both macrosocial contexts believed in their personal control.

For the personality development domain, the observed and expected frequencies differed significantly depending on the macrocontext (East or West) and the three levels of control—"feeling in control," "universally helpless," and "personally helpless" ($x^2(2)=24.44$; $p<.001$). The significant effect was due to the fact that in the Eastern context, fewer adolescents than expected felt universally helpless ($x^2(1)=8.86$; $p<.001$), whereas in the Western context more adolescents than expected felt universally helpless ($x^2(1)=9.30$; $p<.001$).

The pattern in the two other domains—future workplace and school subjects—differed from that of personality development. Again, the overall observed and expected frequencies differed significantly with regard to the macrosocial context and the three types of (no) control (workplace: $x^2(2)=13.88$; $p<.001$; school subjects: $x^2(2)=13.95$; $p<.001$). Importantly, in both domains, more adolescents than expected from Eastern contexts (workplace: $x^2(1))=4.09$; $p<.05$; school subject: $x^2(1)=4.22$; $p<.05$) and fewer adolescents than expected from Western contexts (workplace: $x^2(1)=4.93$; $p<.05$; school subjects: $x^2(1)=4.61$; $p<.05$) felt personally helpless.

Irrespective of the domains, more adolescents attributed a lack of their own control to personal helplessness, (i.e., to a lack of own competencies) than to universal helplessness (i.e., uncontrollability of the situation per se). In the domains concerning the future workplace and school subjects, these effects were even more pronounced for adolescents from Eastern contexts than from Western contexts. However, this effect did not occur for personality development. With respect to the adolescents' macrosocial context, the pattern was different: More adolescents from Western, but fewer from Eastern, contexts felt universally helpless with respect to personality.

Control Expectancy

Before we conducted an ANOVA for each domain, we computed a MANOVA with three between-subject factors—context (East vs. West), age (younger, i.e., up to 14 years vs. older than 14 years), and gender (female vs. male adolescents—two within-subject factors—expected control in the present and in the future, and domain (personality development, workplace, and school subject)—as well as the possible interactions. Only those effects in the subsequent univariate analyses were interpreted that showed significance on the multivariate level. Two between-subject main effects reached significance (Hotelling-Lawley Trace)—macrosocial context ($F_{(2,9352)}=47.09$; $p<.0001$), and gender ($F_{(2,9352)}=5.15$; $p<.01$); the same was true for the within-subject main effects control expectancy ($F_{(1,9353)}=880.61$; $p<.0001$) and domain ($F_{(4,18702)}=372.77$; $p<.0001$), as well as five two-way interactions—age x macrosocial context ($F_{(2,9352)}=6.94$; $p<.001$), age x domain ($F_{(2,18702)}=4.18$; $p<.01$), macrosocial context x domain ($F_{(4,18702)}=7.81$; $p<.0001$), macrosocial context x control ($F_{(1,9353)}=75.19$; $p<.0001$), domain x control expectancy ($F_{(2,9353)}=228.65$; $p<.0001$)—and two three-way interactions—age x macrosocial context x control expectancy ($F_{(1,9353)}=7.70$; $p<.01$) and age x domain x control expectancy ($F_{(2,9353)}=6.81$; $p<.01$). The strongest effect originated from the domain factor. A post hoc analysis (Tukey) confirmed the results mentioned in the previous section, namely that adolescents believe they have the most control over their future workplace, followed by personality development and finally, by school matters. In each domain, we subsequently conducted an ANOVA with three between-subject factors—macrosocial context (East vs. West), age (younger vs. older) and gender—one within-subject factor—expected control in the present and in the future—and the possible interactions.

For personality development, a main effect—macrosocial context ($F_{(1,3151)}=60.20$; $p<.001$)—the context x age interaction ($F_{(1,3151)}=8.42$; $p<.01$), and the within-subject main effect ($F_{(1,3151)}=173.74$; $p<.001$) reached significance. A closer look at the two items tapping control expectancy—control over one's personality development in the present and in the future—revealed that adolescents from Eastern contexts attributed to themselves more control than adolescents from Western contexts, both in the present ($F_{(1,3151)}=23.53$; $p<.001$; $M_{East}=6.92$ vs. $M_{West}=6.37$) and in the future ($F_{(1,3151)}=87.18$; $p<.001$; $M_{East}=7.47$ vs. $M_{West}=6.80$). With respect to expected control in the future, however, there was a significant interaction of macrosocial context x age ($F_{(1,3151)}=23.53$; $p<.001$). Post hoc comparisons indicated that only those adolescents living in Western contexts differed significantly from each other, (i.e., older adolescents from Western contexts expected more control in the future compared to their younger peers [$F_{(1,1542)}=13.84$; $p<.001$]).

As mentioned earlier, the within-subject factor reached significance, too. Adolescents expected more control over their personality development in the future than they had in the present (Fig. 6.1). In addition, the present versus

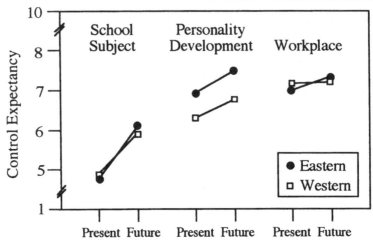

FIG. 6.1. Control expectancy in the present and in the future
by domain and macrosocial context.

future control change score interacted significantly with the macrosocial context ($F_{(1,3151)}=27.13$; $p<.001$). The expected increase in future control was significant in both contexts; however, it was even more pronounced for adolescents from Eastern than for adolescents from Western contexts.

With respect to school subjects and future workplace, there was also an interaction between macrosocial context and present versus future control. It is notable that there were no main effects of context, age, or gender. With regard to school subjects, the difference between present and future control was significant in both contexts, but it was significantly greater for adolescents living in Eastern than for adolescents living in Western contexts ($F_{(1,3118)}=19.87$; $p<.001$). This pattern did not appear for future workplace. In this domain, only adolescents from Eastern contexts expected more control in the future ($F_{(1,1575)}=11.78$; $p<.001$).

Overall, the results for the control expectancy items indicate that control beliefs are domain-specific (i.e., regardless of adolescents' macrosocial context, the participants attributed more control to themselves in the domain of future workplace and of personality development than in the school related domain) and adolescents differ due to their macrosocial context with respect to the amount of personal control they expect for the future. Adolescents from Eastern contexts expect a greater increase in future control than adolescents from Western contexts.

Comparative Control

In accordance with the findings of others (Taylor & Brown, 1988), our results show that adolescents, in general believed they had more personal control than did their peers (i.e., higher comparative control). All means were above 2.5, which indicated having as much personal control as one's peers. This pattern was true for all three domains—for the future workplace (M=2.75), personality development (M= 2.66), and school subjects (M=2.58). To test possible effects of other variables on comparative control, we conducted a three-factorial between-subject ANOVA in each domain with the factors macrosocial context (East vs. West), perceived controllability (being in control, personally and universally helpless), gender (female or male), and the possible interactions.

Adolescents who felt in control of their personality development attributed more control to themselves (than to their peers) relative to adolescents who felt personally and universally helpless ($F_{(2,2938)}$=54.05; p<.001; Tukey test). In addition, adolescents from Eastern contexts reported higher levels of comparative control than did their Western peers ($F_{(1,2938)}$=41.56; p<.001; M_{East}=2.74; M_{west}=2.58), and male adolescents showed higher levels of comparative control than did female adolescents ($F_{(1,2938)}$=7.01; p<.001; M_{female}=2.63; M_{male}=2.70). None of the interactions was significant.

Male adolescents also reported more comparative control over their *future workplace* than did female adolescents ($F_{(1,2820)}$=27.01; p<.001; Mfemale=2.69; Mmale=2.81). In addition, the macrosocial context x perceived controllability interaction reached significance ($F_{(2,2820)}$=5.00; p<.01). Nevertheless, in both contexts, the general picture, with regard to perceived controllability, was the same: Adolescents who felt in control of their future workplace attributed more control to themselves than to their peers, compared to adolescents who felt personally or universally helpless (*East:* $F_{(2,1449)}$=52.09; p<.001; ($M_{in\ control}$=2.82) > ($M_{universally}$ helpless=2.28)=($M_{personally}$ $_{helpless}$=2.32); *West:* $F_{(2,1386)}$=18.10; p<.001; ($M_{in\ control}$= 2.77) > ($M_{universally}$ $_{helpless}$=2.38)=($M_{personally\ helpless}$=2.52); Tukey test). AdolcSCCntS in both macrosocial contexts who felt in control of their future workplace did not differ with respect to their level of comparative control. The same was true for adolescents who felt universally helpless. However, personally helpless adolescents living in Western contexts showed significantly higher levels of comparative control than did personally helpless adolescents from Eastern contexts ($F_{(1,226)}$= 4.88; p<.05; M_{East}=2.32; M_{West}=2.52).

In the school domain, the macrosocial context x perceived controllability interaction was also significant ($F_{(2,2668)}$=12.62; p<.001). In both contexts, the general picture was about the same—adolescents who felt in control of school subjects attributed more control to themselves compared to their peers than did adolescents who felt personally or universally helpless (East: $F_{(2,1388)}$=73.97; p< .001; ($M_{in\ control}$=2.84) > ($M_{universally\ helpless}$=2.41)=($M_{personally}$ $_{helpless}$=2.40); Tukey; West: $F_{(2,1295)}$=18.01; p<.001; ($M_{in\ control}$=2.66) > ($M_{universally}$ $_{helpless}$=2.38)= ($M_{personally\ helpless}$=2.51); Tukey test). In addition, adolescents in Eastern contexts who felt in control reported significantly higher levels of comparative control than their Western peers ($F_{(1,1316)}$=23.39; p<.001; M_{East}=2.84; M_{west}=2.66), whereas Western adolescents who personally felt helpless reported higher levels of comparative control than did their Eastern peers ($F_{(1,829)}$=5.53; p<.05; M_{East}=2.40; M_{West}=2.51).

Control Appraisal

The control appraisal component was assessed by means of two items: domain importance and control motivation. For each domain and with both items, we conducted ANOVAs with the factors macrosocial context, age, gender, and the possible interactions.

Control Motivation. In each domain, the adolescents strived for more control, most for future workplace (M=3.08), followed by personality development (M=2.82), and school subjects (M=2.72). None of the possible interactions, nor the age and gender main effects, reached significance. Nevertheless, the macrosocial context factor was significant for each domain. Adolescents in the Eastern countries reported striving more for control than did their Western peers with respect to their personality development ($F_{(1,3185)}$=108.45; p<.001; M_{East}=2.97; M_{west}=2.65), future workplace ($F_{(1,3070)}$=65.56; p<.001; M_{East}=3.20; M_{West}= 2.95), and school subjects ($F_{(1,3110)}$=21.14; p<.001; M_{East}=2.79; M_{West}=2.64).

Importance of Domains. In general, the adolescents believed that all three domains were important to them. The most important domain was future workplace (M=3.73), followed by personality development (M=3.43) and school subjects (M=3.26). Again, none of the possible interactions, nor the age main effect, reached significance. A main effect of gender found that personality development was regarded as being more important by girls than by boys $F_{(1,3174)}$=51.5 5; p<.001; M_{girls}=3.51; M_{boys}=3.34). However, the adolescents' macrosocial context was not related to the importance of personality development. Nevertheless, the macrosocial context was related to the importance of the future workplace and school subjects. For adolescents from Western contexts, irrespective of age and gender, the future workplace was more important than it was for adolescents from Eastern contexts $F_{(1,311)}$=25.87; p<.001; M_{East}=3.79; M_{West}=3.68). Additionally, Western adolescents estimated control over school subjects to be more important than did Eastern adolescents $F_{(1,3119)}$=47.81; p<.001; M_{East}=3.17; M_{West}=3.35).

National Characteristics and Perceived Control

In addition to the background variables previously mentioned, we examined economic descriptors or indicators of the nations involved in our study (i.e., the nations' Gross National Product, GNP, 1992, country size, population, population density, and degree of urbanization). The correlations between these indicators and perceived control constructs are presented in Table 6.2.

In order to enlarge the scope of the previous analyses, we calculated a Global Perceived Control (GPC) index out of the different control components

TABLE 6.2

Significant Correlations Between GNP, Country Size, Population, Population Density, Degree of Urbanization per Country, and Measures of Control

Measures of Control	Domain	Country Indicators				
		GNP	SIZE	POP	DENS	URB
Control Expectancy (CE)	PD	−.18	.18	.19	−.12	
	WP		.10	.11	−.06	.06
	SS		.32	.30	−.20	
	Mean CE	−.10	.28	.27	−.17	
Comparative Control (CC)	PD	−.13	.10	.12		
	WP		.12	.14	−.07	
	SS	−.05	.17	.19	−.06	
	Mean CC	−.09	.17	.19	−.06	
Control Appraisal (CA)	PD			.09	.08	
	WP	.09				
	SS	.11	−.10	−.06		.05
	Mean CA	.07				
Global Perceived Control		−.07	.23	.24	−.12	
Partial Correlations				.13		−.07

Note. $p<.01$ if $r\geq|.05|$; $2944 <N<3250$. GNP: Gross National Product (1992); SIZE: Country Size; POP: Population, DENS: Population Density; URB: Degree of Urbanization. PD: Personality Development; WP: Future Workplace; SS: School Subject. Mean CE, CC, CA: Composite variable for the respective control dimension across the three domains. Global Perceived Control: Composite variable including control expectancy, comparative control, and control appraisal. Partial Correlations: Controlled for the four country indicators not included in the zero-order correlations.

(control expectancy, comparative control, and control appraisal) across all three domains. As can be seen in Table 6.2, the GNP correlated negatively with GPC. However, this effect was due especially to control expectancy and the comparative control component in personality development. The greater the GNP of a country, the less adolescents believed they had control over their personality development. This effect appeared to a lesser extent for school subjects, but not for the future workplace. The correlation between GNP and control appraisal was different from that between GNP and control expectancy: The greater the GNP, the more positively adolescents appraised control over the future workplace and school subjects.

The results for country size and its population were similar; that is, across all three domains, adolescents from bigger countries and from countries with more inhabitants believed they had more control—for control expectancy and comparative control—than did adolescents from countries that were less populated and smaller in size. However, country size and population did not systematically correlate with the control appraisal component.

The nations' population density and the degree of urbanization generally showed weaker and less consistent effects on the components of control than did the just mentioned indicators. However, all existing relations between population density and control components were negative, indicating that adolescents from countries with high population densities reported less personal control than did adolescents from countries with lower population density. The control appraisal component did not correlate with population density.

The previously mentioned analyses showed that the two strongest correlations were found for the relations between GPC and country size and population. In addition, we identified two lower but significant negative correlations between GPC with GNP, as well as with density. The final set of analyses was conducted to shed light on the unique effects of the country indicators on the control components. For this purpose, the other indicators were partialed out in each analysis, in order to identify the unique effect of the respective indicator on perceived control. Hence, when we partialed out country size, population, population density, and degree of urbanization, the remaining correlation between GPC and GNP was no longer significant. The same occurred for country size and population density. However, population size correlated significantly and positively, and the degree of urbanization correlated significantly and negatively with perceived control. These results of the partial correlations were controlled for the fact that the Euronet sample included heterogenous countries in terms of economic and geographic descriptors (see Table 6.3).

DISCUSSION AND CONCLUSION

All three domains—personality development, future workplace, and school subjects—were rated by our adolescent participants as being important or very important. These importance attributions were barely affected by

TABLE 6.3
Demographic Indicators of Countries in the Euronet Study

Country	GNP	SIZE	POP	DENS	URB
Bulgaria	1330	111	8.5	76	67
Czech Republic	2450	79	10.3	131	76
Finland	21970	338	5.1	15	60
France	22260	552	57.4	106	73
Germany	23030	357	80.6	228	86
Hungary	2970	93	10.3	110	63
Norway	25820	324	4.3	13	76
Poland	1910	313	38.4	123	62
Romania	1130	238	22.7	96	55
Russia	2510	17075	149.0	9	74
Switzerland	36080	41	7.0	169	63
USA	23240	9373	255.6	27	76

Note. GNP: GNP in US $ (for 1991); SIZE: Size in 1000 km²; POP:Population in millions; DENS: Persons per km²; URB: Percentage of people living in urban area.

the macrosocial context. Overall, the future workplace was rated by the adolescents as most important, followed by personality development and school subjects. In addition, adolescents strived for more control in each domain, Eastern adolescents more than Western adolescents. This, too, indicates that these are significant life domains for adolescents.

In both macrosocial contexts, four out of five adolescents perceived themselves as being in control of their personality development and their future workplace. However, in both macrosocial contexts, only one out of two adolescents believed in his or her personal control of what he or she has to learn in school. These results demonstrate that control beliefs differ more among life domains than between the Eastern and Western contexts. However, when adolescents fail to feel in control, they attribute it more to personal incompetence than to the uncontrollability of the task. Another important finding concerns the expected increase in control in the future. Although the adolescents generally expect greater control in the future, those from Eastern contexts expect an even greater increase in control than do adolescents from Western contexts.

In general, our individual participants believed they had more personal control than their peers. This was especially true for the future workplace and for personality development. However, if they felt personally or universally helpless, they attributed less control to themselves than to their peers.

Across the three domains, adolescents from larger countries and from countries with more inhabitants believed they had more control than did adolescents from countries that were less populated and smaller in size. However, when country size, population density, and degree of urbanization were controlled, the correlation between GNP and perceived control disappeared. The same was true for country size and population density, when other variables were controlled. However, the correlation between population size and GPC remained significantly positive, and the correlation between the degree of urbanization and GPC significantly negative.

In general, adolescents from the Eastern and Central European countries seemed to be more optimistic than their Western peers because they attributed to themselves a higher degree of control. This was significantly so for the personality domain, as fewer of the Eastern adolescents showed universal helplessness, more felt superior than did their respective peers, and they anticipated more future control and also claimed greater striving for more control than did their peers from the West.

Because we assume that the objective degrees of freedom were at least not larger in the East, it is not likely that these differences reflect differences in Level 1 (actual controlling). The fact that the difference in perceived control of personality was greater than that for the other domains would reflect a Level 1 difference only if the perceived control in the East were smaller.

Whether the differences are due to perception (Level 2) or to some response bias (Level 3) is less clear. Taking into account the finding of Grob et al.

(chap. 7, this volume)—that the Eastern participants reported lower well-being than the Western participants—it indicates that the adolescents from Eastern contexts are not simply trained to appear positive or optimistic.

There are certainly good reasons to attribute the results to Level 2. Compared with their former situation, the perception of control in the East might indeed have increased by 1992. In addition, because the situation did not change for the best at once, it is also plausible that adolescents living in Eastern contexts anticipated an even better future. They also contended to strive more for a better future than did Westerners. This can only be done on the basis of the belief that they are or will be able to do better. This difference goes hand in hand with the smaller proportion of Eastern participants believing in universal helplessness and the greater proportion of Eastern participants believing in personal, actual helplessness.

These interpretations are preliminary and must be tested in a longitudinal study by referring to historical and intraindividual change. However, being aware of this methodological flaw, the findings of this study show a substantial general picture. Adolescents from two very distinct macrosocial contexts report high levels of personal control and expect even more control in the future. This fact is even more evident for adolescents living in Eastern compared to adolescents living in Western contexts. In addition, adolescents generally overestimate their personal control compared to their peers' control. One may relate this result to the Zeitgeist. At the end of the 20th century, people live in a world where most events are expected to be caused by personal agency and competence: A person is what he or she personally performs. This contemporary understanding of how the world functions is cross-contextually, largely shared by our participants. Further studies might give even more attention to the cross-cultural settings, for example, by investigating whether the personal control optimism is also evident in more distinct contexts than in those included in this study.

REFERENCES

Alloy, L.B., & Abramson, L.Y. (1982). Learned helplessness, depression, and the illusion of control. *Journal of Personality and Social Psychology, 42,* 1114–1126.

Bandura, A. (1977). Self-efficacy: Toward a unifying theory of behavioral change. *Psychological Review, 84,* 191–215.

Flammer, A. (1990). *Erfahrung der eigenen Wirksamkeit Einführung in die Psychologie der Kontrollmeinung [Experiencing self-efficacy. Introduction to the psychology of control beliefs].* Berne, Switzerland: Huber.

Flammer, A. (1995). Developmental analysis of control beliefs. In A.Bandura (Ed.), *Self-efficacy in changing societies* (pp. 69–113). New York: Cambridge University Press.

Flammer, A., & Grob, A. (1994). Kontrollmeinungen, ihre Begründungen und Autobiographic [Control beliefs, their justification, and autobiographical memory]. *Zeitschrift für Experimentelle und Angewandte Psychologie, 41,* 17–38.

Flammer, A., Grob, A., & Lüthi, R. (1989). Swiss adolescents' attribution of control. In J.P. Forgas, & J.M.Innes (Eds.), *Recent advances in social psychology* (pp. 81–94). Amsterdam: Elsevier.

Flammer, A., Grob, A., & Lüthi, R. (1994). *Bernese Questionnaire on Adolescents' Perception of Control.* Research Report No. 1994–1. Institute of Psychology. University of Berne, Switzerland.

Flammer, A., Ito, T., Lüthi, R., Plaschy, N., Reber, R., Sugimine, H., & Zurbriggen, L. (1995). Coping with control-failure in an individual-centered and in a group-centered culture. *Swiss Journal of Psychology, 54,* 277–288.

Grob, A., Flammer, A., & Wearing, A.J. (1995). Adolescents' perceived control: Domain specificity, expectation, and appraisal. *Journal of Adolescence, 18,* 403–425.

Grob, A., Little, T.D., Wanner, B., Wearing, A.J., & Euronet (1996). Adolescents' well-being and perceived control across fourteen sociocultural contexts. *Journal of Personality and Social Psychology, 71,* 785–795.

Langer, E.J. (1975). The illusion of control. *Journal of Personality and Social Psychology, 32,* 311–328.

Oettingen, G. (1995). Cross-cultural perspectives on self-efficacy. In A.Bandura (Ed.), *Self-efficacy in changing societies* (pp. 149–176). New York: Cambridge University Press.

Schneewind, K.A. (1995). Impact of family processes on control beliefs. In A.Bandura (Ed.), *Self-efficacy in changing societies* (pp. 114–148). New York: Cambridge University Press.

Skinner, E.A. (1990). What causes success and failure in school and friendship? Developmental differentiation of childrens' beliefs across middle childhood. *International Journal of Behavioral Development, 13,* 157–176.

Skinner, E.A. (1995). *Perceived control, motivation, and coping.* London: Sage.

Skinner, E.A., Chapman, M., & Baltes, P.B. (1988). Childrens' belief about control, means-ends, and agency: Developmental differences during middle childhood. *International Journal of Behavioral Development, 11,* 369–388.

Taylor, S.E., & Brown, J. (1988). Illusion and well-being: A social-psychological perspective on mental health. *Psychological Bulletin, 103,* 193–210.

Weisz, J.R., Rothbaum, F.M., & Blackburn, T.C. (1984). Standing out and standing in: The psychology of control in America and Japan. *American Psychologist, 39,* 955–969.

Wicki, W., Reber, R., Flammer, A., & Grob, A. (1994). Begriindung der Kontrollmeinung bei Kindern und Jugendlichen [Justification of control beliefs in children and adolescents]. *Zeitschrift für Entwicklungspsychologie und Pädagogische Psychologie, 26,* 241–262.

7

A Cross-National Model of Subjective Well-Being in Adolescence

Alexander Grob
Anna Stetsenko
University of Berne, Switzerland

Colette Sabatier
University of Nanterre, Paris X, France

Luba Botcheva
Center for Interdisciplinary Studies, Sofia, Bulgaria

Petr Macek
Masarik University, Brno, Czech Republic

In recent years, theories of human development have increasingly focused on interactions among individual development, social conditions, and historical contexts (Baltes, 1986; Flammer, 1996; Goulet & Baltes, 1970; Lerner, 1982). This is of special importance in adolescence because during this life period, young people are facing decisive choices regarding their identities and futures, and their emerging developmental pathways are closely tied with the historical, social, and economic conditions of their lives. An important question concerns the factors that can support or impede the transition of young men and women into adulthood. For example, what is the role that subjective well-being plays in successfully managing the life tasks facing adolescents? How much does subjective well-being depend on living conditions and personality characteristics of an individual? These and similar questions have been barely studied in recent research. This study addresses the specific question of how well adolescents feel in different sociocultural context, and whether antecedents of their subjective well-being are the same across these contexts.

SUBJECTIVE WELL-BEING AND ITS DETERMINANTS

Current research defines *subjective well-being* as a complex variable including a lack of self-esteem and dissatisfaction on the negative side as well as happiness and satisfaction with life and oneself on the positive side (e.g., Diener, 1984). In addition, two types of subjective well-being are distinguished, namely *well-being as a personal trait* and *well-being as an actual feeling. Actual well-being* can be reached by evoking short-term positive experiences or reducing aversive states. In this research, we focus on the more stable, more long-term (i.e., enduring) types of subjective well-being.

Following the works of Diener and colleagues (e.g., Diener, 1984; Diener & Diener, 1995), as well as our previous research (see Grob, 1995; Grob et. al., 1991), we differentiate between two components of subjective well-being. The first component encompasses cognitive experiences of well-being. It is assumed that deficits in meeting needs would lead to ill-being and that a good fit, as well as the positive discrepancies between personal aspirations and perceived reality, would result in well-being (Cantril, 1965). This cognitive component of well-being is similar to what Michalos (1985) termed *satisfaction*—a series of judgments about discrepancies between self-perception and peer perception, between self-perception and one's ideal self, as well as between generalized self-perception and actual experience. The second component of subjective well-being focuses on the *emotional side* of satisfaction (see also Bradburn, 1969). Here, the actual feelings are emphasized that are usually experienced by people in the course of their everyday lives.

Taking into account both the cognitive and emotional processes, we have proposed elsewhere (Grob, 1995; Grob et al., 1991) that a set of antecedents might be relevant for subjective well-being. This set includes accomplishing normative and age-specific developmental tasks (see also Havighurst, 1948), accomplishing nonnormative developmental tasks and important life events (see also Grob, 1991), appropriate coping strategies in everyday situations (see also Folkman, Lazarus, Gruen, & DeLongis, 1986; Lazarus & Launier, 1978), adequate social support (see also Argyle, 1989; Barrera, 1988; Cohen, Mermelstein, Karmarck, & Hoberman, 1985), the personal conviction that one is in control regarding important life domains (see also Bandura, 1995; Flammer, 1995; Rotter, 1966,), meaningful purposes in life and future perspectives (see also Emmons, 1986; Nurmi, 1992), and finally, a fit between personal aspirations and the social and cultural context (see also Bronfenbrenner, 1986).

In addition and in view of the previously described considerations, we reasoned that the following indicators might be relevant for subjective well-being: achieving self-chosen and authority-imposed goals, attaining socially defined values, being on the way to attain goals, adapting to one's (social) environment, satisfaction of everyday needs, successful handling of divergent goals, participating in interesting activities, positive evaluation of daily events, meaningful use of time, good health, and accepting oneself.

A Model of Well-Being

With regard to the antecedents of well-being, we distinguish two levels of components: The *background level* and the *agentic level* with the latter mediating the effects of the former on subjective well-being (Fig. 7.1). Specifically, the *background level* comprises variables that are given to an individual independently of his or her actions and decisions, such as gender, age, cultural context, and objective life strains. The *agentic level* includes variables that directly depend on the individual's agency (actions, experiences, and choices), such as sense of control and control expectancies, and effective problem- or emotion-oriented coping behavior.

The literature on subjective well-being suggests that more variables than included in our model might be important in producing effects on this self-related construct (for a review, see Evans, 1994). For example, Lazarus and Launier's (1978) notion of cognitive appraisal could be of some relevance for the model of well-being. Cognitive appraisal is an evaluation by a person of events with regard to their significance for one's well-being. Two other dimensions that have been demonstrated to affect subjective well-being are perceived social support (Barrera, 1988; Cohen et al., 1985) and personality factors (Costa & McCrae, 1980; Diener, 1984). In this study, however, we focused, apart from considering background variables, on those antecedents of subjective well-being that are directly related to a personal sense of control and the ability to cope with situations. We believe that when people consider how they can manage the challenges with which they are

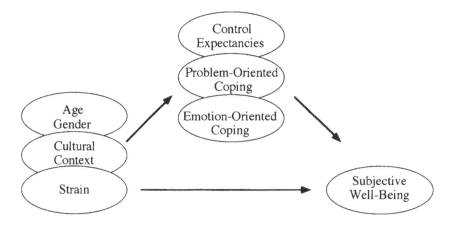

FIG. 7.1. Model of subjective well-being.

confronted, they might refer, in the first place, to skills (general and specific) and to control expectancies (general and specific). We assume that a person who feels in control and has appropriate coping strategies generally feels better than a person who does not have a positive sense of control and self-efficacy expectancies and lacks appropriate coping strategies (see also, e.g., Bandura, 1995; Compas, 1987).

SETTING THE STAGE FOR A
CROSS-NATIONAL COMPARISON

In recent years, there has been a growing recognition of the importance of crosscultural comparison to understand the nature and mechanisms of various psychological phenomena. A consensus emerges that testing the models within a comparative framework is crucial because this gives an opportunity to go beyond the confines of one society type, to expand the range of individual differences, to account for more variables that may be involved in the production of these differences, and ultimately, to achieve higher levels of generality and validity. In the case of studying subjective well-being in adolescence, the impact of sociocultural factors might be particularly strong, as this life period is characterized by growing demands and needs for integration into the surrounding sociocultural, political, and economic structures.

A cross-cultural study including Eastern and Western European countries and the United States represents a unique opportunity to test the generality of the proposed model of subjective well-being, because these countries represent a comparative framework with a sufficient amount of both similarities and differences on various dimensions.

On the one hand, the living conditions (e.g., socioeconomic status) in Eastern European countries differ from those in Western European countries and the United States. Also, this sample of countries represents two different political organizations: an established Western-type democracy and a political system in transition from the former communist regimes toward democracy. Another dimension on which the countries in this sample differ is their sociocultural orientation. This difference, for example, pertains to what has been discussed in the cross-cultural literature as predominantly collectivistic (i.e., Eastern European countries) versus predominantly individualistic cultures (i.e., countries of Western Europe and the United States).

On the other hand, all the countries represented in the sample belong to modern societies with moderate to high levels of industrialization and comparable levels of urbanization, comparable family structures, and levels of education. Furthermore, in terms of ethnicity and religion, the discrepancy between the sampled countries is not very sharp.

This combination of similarities and differences among the countries comprising our comparative framework are potentially relevant for adolescents' well-being. For example, previous cross-national studies revealed that democracy, affluence, and equality are positively related to subjective well-being (Diener & Diener, 1995; Diener, Diener, & Diener, 1995; Headey & Wearing, 1992; Triandis, 1989; Veenhoven, 1991). Also, the analyses of the Euronet data have shown that subjective well-being varies across sociocultural contexts (see Grob, 1998; Grob, Little, Wanner, Wearing, & Euronet, 1996). Although no differences in the structure of subjective well-being were revealed, mean levels of subjective well-being appeared to be different in different countries. Whereas adolescents reported relatively high levels of well-being across all sociocultural contexts, young people living in Western European countries were more satisfied than those living in former socialist countries.

General Expectations

Given the potential importance of sociocultural factors in the production of subjective well-being in adolescents, we wanted to examine whether the particular predictors of subjective well-being differ across the sociocultural contexts and thus, test the generality of our two-level model. In view of the more exploratory nature of our study, our hypothesis was simply that the general model of subjective well-being would be sustained in the face of cultural diversity, although we expected to find certain cross-cultural divergency in the effects of particular variables.

It is important that before the actual analysis of commonalities and differences (if any) in the model of subjective well-being across different contexts could be performed, we wanted to ensure the internal validity of the concepts employed in the study. This purpose was achieved in two steps, on a within-cultural and on a cross-cultural level. At the first level, the intracultural characteristics of the concepts (i.e., consistency values and zero-order intercorrelations) were examined. In the second step, comparisons of the correlation matrices between the cultures were conducted. If both conditions were met (i.e., similar within-cultural consistencies and comparable cross-cultural correlation patterns), the model was tested.

METHOD

The items addressing adolescents' subjective well-being were selected from the *Berne Questionnaire on Adolescents' Well-Being* (BSW–Y; Grob et al., 1991). They represent two first-order scales of satisfaction, namely positive attitudes toward life and self-esteem. The structure of subjective well-being was previously tested and supported in studies using large Swiss samples (Grob, Flammer, & Neuenschwander, 1992). The BSW-Y has evinced satisfactory psychometric properties with respect to internal consistency, stability, and validity (Grob, 1995; Grob et al., 1991). The 13 items were to be answered on a 4-point Likert scale ranging from 1 (*totally false*) to 4 (*very true*). In this section we do not report the consistencies of the

Subjective well-being items nor of the items of the other concepts because they are described in the results.

The *Strain Inventory* covers 11 selected life domains: school, money, girlfriend (for boys)/boyfriend (for girls), other peers and friends, active sports, parents/family, living area/neighborhood, health, leisure opportunities, having access to public information, and having one's own room at home. The adolescents were asked to think about the strains and obstacles with which they were confronted during the last 6 months when answering respective items. Each item was to be answered on a 4-point Likert scale ranging from 1 (not at all difficult) to 4 (very difficult).

The *Coping Reactions questionnaire* consists of 11 items comprising elements from a variety of different instruments from previous research in this field (Folkman et al., 1986; Haan, 1993). The subjects had to indicate how typical a certain reaction was for them when they were faced with difficulties in life. These reactions were grouped into two categories: problem-oriented coping reactions (including the following items: "I try to calm down," "I analyze the situation and try to solve/overcome the difficulty," "I try again and again," and "I seek help from...friends/ ...parents/...siblings") and emotion-oriented coping reactions ("I cry," "I get angry and/or shout," "I am sad and wait until my feelings become better," "I get nervous and anxious," or "I withdraw and hide"). The subjects answered the items on a 4-point Likert scale ranging from 1 (*not at all typical for me*) to 4 (*very typical for me*).

The *Bernese Questionnaire on Adolescents' Perception of Control* (Flammer, Grob, & Lüthi, 1989, 1994) refers to typical life areas of adolescents combined in three groups. In each area, 9 control aspects were differentiated. For our purpose, we included six items to measure the adolescents' global control expectancy (Grob, Flammer, & Wearing, 1995)— the control expectancy at present and in the future in each of three domains (future working place, school subjects, and personality development). The answers to these control aspects ranged from 1 (*I can't influence it at all*) to 2 (*I can influence it completely;* for details, see chap. 6, this volume).

RESULTS

First, we present the consistency coefficients for the concepts under study for each sample. Second, we show the intercorrelations between the concepts on national and cross-national levels, followed by the results of the regression analysis.

Consistency of the Concepts

Table 7.1 shows the standardized consistency coefficients (Cronbach's alpha) for the concepts under study in each country, and pooled over the Eastern and Western countries, respectively. In our model, we use five concepts: A general

TABLE 7.1
*Standardized Cronbachs's Alpha Coefficients for Subjective Well-Being,
Strain, Global Control Expectancy, Emotion-Oriented Coping Reactions,
and Problem-Oriented Coping Reactions, by Country*

Country	Subjective Well-Being	Strain	Global Control Expectancy	Emotion-Oriented Coping	Problem-Oriented Coping
Bulgaria	.75	.67	.70	.61	.53
CSFR	.74	.55	.67	.50	.43
Hungary	.81	.60	.67	.59	.50
Poland	.87	.72	.74	.35	.54
Romania	.73	.59	.72	.45	.48
Russia	.73	.55	.74	.63	.44
Eastern Countries	.79	.62	.71	.56	.49
Finland	.83	.56	.69	.52	.60
France	.78	.60	.59	.65	.52
Germany	.83	.52	.72	.50	.34
Norway	.77	.49	.81	.48	.55
German Switzerland	.79	.62	.64	.54	.39
French Switzerland	.80	.57	.76	.48	.40
USA	.86	.69	.81	.54	.54
Western Countries	.81	.62	.80	.56	.53
Total Sample	.80	.62	.75	.55	.51

measure of strain, a general measure of adolescents' control expectancy, a measure of the subjects' emotion- and problem-oriented coping reactions when confronted with difficulties, and a measure of subjective well-being. The Cronbach's alpha coefficients differed between and within the concepts. The most consistent measure was subjective well-being, with coefficients ranging from .73 for the Romanian and Russian samples, to .87 for the Polish sample. In addition, the global control expectancy measure yielded similar results with the mean consistency coefficient of .75; the lowest consistency coefficient was .59 for the French adolescents, the highest was .81 for the American and Norwegian adolescents. The other scales showed lower reliability coefficients. The coefficients for the strain scale ranged between .49 (Norway) and .69 (United States). The measures for emotion- and problem-oriented coping reactions were not very consistent (.55 and .51, respectively). Therefore, the interpretation of the relations between these two concepts and the other concepts must be made with some caution. However, even the measures with low consistencies that show comparable relational patterns with other variables across countries can be considered as relatively reliable (Little, Lindenberger, & Nesselroade, 1998).

Overall, the consistency coefficients hardly differed across the sociocultural contexts, but differed among the constructs. This result suggests that the same meaning (i.e., mental categories) was implied by the concepts under study.

Correlations Between Predictor Variables and Subjective Well-Being

Table 7.2 presents the intercorrelations of subjective well-being with strain, global control expectancy, and emotion-oriented and problem-oriented coping reactions for each sample and for two macro-contexts (i.e., Eastern and Western countries). A very consistent pattern of interrelations between the concepts emerged across the sociocultural settings. There were significant negative correlations between subjective well-being and strain in all samples. The correlations ranged between $-.30$ for the Czeckoslovakian adolescents and $-.51$ for the German-Swiss adolescents. The more strain adolescents experienced, the worse they felt in general. Although the correlation between subjective well-being and strain for adolescents living in the Western countries (all Western samples pooled together, $r=-.46$) and adolescents living in Eastern countries ($r=-.41$) were about the same, the correlations differed significantly between some samples. For example, Czeckoslovakian adolescents showed significantly weaker negative correlations between subjective well-being and strain than did the adolescents from Romania ($z=2.28$; $p<.05$) or German Switzerland ($z=2.76$; $p<.01$).

TABLE 7.2

Intercorrelations of Subjective Well-Being With Strain, Global Control Expectancy, Emotion-Oriented Coping Reactions, and Problem-Oriented Coping Reactions, by Country

	Strain	Global Control Expectancy	Emotion-Oriented Coping	Problem-Oriented Coping
Bulgaria	$-.39$	.25	$-.34$	ns
CSFR	$-.30$	.28	$-.40$	ns
Hungary	$-.47$	.25	$-.39$	.22
Poland	$-.45$	.22	$-.26$	.38
Romania	$-.48$	.22	$-.26$	.38
Russia	$-.37$	.18	$-.30$	ns
Eastern Countries	$-.41$	.21	$-.31$	.18
Finland	$-.49$	.16	$-.44$	.21
France	$-.42$	ns	$-.38$	.18
Germany	$-.46$	.22	$-.27$	.24
Norway	$-.47$	.21	$-.40$	.19
German Switzerland	$-.51$	.13	$-.24$	.27
French Switzerland	$-.50$	ns	$-.38$	.26
United States	$-.47$	.42	$-.39$	.28
Western Countries	$-.46$	.20	$-.34$	.25
Total Sample	$-.44$	.20	$-.30$	.20

Note. p of all correlations $<.05$.

There were moderate correlations between subjective well-being and control expectancies. Eleven of the 13 correlations between subjective well-being and control expectancy were significant and positive. These correlations ranged between .18 for the Norwegian adolescents and .42 for the American adolescents. The more personal control adolescents expected, the better they felt. In addition, the correlation between global control expectancy and subjective well-being was—with two exceptions, that is, Bulgarian and Czeckoslovakian adolescents—significantly higher for the U.S. adolescents than in the other samples (e.g., $Z_{USA-Hungary}$=2.22; p<.05).

A similar pattern was found in the correlations between emotion-oriented coping and subjective well-being. Again, significant negative correlations emerged in all countries. The more emotionally adolescents reacted when faced with difficulties, the worse they felt in general. The correlations were significant, ranging between –.22 for Romanian adolescents and –.44 for Finnish adolescents. Given the fact that emotion-oriented coping reaction showed lower reliabilities than the other concepts under study, the consistency in the correlational pattern with subjective well-being is important, both statistically and theoretically.

In addition, the problem-oriented coping scale showed a very consistent pattern when related to the well-being scale. Ten of the 13 national samples in this study showed significant positive correlations, ranging from .18 for the French adolescents to .38 for the Polish adolescents. The more problem-oriented strategies adolescents used when dealing with problems, the better they felt. However, in the Bulgarian, Czeckoslovakian, and Russian samples no relations between these two scales were found.

Comparing the correlational pattern between the predictor variables and subjective well-being across the two macrocontexts (Western and Eastern countries), we were able to identify only one statistically significant difference. Namely, problem-oriented coping reactions were significantly more positively related to subjective well-being in the Western context than in the Eastern context (z=2.09; p<.05). However, the three other concepts (strain, control expectancy, and emotion-oriented coping reactions) were related to well-being in a similar way across the macrocontexts.

In summary, strong empirical evidence was obtained concerning the existence of a similar pattern of correlations between subjective well-being and strain, global control expectancies, emotion-oriented coping reactions, and problem-oriented coping reactions across the countries sampled; the coefficients were either positive or negative for all countries. Across all countries, the higher adolescents scored on subjective well-being, the less strain they reported (r=–.44), the more personal control they perceived (r=.20), the less emotion-oriented (r=–.30) and the more problem-oriented (r=.20) they reacted. Eastern and Western samples did not differ in these respects except for problem-oriented coping reactions.

Correlations Between Predictor Variables

As for the predictor variables, their interrelations were generally smaller than their correlation with subjective well-being. In general, there was no correlation between strain and control expectancy, and when a significant relationship emerged, it was negative. That is, the more control adolescents believed they had, the less strain they reported. This was true for the German (r=–.16), Finnish (r=–.16), and American (r=–.24) adolescents.

Only three correlations between control expectancy and emotion-oriented coping were significant. Notably, Norwegian (–.16), American (–.27), and Polish adolescents (–.36) reacted less emotionally in the face of difficulties when they believed they were in control.

Control expectancy correlated more strongly with problem-oriented coping strategies than with emotion-oriented strategies. In four samples (French Switzerland: r=.24, Finland: r=.21, Germany: r=.18, Hungary: r=.16) a positive correlation between problem-oriented coping reactions and control expectancies appeared: The more adolescents preferred problem-oriented coping reactions, the more personal control they believed they had.

Concerning the relation between strain and emotion-oriented coping, again, a clear pattern emerged: Adolescents reported more emotion-oriented coping reactions when they reported higher levels of strain ($r_{Total\,sample}$=.26). However, there was, in general, no relation between a preference for problem-oriented coping and strain, albeit with three exceptions: Germany (r=–.18), Poland (r=–.40), and German Switzerland (r=–.18). For adolescents in these samples, the fewer problem-oriented coping reactions they reported, the more strain they experienced.

Finally, we examined the interrelations between emotion-oriented and problem-oriented coping reactions. With one exception, no significant correlations between emotion- and problem-oriented coping reactions existed. The exception concerned the Polish adolescents (r=–.32).

In general, the pattern of relations within the predictor variables showed high consistencies. The more strain adolescents experienced, the more emotion-oriented coping reactions they showed ($r_{Total\,sample}$=.26), the fewer problem-oriented coping reactions they reported ($r_{Total\,sample}$=–.07), and the less control they expected ($r_{Total\,sample}$=–.07). It is notable that all of these effects were small, but significant, predominantly due to the substantial sample size (n_{min}=3,208). In addition, a significant negative relation between control expectancy and emotion-oriented coping ($r_{Total\,sample}$=–.09) and a positive correlation between problem-oriented coping and control expectancy ($r_{Total\,sample}$=.13) emerged. No relation was found between emotion-oriented coping reactions and problem-oriented coping reactions.

Predicting Subjective Well-Being

To examine how the background and agentic type variables function together in predicting subjective well-being, we conducted a multiple regression analysis using a hierarchical method in which variables were entered in a fixed order.

The order was consistent with the theoretical perspective presented in this chapter: Background type variables were assumed to be hardly changeable units that, nevertheless, might affect adolescents' subjective well-being. Furthermore, we assumed that the background type variables, such as strain and culture, would interact with one another. In the final step, we entered the agentic type variables of control expectancy, emotion oriented-coping reactions and problem-oriented coping reactions, in the regression analysis.

At Step 1 the subjects' gender and age were significant predictors of reported subjective well-being. Both gender and age[1] exhibited a significant beta weight (see Table 7.3). The older adolescents were, the less positive they felt about themselves. Also, male participants reported higher levels of subjective well-being than did female participants. However, the variance explained by these two variables was very small ($R^2=.01$).

At Step 2, we added culture as a predictor. We did not regress each country on subjective well-being, but instead, only two macrocontexts—Eastern and Western blocks. The macrocultural context increased the R^2 significantly by 4 %, demonstrating that adolescents living in Eastern countries had lower levels of subjective well-being than did adolescents living in Western countries, independently of gender and age.[2]

At Step 3, the strain index was entered; it exhibited a substantial effect on subjective well-being in increasing the R^2 by 17 %. This result demonstrates the higher predictive power of the strain index as compared to subjects' gender, age, and macrosocial context. To test the possibility that the meaning of strain is culturally bound, we entered the interaction of strain by culture in the next step (Step 4). Contrary to our assumption, this interaction added nothing to the prediction of subjective well-being.

At Step 5, global control expectancy, emotion-oriented coping reactions, and problem-oriented coping reactions were entered simultaneously to predict subjective well-being. Together, these three variables accounted for 9% of additional predicted variance in subjective well-being. All three regression coefficients were significant: The more control adolescents expected, the more they had problem-oriented coping reactions, and the fewer emotion-oriented reactions they used when confronted with difficulties, the higher levels of subjective well-being they reported.[3]

---

[1]We tested the quadratic effect of age on subjective well-being, too; it did not reach significance.

[2]In another hierarchical regression analysis the countries' GNP in USD, instead of pooling the two macrosocial contexts was regressed on subjective well-being. The increase in explained variance did not differ for *step 2* or with respect to the final model (including five steps). Therefore, we proceeded with the variable which was more illustrative and easier to interpret, i.e., Eastern versus Western countries.

[3]In a sixth step the three interaction terms of Global Control Expectancy, problem-oriented coping reactions, and emotion-oriented coping reactions, respectively, with the adolescents' sociocultural background (Eastern versus Western countries) were regressed on subjective well-being. However, these interaction terms did not increase significantly the amount of explained variance in subjective well-being.

TABLE 7.3

Multiple Regression Results Using Background Type (Age, Gender, Culture, Strain, and Strain X Culture) and Agentic Type Variables (Global Control Expectancy, Problem- and Emotion-Oriented Coping Reactions) to Predict Adolescents' Subjective Well-Being (N=3250).

Variables	b	t	R	R^2	ΔR^2	ΔF
Step 1						
Age	-.06	-3.5***	.10	.01	.01	15.2***
Gender (1 = f; 2 = m)	.08	4.4***				
Step 2						
Culture (1 = e; 2 = w)	.21	12.1***	.23	.05	.04	146.4***
Step 3						
Strain	-.42	-26.3***	.47	.22	.17	690.9***
Step 4						
Culture x strain	-.15	-1.8	.47	.22	.00	3.1
Step 5						
Global control expectancy	.14	9.3***	.56	.31	.09	140.4***
Problem-oriented coping reactions	.18	12.2***				
Emotion-oriented coping reactions	-.19	-11.9***				
Final bs						
Age	-.05	-3.1**				
Gender	.03	2.0*				
Culture	.25	3.5***				
Strain	-.30	-6.5***				
Culture strain	-.03	-0.9				
Global control expectancy	.14	9.3***				
Problem-oriented coping reactions	.18	12.2***				
Emotion-oriented coping reactions	-.19	-11.9***				

Note. *$p<.05$; **$p<.01$; ***$p<-001$; *b:* standardized beta coefficients, f: female; m: male; e: Bulgaria,, CSFR, Hungary, Poland, Romania, and Russia; w: Finland, France, West Germany, Norway, French Switzerland, German Switzerland, United States.

Together, the background and agentic type variables accounted for 31% of the variance in reported subjective well-being, with the strain index the most important, and gender and age being the least important predictors of subjective well-being.

DISCUSSION AND CONCLUSION

This study supports the generality of the proposed two-level model of subjective well-being in adolescence by providing evidence of its cross-cultural invariance. Given sociocultural, political, and economic differences between the countries sampled in this study and their possible impact on self-related constructs in adolescents, the cross-cultural consistency in the structure of well-being, with respect to the underlying measurement model (for details, see Grob et al., 1996), was remarkable. Specifically, the analyses revealed similar reliability coefficients of the scales employed in the study across the sociocultural settings, which suggests that the meaning of the scales was the same for the adolescents throughout the settings. Moreover, there were consistent patterns in predictive effects from the variables of both levels (i.e., background and agentic) on subjective well-being in adolescents across all of the samples.

The amount of daily strain had a strong impact on adolescents' well-being regardless of the macrosocial contexts. That is, the more hassled adolescents felt they were, the lower the level of their subjective well-being. At the same time, the adolescents' well-being was hardly affected by gender and age. In addition, across all of the countries, the agentic type variables strongly predicted subjective wellbeing: The adolescents' well-being was predicted by a low preference for emotion-oriented coping reactions and a high preference for problem-oriented coping reactions, as well as by a positive belief in personal control (i.e., by high control expectancies).

A high overall mean level of subjective well-being was found, confirming findings from other research (see, e.g., Diener & Diener, 1995; Headey & Wearing, 1992): In general, adolescents felt well, and in each context, the mean level of subjective well-being was above the theoretical average indicated by the scale. The adolescents reported on their future as looking good and that they were able to do things as well as other people can. However, differences between the countries exist, even although they are not large. Considering the theoretical range of the well-being scale (1–4), the highest level of subjective well-being (German-speaking Switzerland) is only 13 % higher than the lowest level (CSFR).

These mean level differences were nearly always consistent with the distinction between the two macrocontexts, the countries of Eastern and Central Europe (i.e., former socialist countries) on the one hand, and countries of Western Europe and the United States (i.e., Western type democracies) on the other. Except for the French samples, every Western country is higher on subjective well-being than every former socialist country.

Because the economic situation in these two macrocontexts was very different at the time of the study with the economies of Eastern European countries being much weaker than those of Western countries, we regard this finding as further support for the assumption that subjective well-being of adolescents is also linked to the income levels or wealth of the country where they live (Diener et al., 1995). The few exceptions to this rule (e.g., French sample) suggest that other macrolevel factors than economic affluence have an impact on the levels of subjective wellbeing in adolescents. These factors are difficult to trace in the present study, but further research could shed light on this question.

Although the data suggest that security and economic stability favor subjective well-being, they demonstrate an additional process, namely that everyday strain on the one hand impairs subjective well-being, and individual properties, such as having a positive sense of personal control, and the tendency to react in the face of difficulties by analyzing the situation enhance subjective well-being. Taken together, strain and the three agentic type variables (control expectancy and emotion-and problem-oriented coping reactions) accounted for 26% of the 31 % explainable variance in subjective well-being. These data support the hypothesis that both sociohistorical conditions and personal competencies affect subjective well-being substantially.

In conclusion, the broad comparative framework allows us to escape the confines of a one-society perspective. This approach is of special importance because self-related cognitions in adolescents, which serve as a prerequisite for their future decisions and therefore guide their future paths, are of great significance. The impact of sociocultural factors might be quite strong as this life period is characterized by growing demands and needs of integration into given societal, political, and economic structures. All the countries represented in the sample belong to modern societies in that they have comparable levels of industrialization, urbanization, family structure, and education. Simultaneously, they differ significantly from one another, for example, with respect to economics, political traditions, or intracultural diversity. Given these culturally determined differences and similarities, the adolescents showed a highly similar predictive pattern of subjective well-being across all the cultural units.

These results have sociopolitical implications. There is the question of how the well-being of adolescents, in general, and the well-being of adolescents who are living in the countries moving toward new democratic structures, specifically, can be supported with the purpose to establish positive life perspectives. To answer this question, it is notable that although the macrosocial context per se was predictive of adolescents' subjective well-being, there were other factors with even greater importance for subjective well-being.

REFERENCES

Argyle, M. (1989). *The psychology of happiness*. London: Routledge and Kegan Paul.

Baltes, P.B. (1986). Theoretical positions of life-span developmental psychology: On the dynamics between growth and decline. *Developmental Psychology, 23*, 611–626.

Bandura, A. (1995). *Self-efficacy: The exercise of control*. New York: Freeman.

Barrera, M. (1988). Models of social support and life stress. In L.H.Cohen (Ed.), *Life events and psychological functioning. Theoretical and methodological issues* (pp. 211–236). Beverly Hills, CA: Sage.

Bradburn, N.M. (1969). *The structure of psychological well-being*. Chicago: Aldine-Atherton.

Bronfenbrenner, U. (1986). Ecology of the family as a context for human development: Research perspectives. *Developmental Psychology, 22*, 723–742.

Cantril, H. (1965). *The pattern of human concerns*. New Brunswick, NJ: Rutgers University Press.

Cohen, S., Mermelstein, R., Karmarck, T., & Hoberman, H.M. (1985). Measuring the functional components of social support. In I.G.Sarason & B.R.Sarason (Eds.), *Social support: Theory, research and applications* (pp. 73–94). Dordrecht, the Netherlands: Nijhoff.

Compas, B.E. (1987). Coping with stress during childhood and adolescence. *Psychological Bulletin, 101*, 393–403.

Costa, P.T., Jr., & McCrae, R.R. (1980). Influence of extraversion and neuroticism on subjective well-being: Happy and unhappy people. *Journal of Personality and Social Psychology, 38*, 668–678.

Diener, E. (1984). Subjective well-being. *Psychological Bulletin, 95*, 542–575.

Diener, E., & Diener, M. (1995). Cross-cultural correlates of life-satisfaction and self-esteem. *Journal of Personality and Social Psychology, 68*, 653–663.

Diener, E., Diener, M., & Diener, C. (1995). Factors predicting the subjective well-being of nations. *Journal of Personality and Social Psychology, 69*, 851–864.

Emmons, R.A. (1986). Personal strivings: an approach to personality and subjective well-being. *Journal of Personality and Social Psychology, 51*, 1058–1068.

Evans, D.R. (1994). Enhancing quality of life in the population at large. *Social Indicatiors Research, 33*, 47–88.

Flammer, A. (1995). Developmental analysis of control beliefs. In A.Bandura (Ed.), *Self-efficacy in changing societies* (pp. 69–113). New York: Cambridge University Press

Flammer, A. (1996). *Entwicklungstheorien* [Theories of development] (2nd ed.). Berne, Switzerland: Huber.

Flammer, A., Grob, A., & Lüthi, R. (1989). Swiss adolescents' attribution of control. In J.P. Forgas, & J.M.Innes (Eds.), *Recent advances in social psychology: An international perspective* (pp. 81–94). Amsterdam: Elsevier.

Flammer, A., Grob, A., & Lüthi, R. (1994). *Bernese Questionnaire on Adolescents' Perception of Control (BAG)* (Research Report No. 1994–1). Institute of Psychology, University of Berne, Switzerland.

Folkman, S., Lazarus, R.S., Gruen, R.J., & DeLongis, A. (1986). Dynamics of a stressful encounter: Cognitive appraisal, coping, and encounter outcomes. *Journal of Personality and Social Psychology, 50*, 992–1003.

Goulet, L.R., & Baltes, P.B. (Eds.). (1970). *Life-span developmental psychology: Research and theory*. New York: Academic Press.

Grob, A. (1995). Subjective well-being and significant life-events across the life-span. *Swiss Journal of Psychology, 54*, 3–18.

Grob, A. (1998). Adolescents' well-being in 14 cultural contexts. In J.-E.Nurmi (Ed.), *Adolescents, cultures and conflicts—Growing up in Europe* (pp. 21–42). New York: Garland.

Grob, A., Flammer, A., & Neuenschwander, M. (1992). *Kontrollattributionen und Wohlbefinden von Schweizer Jugendlichen III* [Control attributions and subjective well-being of Swiss adolescents III]. (Research Report No. 1992–4). Institute of Psychology, University of Berne, Switzerland.

Grob, A., Flammer, A., & Wearing A.J. (1995). Adolescents' perceived control: Domain specificity, expectancy, and appraisal. *Journal of Adolescence, 18,* 403–25.

Grob, A., Little, T.D., Wanner, B., Wearing, A.J., & Euronet (1996). Adolescents' well-being and perceived control across fourteen sociocultural contexts. *Journal of Personality and Social Psychology, 71,* 785–795.

Grob, A., Lüthi, R., Kaiser, F.G., Flammer, A., Mackinnon, A., & Wearing, A.J. (1991). Berner Fragebogen zum Wohlbefinden Jugendlicher (BFW) [Berne questionnaire of adolescents' subjective well-being (BSW–Y)]. *Diagnostica, 37,* 66–75.

Haan, N. (1993). The assessment of coping, defense and stress. In L.Goldberger & S.Breznitz (Eds.), *Handbook of stress: Theoretical and clinical aspects* (2nd ed., pp. 258–273). New York: Free Press.

Havighurst, R.J. (1948). *Developmental tasks and education.* New York: McKay.

Headey, B.W., & Wearing, A.J. (1992). *Understanding happiness.* Melbourne: Longman Cheshire.

Lazarus, R.S., & Launier, R. (1978). Stress-related transactions between person and environment. In L.Pervin & M.Lewis (Eds.), *Perspectives in international psychology* (pp. 287–327). New York: Plenum.

Lerner, R.M. (1982). Children and adolescents as producers of their own development. *Developmental Review, 2,* 309–333.

Little, T.D., Lindenberger, U., & Nesselroade, J.R. (1998). *On selecting indicators for multivariate measurement and modeling with latent variables.* Manuscript submitted for publication.

Michalos, A.C. (1985). Multiple discrepancy theory. *Social Indicators Research, 16,* 347–13.

Nurmi, J.-E. (1992). Age differences in adult life goals, concerns, and their temporal extension: A life course approach to future-oriented motivation. *International Journal of Behavioral Development, 15,*487–508.

Rotter, J.B. (1966). General expectancies for internal vs. external locus of control of reinforcement. *Psychological Monographs, 80,* 1–28.

Triandis, H.C. (1989). The self and social behavior in differing cultural contexts. *Psychological Review, 96,* 506–520.

Veenhoven, R. (1991). Is happiness relative? *Social Indicators Research, 24,* 1–34.

8

Adolescents' Preferences for Their Homeland and Other Countries

Connie Flanagan
Pennsylvania State University

Luba Botcheva
Center for Interdisciplinary Studies, Sofia, Bulgaria

The world is becoming more international at a breathtaking pace. Global reorganization has reduced the economic importance of national borders and has sparked intense national debates about the dangers to cultural diversity that political and economic reorganizations pose. Technology has expanded opportunities for cross-national communication and understanding, but it has also increased the hegemony of Western, especially U.S. culture in the images presented in advertising, entertainment, and lifestyle. For example, Dixon (1977) contended that, more than any other source of cultural stereotypes, comics published in the United States and Britain promote prejudice toward foreigners and extranationals. Almost three decades have passed since McLuhan's premonition that the medium of telecommunications would reshape our concepts of the world as a global village and consequently our self-concepts (McLuhan & Fiore, 1967). Yet it remains an open question whether this medium has had a homogenizing effect or has been a means of increasing international understanding and perspective-taking. Has the arrival of the global village had an impact on young people's interest in other cultures? This chapter provides some insights into that question.

The issue is both developmental and historical. It is historical insofar as the medium has transformed opportunities for younger generations to learn about cultures other than their own. But the question is also developmental because it is based on the assumption that concepts such as *homeland, other countries* or *compatriots, foreigners* are meaningful to children. As Piaget (Piaget & Weil, 1951) ascertained, mastery of the concepts of *homeland* or *other countries* involves a process of decentering, of transition from egocentricity to reciprocity. His interviews with Swiss children revealed that young children conceived of foreigners in absolute terms and not only preferred their own homeland to all others but could

131

not understand why French or English children might also prefer their homelands. With age, however, children became aware that foreigners might have an affection for their own homelands. However, as Piaget noted, the implications of this capacity for reciprocity will vary according to whether the child's social environment is tolerant or critical of foreigners and other outgroups.

In general, developmental theory posits an age-related decline in in-group bias. Studies of U.S. youth are generally supportive of such trends. Tolerance of persons and groups with whom one disagrees or who promote offensive ideas increases between childhood and adolescence and appears to peak in late adolescence (Owen & Dennis, 1987; Sigelman & Toebben, 1992). This developmental trend is qualified by the fact that adolescents are less likely to accord rights to groups they dislike (Zellman & Sears, 1971), although tolerance can be enhanced by learning more about such groups (Avery, 1992). Tolerance may be unrelated to children's interests in social interaction with others. According to Sigelman and Toebben (1992), despite an age-related increase in political tolerance and in defending free speech, there is no such change in children's desire to interact with persons with whom they disagree. Not surprisingly, there are also age-related increases in children's awareness of nations and of dimensions of difference between nations. However, insofar as older youth are more capable of identifying with the polarities that exist between their own nation and others (Lambert & Klineberg, 1967; Middleton, Tajfel, & Johnson, 1970; Targ, 1970), the potential for nationalism may also increase with age. Other work has shown that national and international images are affected by socialization practices and that these images become more differentiated with age (LeVine, 1965). Major world events and interpretations of those events, shaped inevitably by the media, affect public images of the nations involved (Deutsch & Merritt, 1965). Unfortunately, although mass-mediated communication is related to adult tolerance, it seems to be less effective in instilling tolerant attitudes in children (Owen & Dennis, 1987).

There have been relatively few studies of children's attitudes toward their homeland and toward other countries. Exceptions are seen in two studies in the United States that approached the issue with very different methodologies and arrived at similar conclusions. Sinatra, Beck, and McKeown (1992) were interested in whether 2 years of instruction in U.S. history would have any effect on children's characterization of their own and other countries. They conducted interviews with fifth and eighth graders and found that the children's perceptions of their own country were quite positive and, by comparison, their perceptions of other nations were quite negative. Although simplistic and absolute categorization of countries as either good or bad decreased somewhat as children got older, their longitudinal data revealed that students' views of their homeland and other nations became more stable over time and after instruction.

In the second of these studies, Zevin (1995) administered a semantic differential to middle and high school students to assess their attitudes toward the United States, Canada, and Russia and related those attitudes to the sources of information students said were the basis of their feelings. A bias in favor of one's homeland was apparent. Futhermore, time spent viewing television news was associated with positive views of one's own national identity as well as with the belief that Russia was an untrustworthy nation.

Comparative studies of children's national preferences are quite rare. One notable exception is work by Tajfel, Nemeth, Jahoda, Campbell, and Johnson (1970) conducted in six European countries. When 6- to 12-year-olds were asked to choose from a set of standardized photographs those people they liked or disliked, the children overwhelmingly preferred people whom they believed were compatriots. This preference decreased as children got older except in Louvain where the preference for compatriots increased with age, an exception the investigators speculated may have been due to the lack of a unique national label for the Flemish children.

We took the opportunity of the cross-national collaboration to gain some insights into adolescents' interest in their homeland as well as their interest in other cultures and peoples. We presented youth with a list of the countries participating in the study and asked to what extent they would like to have contact with people in each of those countries. Three sets of issues were addressed. The first was whether there would be a tendency among all adolescents to indicate a preference for compatriots over foreigners. Based on convergent evidence from the literature, we predicted a main effect for homeland preference; that is, regardless of national origins, we expected adolescents would prefer contact with compatriots over foreigners.

Second, we expected to find a common underlying structure of adolescents' national preferences, affected in large part by the hegemony of Western media and advertising. Of the 25 largest advertising companies in the world, 15 are American (Barber, 1995). To get an idea of the global impact of advertising we can imagine the statistic that one fifth of the human race views the same Pepsi-Cola ad put out by the world's largest advertising company (Bagdikian, 1992). Based on this Western and particularly U.S. media monopoly, we expected youth would conceive of those lifestyles as more modern and desirable. Accordingly, we predicted a "Western" bias; that is, across countries, adolescents would express more interest in contact with the United States and western Europe than with eastern/central Europe or Russia. A logical extension of this hypothesis was that youth from western Europe and Scandinavia would express greater interest in the United States than in other countries. Despite high standards of living in their own countries, we expected that American lifestyles, symbols, and pop culture would pique the interests of youth.

Third, we predicted specific regional, gender, and age differences in the preference patterns of youth. Regional differences were expected to reflect (a) enemy images promulgated by Cold War relations between the United States and Russia and (b) the sociopolitical constraints imposed on nations of the former Soviet bloc. With respect to the latter, we predicted first, that youth from eastern/central Europe and Russia would express the highest overall interest in meeting foreigners. Although constraints on travel and information exchange varied among the nations of eastern and central Europe, there were undeniable restrictions on commerce with outsiders in all of these nations. Considerable efforts by schools, media, and youth organizations were aimed at homogeneity rather than autonomy in the population (Karpati, 1996; Pastuovic, 1993). In a context where official propaganda censored music and news from Western sources, pop culture from such sources was even more alluring. As Wicke (1985) pointed out, as early as the 1960s the technology of the simple transistor radio gave young people in the German Democratic Republic the autonomy of making their own media decisions. The developmental import of Wicke's point is echoed in work by Larson, Kubey, and Colletti (1989). Their research with an early adolescent U.S. population suggests that the shift from television viewing to listening to music signals a change in value orientations from parent to peer.

Manaev (1991) reported on the patterns of listening to Western radio among 2,000 young Belorussians; surveys in the late 1980s revealed this was a mass phenomenon. Listening habits were related to youths' reports that, after listening to Western radio, they changed their opinions on issues. In addition, listening habits in terms of the choice of music and information became an integral part of the social construction of the youths' interactions, identities, and ultimately their beliefs.

At the time we were collecting data for this study, limitations on information exchange and travel were being lifted and communication and contact with foreigners was just becoming possible. In this historic context we expected youth from the eastern and central European nations to be eager for more information and contact with people outside their borders. Counterbalancing this general interest in foreigners, we expected the adolescents from eastern/central Europe to want less contact with Russia itself. The end of an era of Soviet occupation in their countries and a chance for autonomy in the region was marked in 1990. One could argue that during the 40 years of Soviet occupation contact with Russia came at a cost to the citizens of these countries. In terms of national identity, that cost included a revision of their history and a prohibition on many cultural traditions. In light of this recent history of relations with Russians, we expected youth from the eastern and central European countries to want very little contact with Russia. Our third hypothesis with respect to regional differences was that U.S. youth would be more interested than others in having contact with Russians. Because data were being collected at a relatively early point in the Cold War thaw, relations between the two superpowers were being redefined and enemy images refrained by the media. Although U.S. youth are notorious for their poor command of geography, every young American has some knowledge, however stereotypical, of Russia.

Our final questions were developmental ones. We expected that (a) older adolescents would be more interested than their younger counterparts in having contact with foreigners, and (b) females would express more overall interest than males in meeting foreigners. As noted earlier, tolerance appears to peak during late adolescence. Furthermore, compared to children and early adolescents, older adolescents have access to different sources of information and communication and enjoy more independence (e.g., freedom to travel), factors that facilitate cross-national contact. In addition, as youth approach the transition to adulthood they should be more cognizant of the importance of international communication in a global world. With respect to gender differences, research on attitudes toward ethnic and racial groups indicates that among White youth, females tend to be more open and tolerant than males toward groups other than their own (Phinney & Cobb, 1993). Based on this work, we expected that females in our study would express more interest than males in meeting people from other countries.

METHOD

The variables used in the analyses were adolescents' reports of how much contact they would like to have with people in 10 different countries. For this purpose we used a Likert-type scale ranging from 1 *(no contact)* to 4 *(very frequent contact)*. The following countries were included in the list: Bulgaria, Czechoslovakia, Finland, France, Germany, Hungary, Poland, Russia, Switzerland, and the United States. Participants from eight of these countries had the option of choosing contact with others in their own country. Note, however, that the option to choose one's own country was not available in the Finnish or Hungarian versions of the survey.

Regional composites were created to be used as independent variables. These were based on the 10 original countries with the addition of Norway, Romania, and a sample of French-speaking Swiss. The following regional composites were formed: (a) Western Europe, which included samples from the French- and German-speaking parts of Switzerland, Germany, and France; (b) Scandinavia, which was comprised of the samples from Finland and Norway; (c) Eastern and Central Europe, which consisted of Bulgaria, the Czechoslovakian Federal Republic (CSFR), Hungary, Poland, and Romania; (d) Russia; and (e) the United States. The decision to separate Scandinavia from Western Europe was based on considerations of geographical proximity, linguistic differences, and the likelihood that youth would be more comfortable with nations, customs, language, and people from their own geographical region. Geographically, Norway and Finland, like the rest of Scandinavia, are separated from the European continent. As a result, travel to these destinations, especially by car or train, is neither as easy nor as quick as it is to countries on the mainland of Europe. Thus, we expected that youths' interest in this region would differ from their interest in Western Europe. Note that we were able to create this grouping only for the independent variable because Norway was not an option in the list of countries that comprised the dependent variable. The decision to separate Russia from the other nations in the former Soviet-bloc was based on the arguments presented earlier. An additional refinement of the independent variable was made for the analysis of adolescents' interest in meeting people from Russia. For that analysis only, the composite of Eastern/Central Europe was divided into two regions with the CSFR, Hungary, and Poland categorized as Central Europe and Bulgaria and Romania as Eastern Europe.

Regional composites also were created to be used as dependent variables. The dependent variable, Western Europe, was comprised of the mean level of adolescents' reported interest in having contact with France, Germany, Finland, and Switzerland. The dependent variable, Eastern/Central Europe, was comprised of the mean level of interest in having contact with Bulgaria, CSFR, Hungary, and Poland. In constructing these regional composites we adjusted for the fact that some samples (i.e., Hungary and Finland) did not have the option of their own country as a preference. Thus we made the preference for one's own country missing for all cases. (Note that the independent and dependent variable composites differ slightly due in part to the addition of three samples, that is, Norway, Romania, and French-speaking Swiss, after initial survey construction). Analysis of variance (ANOVA) with repeated measures was used to test for an overall preference for meeting people from Western over Eastern European countries. Following that, three-way (age×gender×geographical region) ANOVAS were run. Considering the large number of cases and the number of analyses to be conducted, significance levels were set at $p < .01$.

RESULTS

Adolescents' Preferences for Their Homeland and for Other Countries

Before transforming any variables, descriptive statistics were run to assess adolescents' level of interest in having contact with people from their own and other countries. Table 8.1 presents the means and standard deviations for (a) adolescents' preferences for meeting compatriots and (b) the other country of highest interest to each group of adolescents. Recall that methodological constraints meant that the following groups did not have the option of selecting their own country: Finland, Hungary, Norway, and Romania. As expected, adolescents expressed high interest in having contact with compatriots;

TABLE 8.1
Adolescents' Preferences for Meeting Other People

| Country | Interest in Own Country | | Highest Interest in Another Country | | Other Country of |
	M	SD	M	SD	Highest Interest
Bulgaria	3.32	.91	3.56	.76	United States
CSFR[1]	3.54	.73	3.26	.90	United States
Finland	no option		3.21	.85	United States
France	3.45	.88	3.54	.70	United States
Germany	3.62	.73	3.27	1.01	United States
Hungary	no option		3.20	.88	United States
Norway	no option		3.38	.80	United States
Poland	3.86	.55	3.08	.81	United States
Russia	3.71	.75	3.21	.85	United States
German Switzerland	3.60	.76	3.20	.94	United States
French Switzerland	3.40	.87	3.44	.78	United States
Romania	no option		3.51	.79	United States
United States	3.68	.80	2.72	1.05	France

[1]CSFR=Czechoslovakian Federal Republic.

however, they also showed relatively high interest in having contact with foreigners. Among the countries that had the preference for compatriots option, only youth from Bulgaria and France failed to choose compatriots over other groups, although the mean preference for their compatriots was not significantly lower than their top rated choice. Youth in all countries ranked the United States either first or second only to their own country.

Omnibus tests were conducted to address the Western bias in adolescents' preferences, followed by more discrete analyses. A repeated measures ANOVA was conducted with the preferences for Western and Eastern/Central European countries as the repeated measure and the five regional composites listed previously as the between-subjects factor. (Note that the United States and Russia were excluded from these composites.) The results indicated a significant effect of the repeated measure, $F(1,3204)=2623.60$, $p<.0001$. As expected, youth voiced stronger preferences for having contact with people in Western ($M=2.72$, $SD=.71$), when compared to Eastern or Central European ($M=1.80$, $SD=.66$), countries.

Adolescent Differences in Preference Pattern Toward Other Countries

Turning next to our expectations for regional differences in preference patterns, we first examined whether, when compared to other regional groups, youth from the former Soviet bloc would express higher overall interest in meeting foreigners. To assess this question, a mean interest level, based on the average for the 10 original countries, was computed, and a 5 (region)×2 (gender)×2 (adolescent age group) ANOVA run. The results indicated main effects of region and gender, and interactions of region with gender. Posthoc Scheffe tests supported our thesis that, compared to youth in the other three regions, those from Russia and Eastern and Central Europe would be significantly more interested in having contact with foreigners. The results of the gender differences by region are presented in Table 8.2. Whereas there were no gender differences in Russia, the United States, or the Eastern and Central European countries, compared to their male peers, female adolescents from Scandinavia and Western Europe were more interested in having contact with foreigners. Contrary to our expectation, older adolescents did not express more interest than their younger peers in having contact with foreigners.

Adolescent Differences in Preference Pattern Toward Western and Eastern/Central Europe

Tables 8.3 and 8.4 summarize the results of the three-way ANOVAS for interest in Western and Eastern/Central Europe respectively.

The analysis of students' interest in meeting people from Western Europe revealed a main effect of region, $F(4,3217)=70.39$, $p<.0001$, and an interaction of region with age, $F(4,3217)=4.40$, $p<.01$. Consistent with

TABLE 8.2
Adolescents' Interest in Having Contact with Foreigners: Gender Differences by Region

	Females		Males		
Region	M	SD	M	SD	F
Eastern/Central Europe	2.48	.52	2.46	.58	ns
Russia	2.51	.43	2.50	.61	ns
Scandinavia	2.37	.53	2.17	.52	18.64*
Western Europe	2.24	.54	2.08	.51	19.04*
United States	2.11	.69	2.04	.76	ns

Note, ns=nonsignificant.
*$p<.0001$.

TABLE 8.3
Adolescents' Interest in Having Contact With People in Western European Countries: Age Differences by Region

	Younger Adolescents		Older Adolescents		
Region	M	SD	M	SD	F
Eastern/Central Europe	2.92	.71	2.90	.64	ns
Russia	2.90	.69	2.89	.64	ns
Scandinavia	2.48	.70	2.72	.68	14.70**
Western Europe	2.48	.64	2.52	.65	ns
United States	2.19	.82	2.44	.83	4.38*

Note, ns=nonsignificant.
*$p<.05$, **$p<.0001$.

TABLE 8.4

Adolescents' Interest in Having Contact With People in Eastern/Central European Countries: Gender Differences by Region

Region	Girls		Boys		
	M	SD	M	SD	F
Eastern/Central Europe	1.88	.65	1.83	.69	ns
Russia	1.90	.53	1.94	.71	ns
Scandinavia	1.96	.62	1.68	.56	29.20*
Western Europe	1.78	.66	1.55	.59	26.38*
United States	1.78	.67	1.78	.78	ns

Note. ns=nonsignificant.
*$p<.0001$.

the results presented in Table 8.2, youth from Russia ($M=2.90$, $SD=.65$) and Eastern/Central Europe ($M=2.91$, $SD=.67$) expressed more interest in meeting people from Western Europe than did other groups. In addition, as Table 8.3 shows, older adolescents from Scandinavia and the United States expressed more interest in meeting Western Europeans than their younger counterparts, although there were no age differences in the other regions.

The analysis of adolescents' interest in meeting people from Eastern/Central Europe revealed main effects of region, $F(4,3192)=12.42$, $P<.0001$; main effects of gender, $F(1,3192)=24.29$, $p<.0001$; and interactions of gender with region, $F(4, 3192)=5.43$, $p<.001$. Post hoc tests supported our expectation that girls ($M= 1.86$, $SD=.64$) would express more interest in meeting people from Eastern/Central Europe than boys ($M=1.74$, $SD=.67$). In addition, youth from Western Europe were less interested in meeting Eastern/Central Europeans than their peers from Eastern Europe, Scandinavia, or Russia. Table 8.4 summarizes the gender differences for each region. As can be seen, male adolescents from Western Europe and Scandinavia expressed significantly less interest in meeting Eastern/Central Europeans than their female peers, whereas there were no gender differences among youth from the other three regions.

Adolescent Differences in Preference Pattern Toward the United States and Russia

We turn next to the analyses for specific interest in the United States and Russia. In terms of interest in the United States, the three-way ANOVA revealed a main effect of gender, $F(1,3008)=6.80$, $p<.01$, and an interaction of gender with age, $F(1,3008)=7.43$, $p<.01$. There were no regional differences in adolescents' expressed interest in having contact with the United States. As shown in Table 8.1, such interest was quite high in all countries (above 3.0 on a 4-point scale). The age by gender interaction was due to the fact that, among early adolescents, girls ($M= 3.41$, $SD=.81$) expressed more interest than boys ($M=3.24$, $SD=.92$), whereas there were no gender differences among older adolescents (Table 8.5).

Finally, our expectations for regional differences in adolescents' interest in Russia were only partially confirmed. Recall that Eastern/Central Europe was subdivided for this analysis. The results of the three-way ANOVA indicated significant effects of age, $F(1,2983)=22.50$, $p<.0001$; significant effect of region, $F(4,2983)=13.50$, $p<.0001$; and a gender by region interaction, $F(4,2983)=4.06$, $p<.01$. As expected, interest in Russia was low among youth from Central ($M=1.71$, $SD=.82$) and Eastern Europe ($M=1.79$, $SD=.92$). However, Scandinavian youth also expressed very low interest in contact with Russia ($M=1.77$, $SD=.84$). The results of Scheffe tests indicated that U.S. and Western European youth expressed more interest in having contact with Russia than their peers in Scandinavia, Central, and Eastern Europe. A closer look at the gender by region interaction did not yield any consistent pattern. Whereas girls from Central Europe and Scandinavia expressed more interest in Russia than did their male peers, girls from Eastern Europe were less interested than were the boys in that region. Gender had no effect on interest levels in the United States or Western Europe.

In summary, we addressed three sets of questions. With respect to the first, adolescents showed a preference for contact with compatriots, although they also expressed a high level of interest in meeting certain groups of foreigners. Second, regardless of their national origin there was a common structure underlying youth preference patterns. A western bias was clearly revealed. Not only did youth show a marked preference for contact with Western over Eastern/Central Europe, they also ranked contact with people in the United States higher than contact with any other group, except their own. Our third set of hypotheses were only partially confirmed. Youth from Eastern/Central Europe and Russia were, on average, more interested in foreign contacts than were youth in other regions. In addition, youth from the former Soviet bloc did some discriminating between countries because they expressed relatively less interest in Russia. The results presented some surprises as well. The comparatively low interest Scandinavian youth had in Russia was unexpected, and our hypotheses of gender and age differences were supported in some regions but not in others.

TABLE 8.5

Adolescents' Interest in Having Contact With People in Russia: Gender Differences by Region

Region	Girls		Boys		
	M	SD	M	SD	F
Central Europe	1.78	.82	1.66	.82	5.89*
Eastern Europe	1.69	.81	1.93	1.02	7.08**
Scandinavia	1.87	.84	1.68	.83	6.90**
Western Europe	1.95	.96	1.91	.98	ns
United States	2.12	1.07	2.22	1.11	ns

Note, ns=nonsignificant.
*$p<.05$, **$p<.01$.

DISCUSSION AND CONCLUSION

The political, economic, and social landscape that contemporary youth will enter as they move into adulthood is vastly different from the one their parents knew. Increasingly, the world is interconnected. Issues from acid rain and destruction of the ozone to migration, economic, and cultural exchange transcend national borders. Citizenship for today's youth will be defined in global, not just national, terms. In the late 1960s, Erikson (1968) pointed out that tolerance and interdependence are essential aspects of democratic identities and, as far back as Aristotle, friendship was considered a foundation of the polity. Friendship, of course, depends on the opportunity for contact with and understanding of others. The data from our study suggest that youth are open to learning more about foreigners but typically prefer contact with compatriots. This preference is consistent with the preponderance of evidence from social science suggesting that people tend to seek contact with similar others. However, a preference for that which is familiar is a rather inadequate standard of preparation for an increasingly global world. Proactive steps may be called for and there is evidence pointing to the kinds of measures that should be taken. For example, comparative studies with secondary school students indicate that students' interest in and knowledge about current events and politics is enhanced by an open classroom climate where exchange of ideas and opinions is encouraged (Torney-Purta & Lansdale, 1986). Such proactive interventions would seem to be an imperative in light of the other results of this study.

We suggest several inferences to explain the Western and particularly U.S. bias in young people's preferences. First, although we cannot directly test this with the data, we believe the media and advertising play a powerful role in shaping such preferences. The popular image of personal freedom and material success supposedly enjoyed by the average U.S. citizen is attractive to youth. Physical appearance is prominent in the list of factors contributing to an adolescent's social status (Langlois, 1986), and adolescent subculture and fashion has been traditionally of western origin. Second, the low level of interest in Eastern/Central Europe, especially as expressed by youth from Western Europe, suggests that these nations may still be considered outgroups, hardly surprising when the nations themselves, at the end of the 20th century, have been assigned a second-class status vis-à-vis the European Community. One of the reasons for this low interest might be a lack of information about the characteristics of the individuals in these countries. The image of an Eastern bloc may have been strong in the minds of participants at the time of the study. In time this schema should be accommodated to include the diversity of cultures, customs, languages, and peoples in the Central and Eastern European region, but the stereotype will change only if increased opportunities for travel and information exchange motivate such reappraisals.

The possibilities of distance learning via the technology of telecommunications and the Internet provide such tools but, to be effective, these technologies have to be broadly available to young people. Torney-Purta's (1990, 1992) work provides evidence of the potential of technology to enlarge adolescents' schema about international relations. As part of the Maryland Summer Center for International Studies (MSCIS), she employs a computer-assisted foreign policy simulation with 13- to 17-year-olds. In the course of an intense 2 weeks, Torney-Purta demonstrates impressive changes in adolescents' knowledge of international affairs, perspective-taking, and appreciation of political and economic reciprocity in international relations. In a similar vein, international education has been promoted for its potential to promote young people's openness to other countries and groups (Reischauer, 1973; UNESCO, 1989).

Finally, the results of our study point to the role of historical change and political policies of specific nations as these impact the preference patterns of their youth. The fact that adolescents from Central/Eastern Europe and Russia were especially eager to meet foreigners can be understood in the context of the political changes occurring in those nations at the time of the study. After several decades of censure, opportunities for travel and a free exchange of information were suddenly opening up. The importance that young people under those circumstances assigned to meeting foreigners may reflect the novelty of the opportunity. (In a similar vein, Schlegel, 1995, describes an upsurge of interest in St. Valentine's Day among adolescents in the gymnasia of Poland. The addition of this holiday to the social calendar of teenagers is a phenomenon instigated by the teens and one that, because of its Western connotation, marks them as "in the know.") As historical conditions change and youth in the nations of central and eastern Europe adapt to yet a new social order, we would expect to find parallel changes in their preference patterns. Our prediction would be that, until standards of living increase in these countries, the desire to know more about Western styles and mores will not diminish.

Some scholars have sounded a pessimistic tone with respect to the failure of information technology to promote civic interest and involvement. Greider (1992) argued that whereas in principle the proliferation of broadcasting and technology should enrich the democratic process, in practice it has impoverished civic participation. If today's youth are going to be competent global citizens they will need both access to the tools of modern communication as well as the motivation to utilize those tools to promote global understanding.

REFERENCES

Avery, P.G. (1992). Political tolerance: How adolescents deal with dissenting groups. In H.Haste & J.Torney-Purta (Eds.), *New directions for child development: The development of political understanding: A new perspective* (pp. 39–51). San Francisco: Jossey-Bass.

Bagdikian, Ben H. (1992). *The media monopoly* (4th ed.). Boston: Beacon Press.

Barber, B.R. (1995). *Jihad vs. McWorld*. New York: Random House.

Deutsch, K.W., & Merritt, R.L. (1965). Effects of events on national and international images. In C.H.Kelman (Ed.), *International behavior: A social-psychological analysis* (pp. 132–187). New York: Holt, Rinehart & Winston.

Dixon, B. (1977). *Catching them young 2: Political ideas in children's fiction*. London: Pluto Press.

Erikson, E.H. (1968). *Identity: Youth and crisis*. New York: Norton.

Greider, W. (1992). *Who will tell the people? The betrayal of American democracy*. New York: Simon & Schuster.

Karpati, A. (1996). Hungarian adolescents of the 1990's: Ideals, beliefs and expectations. In D. Benner & D.Lenzen (Eds.), *Education for the new Europe* (pp. 29–42). Providence, RI: Berghahn Books.

Lambert, W.E., & Klineberg, O. (1967). *Children's views of foreign peoples: A cross-national study*. New York: Appleton-Century-Crofts.

Langlois, J.H. (1986). From the eye of the beholder to behavioral reality: Development of social behaviors and social relations as a function of physical attractiveness. In C.P.Herman, M.P. Zanna, & E.T.Higgins (Eds.), *Physical appearance, stigma and social behavior: The Ontario symposium* (Vol. 3), (pp. 23–47) Hillsdale, NJ: Lawrence Erlbaum Associates.

Larson, R., Kubey, R., & Colletti, J. (1989). Changing channels: Early adolescent media choices and shifting investments in family and friends. *Journal of Youth and Adolescence, 18,*583–599.

LeVine, R.A. (1965). Socialization, social structure, and intersocietal images. In C.H.Kelman, (Ed.), *International behavior: A social-psychological analysis,* (pp. 45–69). New York: Holt, Rinehart & Winston.

Manaev, O. (1991). The influence of western radio on the democratization of Soviet youth. *Journal of Communication, 41(2),* 72–91.

McLuhan, M., & Fiore, Q. (1967). *The medium is the message*. New York: Bantam.

Middleton, M.R., Tajfel, H., & Johnson, N.B. (1970). Cognitive and affective aspects of children's attitudes. *British Journal of Social and Clinical Psychology, 9,* 122–134.

Owen, D., & Dennis, J. (1987). Preadult development of political tolerance. *Political Psychology, 8,541–561.*

Pastuovic, N. (1993). Problems of reforming educational systems in post-communist countries. *International Review of Education, 39,* 405–418.

Phinney, J.S., & Cobb, N.J. (1993, March). *Adolescents' reasoning about discrimination: Ethnic and attitudinal predictors*. Paper presented at the biennial meeting of the Society for Research in Child Development, New Orleans, LA.

Piaget, J., & Weil, A.M. (1951). The development in children of the idea of homeland, and of relations with other countries. *International Social Science Bulletin, 3,* 561–578.

Reischauer, E. (1973). *Toward the 21st century: Education for a changing world*. NY: Alfred A. Knopf.

Schlegel, A. (1995). The globalization of adolescent culture. Unpublished manuscript, University of Arizona, Tucson.

Sigelman, C., & Toebben, J. (1992). Tolerant reactions to advocates of disagreeable ideas in childhood and adolescence. *Merrill Palmer Quarterly, 38, 542–557.*

Sinatra, G.M., Beck, I.L., & McKeown, M.G. (1992). A longitudinal characterization of young students' knowledge of their country's government. *American Educational Research Journal, 29*, 633–661.

Tajfel, H., Nemeth, C., Jahoda, G., Campbell, J.D., & Johnson, N. (1970). The development of children's preferences for their own country: A cross-national study. *International Journal of Psychology, 5*, 245–253.

Targ, H.R. (1970). Children's developing orientations to international politics. *Journal of Peace Research, 7*, 79–97.

Torney-Purta, J. (1990). From attitudes and knowledge to schemata: Expanding the outcomes of political socialization research. In O.Ichilov (Ed.), *Political socialization, citizenship, education, and democracy* (pp. 98–115). New York: Columbia University Press.

Torney-Purta, J. (1992). Cognitive representations of the political system in adolescents: The continuum from pre-novice to expert. In H.Haste & J.Torney-Purta (Eds.), *New directions for child development, The development of political understanding: A new perspective* (Vol. 56, pp. 11–25), San Francisco: Jossey Bass.

Torney-Purta, J., & Lansdale, D. (1986, April). *Classroom climate and process in international studies: Data from the American schools and the world project.* Paper presented at the annual meeting of the American Educational Research Association, San Francisco, CA.

UNESCO. (1989). *Education for International Understanding, Co-operation, Peace and Human Rights.* APEID. Bangkok, Thailand: Principal regional office for Asia and the Pacific.

Wicke, P. (1985). Young people and popular music in East Germany: Focus on a scene *Communication Research, 12*, 319–325.

Zellman, G., & Sears, D.O. (1971). Childhood origins of tolerance for dissent. *Journal of Social Issues, 27*, 109–136.

Zevin, J. (1995). *Perceptions of national identity: How adolescents view their own and other countries* (ERIC Document 380394). Report No. Ed 380 394 (EDRS) 50024 852.

9

Being a Minority: Hungarian Adolescents in Transylvania, Romania

Benö Csapó
Erzsébet Czachesz
Attila József University, Szeged, Hungary

Aurora Liiceanu
Institute of Psychology, Bucharest, Romania

Sándor Lázár
Babes-Bólyai University, Cluj, Romania

In recent decades, multiculturalism has become a key term in the educational and psychological literature. Typically, *multiculturalism* means the acknowledgment of cultural pluralism. It involves supporting cultural variety, maintaining diversity, sometimes, this involves actively protecting minority cultures from unification tendencies. However, this term has different connotations in different regions of Europe. For example, in Switzerland, multiculturalism has been the way of life for centuries. In some Western European countries, coexistence with immigrants from other cultures inspired the elaboration of multicultural education. In recent years, multiculturalism is most often mentioned in relation to the European unification process, which resulted in unprecedented communication among Western European nations.

In some Central European countries, that have tight historical links to the West and are eager to join the European Union, the idea of multiculturalism is well-accepted and the legislation and educational systems are getting ready to adopt Western norms. The idea of peaceful coexistence of different cultures is far less welcome in the Eastern European countries, however, and the rights of minorities are far less accepted. For example, using bilingual street names and other bilingual public signs, which is a norm in the regions of Scandinavian countries populated by ethnic minorities, is unimaginable or is subject to intense political debate in Eastern Europe. The political systems under Soviet dominance suppressed ethnic and minority conflicts during the post-World War II era and the collapse of the Soviet regime unleashed hostilities caused by these unsolved problems. In the 1990s, the multitude of ethnic conflicts range from political dispute within a parliamentary system to violent extremist demonstrations to a full-scale bloody war.

Transylvania, a large geographical and economic region in the Carpatian basin, has been home to a few nationalities—Hungarians, Romanians, and Germans—for centuries. During its stormy history, it was part of the Hungarian Kingdom (11th–16th centuries), became an autonomous principality when the Turks occupied central Hungary (16th-17th centuries), and then it became part of the Austro-Hungarian Monarchy. Finally, in 1920, in accord with the Treaty of Trianon closing World War I, Transylvania was ceded to Romania and around 3 million Hungarians remained there as the largest national minority of Europe.

Although during the Cold War era the Central and Eastern European countries were often referred to by western politicians and journalists as a "bloc" (Ostblock, Eastern bloc, Soviet bloc, countries behind the Iron Curtain, the satellite states, etc.), they did not really form a coherent bloc. These countries had different cultures and different traditions; furthermore, the political atmosphere of the period that they spent behind the Iron Curtain was quite different from country to country. Thus, those adolescents who were the participants in this study have spent their adolescent years in different political and social climates on the two different sides of the border, and the political changes have also affected them in different ways. Therefore, it is not only their minority status that made the social environment of the Hungarian adolescents in Transylvania different from that of those living in Hungary.

In Hungary, political and economic reforms started at the end of the 1960s, introducing elements of market economy into the principally central planning system. The reforms accelerated in the 1980s, resulting in a modest form of welfare. Journalists and political scientists were quite creative in finding telling expressions (the merriest barrack in the camp, goulash communism, soft dictatorship, etc.) to describe the peculiar social system of Hungary in the 1970s and 1980s. By that time, there was also a broad underground movement, the so-called *democratic opposition,* which became a negotiating partner of the old regime in elaborating the way of transition. Thus, the political turn in Hungary took place through round-table negotiations and resulted in the modification of the constitution (defining Hungary as a parliamentary democracy) in October 1989 and the parliamentary elections in the spring of 1990. At the time of our data collection, adolescents lived in a working multiparty democracy with privatization in progress, but the negative effects of the transition (unemployment, inflation, growing social inequalities, drug abuse, crime, etc.) were also experienced.

In Romania, modest steps of distancing its politics from the mainstream Soviet political measures in international issues earned some respect for the country during the 1970s, but at the same time, inner politics went wild and by the 1980s, the Ceausescu regime became the symbol of a paranoiac dictatorship and a cult of the self. A strict ban on abortion, combined with nationalistic propaganda promoting the increase of the population, resulted in the birth of thousands of unwanted children later left in orphanages. The last years of the regime were marked by food, fuel, and electricity rationing and an acute shortage of basic goods. Religious and historic buildings in the capital were destroyed and within the framework of so-called systematization, thousands of villages were targeted for demolition. One aim of this systematic attempt to destroy traditional values was to dissolve compact minority communities that had been preserving their own traditional culture. The change of the political system then took place in a sudden eruption in December 1989, accompanied by street fighting, assaults, and brutal scenarios and ending in the killing of dictators. In terms of democratization and improving living conditions, modest changes took place afterward. However, the situation of minorities did not improve; the new constitution (approved in 1992) defined Romania as a "unitary and national state," ignoring the existence of national minorities (for an authentic description of the 1989 revolutions, see Prins, 1990).

The coexistence of ethnic groups and the acculturation of national minorities are undoubtedly the most crucial issues that Eastern Europe faces at the end of this century. Berry describes four varieties of acculturation (integration, separation, assimilation, and marginalization; see Berry, Poortinga, Segall, & Dasen, 1992). In this chapter, we show how some features of acculturation can be characterized and how the type of acculturation can be identified by means of our questionnaire.

METHOD

Three samples are compared in this chapter. The Transylvanian sample ($N=594$, Hungarians in Romania) was drawn from schools for Hungarian minorities in Cluj-Napoca. The same principles of sampling were used there as in all other countries (see chap. 2, this volume). Altogether, 24 classes were included, proportionally representing the Hungarian classes in the schools of the city. The structure and management of the minority schools are identical to those of the Romanian schools. The Hungarian sample (living in Hungary) is representative of the schools of Szeged and its metropolitan area ($N=572$). The same Hungarian translation of the questionnaire was administered to the two Hungarian-speaking samples. These two samples are compared to the Romanian sample, which is comprised of students in the capital, Bucharest ($N=215$; for further information on the Romanian and Hungarian samples, see chap. 2, this volume).

The sites where the Hungarian and Transylvanian adolescent groups live are quite comparable in terms of the size of the cities and their relative status within the region. Szeged is located in the southeast of Hungary, whereas Cluj-Napoca (in short, Cluj, or in its Hungarian name, Kolozsvár) is in the western part of Transylvania. Both cities are cultural centers in their region, with theaters and several high schools; both are hosts to a university. Furthermore, both downtown areas have the same typical atmosphere, so characteristic of many Central European cities, with a distinct type of architecture, cafés, squares, parks, and walking areas. This atmosphere, primarily shaped around the end of the last century within the Austro-Hungarian monarchy, is still clearly recognizable in Cluj, despite the many forces acting against it in this century. Furthermore, there is a specific historical relation between Cluj and Szeged. When Transylvania became part of Romania and the town Kolozsvár was renamed Cluj, the lives of the Hungarian faculty at the university became difficult. A new university was established then at Szeged and the Hungarian-speaking faculty of the former Kolozsvár University were invited to Szeged.

For the ease of expression, hereafter, the three groups will be referred to as *Hungarians* or the Szeged group (Hungarians living in Hungary), *Transylvanians* or the Cluj group (Hungarians living in Romania) and *Romanians* or the Bucharest group (Romanians living in Romania) and their names will be abbreviated as H, T, and R, respectively.

Among the three samples, we can identify three types of relations. Each relation links two of the three groups and separates them from the third group. Language and culture form a link between the adolescents living in Hungary (Szeged) and in Transylvania (Cluj). Transylvanian adolescents share citizenship, living circumstances, and broader social and political surroundings with their Romanian counterparts who live in Bucharest. Their minority status makes the situation of Transylvanian adolescents different from the other two groups, so nonminority status forms a link between the Szeged and Bucharest students.

We might expect that the responses given by Transylvanian adolescents to the questions in our questionnaire, being influenced by two cultures, would fall somewhere between those of the Romanian and Hungarian children. However, in some cases, they could be closer to one of these groups, thus showing the greater influence of that cultural group. Finding a pattern other than this, namely, that responses of the Transylvanian adolescents were outside the range of the two other samples, might suggest a specific effect of their minority status.

As a first overview of the similarities and differences between the groups just described, we have calculated the means for each of the three samples for future expectations, daily hassles, coping strategies, well-being, intercultural attitudes, and personal control items. Then, for each variable, we examined the differences between the means of the three samples to find out whether two of them were much closer to each other than to the third one. If two of the samples showed no significant difference, were obviously close to each other in terms of mean scores, and each differed significantly from the third sample, we marked them as being similar with respect to the given item. Thus, when in the next sections we speak about the similarity of two samples, we mean that there was not a significant difference between these two samples, but at the same time, that both differed significantly from the third sample.

There are several possible statistical methods for an accurate analysis of the effects of the three relations among the groups previously mentioned, but unfortunately, none of them alone is satisfactory and each requires lengthy tables for their presentation. So, here, we summarize the statistical procedures we carried out and only present the results of one (and in a certain way, the most conservative) statistical test for each item examined.

First, we introduced three new dichotomous variables to characterize the three types of relations. The value of the language and culture (L) was the same for the Hungarian and Transylvanian groups, the country and citizenship (C) were identical for the Transylvanian and Romanian groups, whereas *minority status* (M) had the same value for the two nonminority groups—the Hungarian and Romanian adolescents. Then, we carried out separate multivariate analyses of variance (MANOVAs), using these three variables as independent variables and sets of items as the dependent variables. The items were grouped according to the concepts they measured (i.e., future expectations, well-being, and so on). When the multivariate F values were highly significant ($p<.0001$), we went further and carried out univariate analyses (ANOVAs) in order to examine which variables were responsible for the overall differences. At this level, we carried out the conservative Scheffé test to show which groups were significantly different. The results of the Scheffé tests are summarized in Table 9.1. Out of the three groups, three pairs can be formed (H–R, H–T, R–T) and the Scheffé test simultaneously examines the significance of the differences between the members of the pairs. Significant differences are indicated with an "*" in the table. From no significant difference at all, through one difference in one of the pairs to three differences, eight patterns of differences are possible. From our point of view, those patterns where exactly two significant differences were found are the most interesting. For example, if there were significant differences in the H–R and in the R–T pairs but not in the H–T pair, this means that the Hungarian and the Transylvanian adolescents were similar in the respective variable.

With Scheffé tests, there is also a problem that we should mention. The Hungarian and Transylvanian samples were much larger than that of the Romanian. Because statistical significance is a function of sample sizes as well, this test indicated relatively more significant differences between the Hungarian and Transylvanian groups than could have been expected with equal sample sizes. Thus, fewer language and culture (L) type similarities appeared than were observed by just comparing the group means. However,

TABLE 9.1

Differences Among the Hungarian, Transylvanian, and Romanian Samples

Variable	Mean H	Mean T	Mean R	F	n	p	H-R	H-T	R-T	Relation
Future expectations										
Getting married/living permanently with partner	3.33	3.41	3.29	2.74	1368	ns				—
At what age do you expect to reach this goal?	23.5	23.3	25.3	20.71	1333	.0001	*		*	L
Acquiring a good profession	3.73	3.75	3.85	4.46	1379	.05	*		*	L
At what age do you expect to reach this goal?	21.4	21.2	22.2	8.26	1322	.001	*		*	L
Earning much money	3.09	3.17	3.33	8.52	1373	.05	*		*	L
Having children	3.44	3.52	3.10	22.73	1367	.0001	*		*	L
At what age do you expect to reach this goal?	25.5	25.4	27.3	19.47	1309	.0001	*		*	L
Good health	3.86	3.93	3.96	10.78	1375	.001	*	*		C
Being liked by other people	3.53	3.45	3.14	23.62	1364	.0001	*		*	L
Getting a good education	3.40	3.47	3.88	46.66	1376	.0001	*		*	L
Enjoying my vacations and leisure time	3.56	3.58	3.65	2.08	1375	ns				—
Taking responsibility for my parents	3.64	3.70	3.57	4.01	1368	.05			*	—
At what age do you expect to reach this goal?	24.5	24.7	31.6	41.34	1174	.0001	*		*	L
Having a good time with my friends	3.46	3.54	3.43	3.13	1377	ns				—
Being useful for my country	2.81	2.81	3.07	8.11	1361	.001	*		*	L
At what age do you expect to reach this goal?	24.1	23.2	26.9	11.9	1122	.001	*		*	L
Becoming an important professional	2.89	3.19	3.67	74.26	1372	.0001	*	*	*	—
At what age do you expect to reach this goal?	25.6	24.9	27.1	9.52	1186	.05	*		*	L
Becoming famous	1.92	2.33	2.80	75.71	1369	.0001	*	*	*	—
At what age do you expect to reach this goal?	27.2	28.8	30.8	8.11	1007	.001	*	*		—
Travelling a lot	2.94	3.11	3.26	12.48	1372	.01	*	*		C
At what age do you expect to reach this goal?	21.0	20.5	23.1	8.06	1147	.05	*		*	L

Variable	Mean H	Mean T	Mean R	F	n	p	H-R	H-T	R-T	Relation
Daily hassles										
School	2.78	2.75	2.31	32.88	1380	.0001	*		*	L
Money	2.39	2.38	1.88	30.35	1365	.001	*		*	L
Girlfriend (for boys)/boyfriend (for girls)	2.00	2.09	1.90	3.24	1351	ns				–
Remaining peers and friends	1.66	1.61	1.68	1.13	1367	ns				–
Active sports	2.05	1.93	1.41	38.14	1341	.0001	*		*	L
Parents/family life	2.01	2.06	1.77	7.51	1376	.01	*		*	L
Living area/ neighborhood	1.58	1.59	1.47	1.52	1369	ns				–
Health	1.77	1.73	1.62	2.86	1374	ns				–
Leisure opportunities	1.73	1.83	2.11	12.12	1374	.01	*		*	L
Getting public information	2.04	2.01	1.79	7.62	1361	.01	*		*	L
The own room at home	1.70	1.58	1.41	7.85	1356	.001	*			–
Coping strategies										
I cry.	1.86	2.18	2.04	17.79	1376	.05	*	*		C
I try to calm down.	2.79	2.90	3.07	8.40	1368	.05	*		*	L
I get angry and/or shout.	2.44	2.42	1.84	32.89	1366	.0001	*	*	*	L
I analyze the situation and try to solve/ overcome the difficulty.	2.81	3.10	3.44	51.66	1370	.0001	*	*	*	–
I pray and hope for the better.	2.01	2.79	3.00	104.98	1372	.0001	*	*		C
I try to forget the difficulties by doing/ thinking something else.	2.44	2.61	2.75	8.8	1375	.05	*	*		C
I'm sad and wait until my feelings become better.	1.91	2.24	2.51	33.42	1375	.0001	*	*		C
I get nervous and anxious.	2.50	2.47	2.20	7.33	1373	.01	*		*	L
I try again and again.	2.72	2.83	3.09	12.09	1365	.01	*		*	L
I give up and try to do something else.	1.75	1.99	1.99	11.88	1373	.01	*	*		C
I often find out that I had wrong aspirations and that the difficulties led me to go better ways.	2.46	2.60	2.58	3.56	1357	.05		*		–

Variable	Mean H	Mean T	Mean R	F	n	p	H-R	H-T	R-T	Relation
I try to forget my problems by taking alcohol and other drugs.	1.22	1.14	1.21	3.05	1373	ns				–
I withdraw and hide.	1.78	1.77	1.66	1.40	1369	ns				–
I seek help from friends.	2.25	2.35	2.11	5.66	1371	.01			*	–
I seek help from parents.	2.27	2.59	2.41	15.87	1372	.0001		*	*	–
I seek help from siblings.	1.98	2.24	1.82	17.07	1312	.0001		*	*	M
Well-being										
My future looks good.	2.83	2.88	3.11	11.57	1371	.001	*	*	*	L
I enjoy life more than most people.	2.38	2.54	2.94	32.33	1375	.0001	*	*	*	L
I'm not happy with the way my life plans have developed.	2.93	2.76	2.70	6.60	1371	.05	*	*		C
I accept the things in my life that cannot be changed	2.65	2.82	2.77	4.62	1375	.05		*		–
Whatever happens, I can see the bright side.	2.76	3.05	3.26	34.59	1368	.0001	*	*	*	C
I'm happy to live.	3.40	3.53	3.49	3.67	1368	.05	*	*		–
My life has not enough meaning.	3.30	3.21	3.56	11.89	1366	.01	*		*	L
My life runs on the right track.	2.60	2.54	3.34	80.35	1368	.0001	*	*	*	L
I'm able to do things just as good as other people can	2.95	2.91	2.58	20.8	1374	.0001	*	*	*	L
I feel less worthy than others.	3.06	2.72	3.07	23.83	1374	.0001	*	*	*	M
I have an overall positive attitude towards myself.	3.06	3.18	2.92	8.58	1370	.0001		*	*	–
I feel myself alone, even when I do not want to be.	3.04	2.96	2.80	4.98	1373	.01	*			–
Sometimes I feel that something is wrong with me.	2.46	2.14	2.06	22.97	1372	.0001	*	*		–
Intercultural attitudes										
Bulgaria	1.66	1.55	1.59	4.04	1363	.05		*		
Czechoslovakia	1.78	1.77	1.73	0.48	1359	ns				

Variable	Mean H	Mean T	Mean R	F	n	p	H-R	H-T	R-T	Relation
Finland	2.53	2.36	2.28	8.52	1363	.01	*		*	C
France	2.92	2.56	3.20	47.07	1367	.0001		*	*	M
Germany	3.04	3.11	3.33	8.86	1365	.01	*		*	L
Italy	2.87	2.90	3.25	13.96	1361	.0001	*		*	L
Poland	1.71	1.82	1.81	3.65	1349	.05		*		·
Russia	1.63	1.43	1.69	15.51	1354	.0001		*	*	M
Switzerland	3.07	2.92	3.30	13.71	1362	.01	*		*	L
United States	3.20	3.40	3.51	12.66	1370	.001	*	*		C
Personal control - development										
Do you think that you can influence the way you are and how you behave?	1.79	1.77	1.79	.43	1370	ns				–
Indicate to what extent you can influence the way ...	6.53	6.74	7.57	18.6	1364	.0001	*		*	L
Indicate to what extent you can influence the way ... in 3 up to 5 years.	7.01	7.66	7.76	18.56	1355	.0001	*	*		C
Who or what influences the way ...										
I do	1.93	1.92	1.54	4.77	903	.05	*		*	L
Peers (e.g. fellow-students, siblings, friends)	2.88	3.41	3.76	17.06	872	.001	*	*		C
Authority (e.g. parents, master of a trade, teacher)	3.40	2.82	3.32	12.93	868	.01		*	*	M
Institutions (e.g. school, place of work)	4.7	3.68	4.35	43.78	856	.0001	*	*	*	M
Society (e.g. publicity, fashion)	5.08	4.30	4.67	21.46	858	.0001	*	*		–
Natural laws (e.g. weather, good luck, bad luck)	4.64	4.87	4.41	4.97	866	.01				–
Compare your influence with the one of the friends of your age.	2.59	2.60	2.72	2.78	1323	ns				–
Do you try to get more influence on the way ...	2.57	2.72	2.99	18.16	1351	.0001	*		*	L
How important do you find the way ...	3.34	3.41	3.64	15.54	1351	.0001	*		*	L
Do you think that anybody can influence the way ...	3.26	3.14	2.62	19.09	498	.0001	*		*	L

Variable	Mean H	Mean T	Mean R	F	n	p	H-R	H-T	R-T	Relation
Personal control - learning										
Do you think that you can influence what you are required to learn?	1.35	1.56	1.53	26.99	1350	.0001	*	*		C
Indicate to what extent you can influence what ...	3.90	5.39	5.46	49.99	1349	.0001	*	*		C
Indicate to what extent you can influence what ... in 3 up to 5 years.	5.76	9.97	6.17	28.64	1339	.01	*	*	*	M
Who or what influences what ... I do	2.98	2.72	2.13	10.89	904	.01	*	*	*	L
Peers (e.g. fellow-students, siblings, friends)	4.87	4.11	4.32	18.25	876	.01	*	*	*	C
Authority (e.g. parents, master of a trade, teacher)	2.66	2.59	3.14	7.96	878	.01	*		*	L
Institutions (e.g. school, place of work)	2.68	2.76	3.69	22.94	872	.0001	*		*	L
Society (e.g. publicity, fashion)	5.28	3.91	5.05	68.92	861	.0001		*	*	M
Natural laws (e.g. weather, good luck, bad luck)	5.88	5.00	4.99	36.78	862	.0001	*	*	*	C
Compare your influences with the one of the friends of your age.	2.53	2.53	2.60	.92	1291	ns				–
Do you try to get more influences on what ...	2.57	2.78	2.86	12.28	1330	.001	*	*		C
How important do you find what ...	3.12	3.19	3.32	7.08	1327	.01	*		*	L
Do you think that anybody can influence what ...	2.68	2.75	2.67	.51	741	ns				–
Personal control - work										
Do you think you can influence what employment you will get?	1.85	1.75	1.77	8.27	1329	.001		*		–
Indicate to what extent you can influence what employment ...	6.83	6.35	7.21	11.83	1329	.01		*	*	M
Indicate to what extent you can influence what employment ... in three up to five years.	6.90	7.13	7.15	1.68	1317	ns				–

Variable	Mean H	Mean T	Mean R	F	n	p	H-R	H-T	R-T	Relation
Who or what influences what employment ...										
I do	1.71	2.13	1.59	10.30	893	.01		*	*	M
Peers (e.g. fellow-students, siblings, friends)	5.12	4.36	4.46	20.57	867	.0001	*	*		C
Authority (e.g. parents, master of a trade, teacher)	3.53	2.98	3.43	11.31	879	.01	*	*	*	M
Institutions (e.g. school, place of work)	3.26	3.02	4.45	46.92	849	.0001	*		*	L
Society (e.g. publicity, fashion)	4.96	3.52	5.03	78.36	853	.0001		*	*	M
Natural laws (e.g. weather, good luck, bad luck)	5.58	4.95	5.11	14.74	859	.01	*	*	*	C
Compare your influence with the one of the friends of your age.	2.70	2.71	2.81	2.19	1275	ns				–
Do you try to get more influence ...	2.91	2.96	3.21	8.95	1319	.01	*		*	L
How important do you find what employment ...	3.53	3.53	3.83	21.07	1321	.0001	*		*	L
Do you think that anybody can influence what employment ...	3.08	2.66	2.56	12.41	433	.001	*	*		C

Note. H: Hungarians in Hungary; T: Hungarians in Transylvania; R: Romanians; H-R, H-T, and R-T abbreviate the two groups compared; L: language and culture; C: country and citizenship; M: minority status.
*Significant difference between the two groups indicated in the column header.

the result of this test (the number of significant L-type similarities was large enough) is completely consistent with the other statistical analyses and other observations.

In the next section, we examine the three types of relations in detail. Only the significant differences ($p<.05$) are discussed, so we do not quote the significance level there. We focus on the content of the items, and in some cases, the direction and magnitude of the differences are illustrated with figures.

RESULTS

Language and Culture

By examining the significance of differences, we found that in most cases, the two Hungarian-speaking samples (H and T) proved to be alike. Forty-three out of the 78 two-difference patterns fell into this type. We may attribute this mostly to the common language and cultural background shared by these two groups. However, we must consider that the geographic area also plays some role in the differences and that those Romanian adolescents who live in the more 'westernized' western region of Transylvania may also be different from their peers living in Bucharest. This is why we took a closer look at the content of the questions that distinguish the Romanian adolescents from both Hungarian groups.

The similarities between the Hungarian and Transylvanian samples were most obvious in the *future expectations* items, which asked adolescents to rate the importance of different goals in their future (Fig. 9.1). The Romanian children placed higher importance on having a good profession, making money, getting higher education and being useful to their country than did the Transylvanian and Hungarian adolescents. Three out of these four items are rather practical and rational and reflect clear and ambitious future goals, whereas the fourth one—"being useful to the country"—involves patriotic feelings. We do not know exactly what the minority children understood by "country." However, interestingly, the Transylvanian adolescents considered "being useful to the country" exactly as important ($M=2.81$) as the adolescents in Hungary ($M=2.81$). The two domains where the Hungarian and Transylvanian adolescents placed more importance than did the Romanians were rather emotional (raising one's children and being liked by others). Because modernization and industrialization usually weaken the importance of family and personal relationships and increase the role of materialistic values, this finding contradicts our expectations; however, it seems to support the stereotype about the emotional characteristics of Hungarians.

The age when the young become socially mature and more or less independent from their parents and achieve their own goals is usually a characteristic of the respective culture. Our results support this presumption. In seven out of the eight questions, the Hungarian and Transylvanian groups

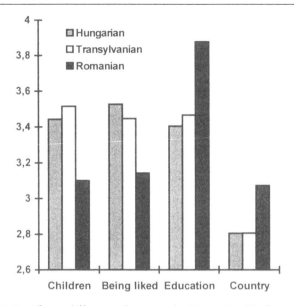

FIG. 9.1. Significant differences between the Romanian (Bucharest) group and the other two groups on the importance of attaining these goals in the future (future expectations).

gave very similar estimations of the age at which they anticipate fulfilling their future expectations, whereas the Romanian adolescents indicated ages that were 1 to 7 years older. There were minor differences between the Hungarian-speaking (H and T) and the Romanian adolescents in the questions about marriage and profession; larger differences in raising children (H: 25.49, T: 25.43, R: 27.33) and in being useful to the country (H: 24.09, T: 23.17, R: 26.90); and very large differences concerning being responsible for parents (H: 24.51, T: 24.68, R: 31.62). Because the questions on age are the most concrete items on the questionnaire and the least affected by translation, these data are the most convincing examples that the minority children belong to another culture than that of the majority in Romania.

The patterns we found in the daily hassles items are very similar to those found for future expectations; however, these results highlight another phenomenon. Future expectations can be quite independent of present conditions, so it is not surprising if they are rather determined by the broader culture or ethnic identity. We would have expected that when thinking about daily hassles, adolescents would be more influenced by their immediate living conditions; however, we did not find this to be so in this study. Although the everyday living conditions of Transylvanian adolescents are much closer to those of the Romanian than to those of Hungarian adolescents, in their responses, they were closer to the Hungarian adolescents. In 6 out of the 11 daily hassles items, adolescents in Transylvania and Hungary responded alike and differently from the Bucharest sample, and in the other 5 items, no significant differences were found (Fig. 9.2).

Interestingly, on most of the questions (free time was the only exception), Romanian adolescents reported far fewer hassles than the two Hungarian-speaking (H and T) groups. On some items, the two Hungarian-speaking samples were strikingly close to each other, whether the source was hassles related to school (Hungarian: 2.78, Transylvanian: 2.75), money (Hungarian: 2.39, Transylvanian: 2.37), or parents (Hungarian: 2.01, Transylvanian: 2.06). These responses suggest that what really made the results different for the Romanian adolescents was not the actual everyday experiences, but rather the subjective perception of hassles and the willingness to report them in the questionnaire. In these terms, it might be concluded that Hungarians are more likely to complain, whereas Romanians tend to hide their problems.

Regarding coping strategies, fewer similarities were found between the Hungarian and Transylvanian samples. Statistically significant associations were observed in only 4 out of the 16 items in the two samples and were really close to each other on only 3 items. Hungarian-speaking adolescents indicated a higher likeliness of affective reactions (getting angry and getting nervous), whereas Romanians seemed to prefer more rational solutions (trying to calm down and trying again).

Among the well-being and self-esteem items, there were five items where the two Hungarian (H and T) samples were similar (Fig. 9.3). Consistent with their responses to questions about everyday hassles, Romanians were also more likely to report their positive feelings ("My future looks good," "I

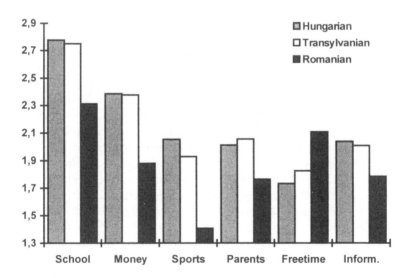

FIG. 9.2. Significant differences between the Romanian (Bucharest) group and the other two groups in daily hassles.

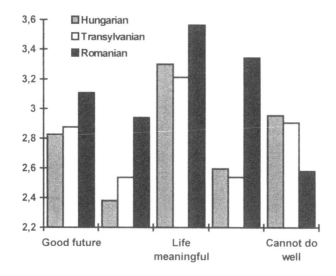

FIG. 9.3. Significant differences between the Romanian (Bucharest) group and the other two groups on well-being items.

enjoy life more than others," "My life runs in the right direction"), whereas Hungarians reported more pessimistic feelings ("My life does not have meaning") but higher self-esteem ("I am able to do things as well as others"). In two items ("My life runs in the right direction" and "My life does not have meaning"), the unusual patterns (the Transylvanian adolescents were not between the two other samples) might indicate a slight negative effect of minority status on psychological well-being.

The personal control items were those in which language and culture did not have a much larger impact than citizenship and minority status. Although the responses of the Hungarian and Transylvanian groups were alike only in one third of the questions, a few consistent tendencies could be observed. For example, Romanian adolescents thought that they had stronger control over their everyday behavior, and in each situation, Romanian adolescents attributed larger importance to the way they behave, what they learn, or what kind of job they will find.

Country and Citizenship

The Hungarian adolescents living in Transylvania are citizens of Romania and they have been experiencing the same economic and political constraints as the Romanian adolescents in Bucharest. This relation proved to be weaker than language and culture. We have found fewer similarities between the two groups living in Romania; however, these similarities are quite characteristic and can be interpreted as the impact of their common fate. In this section, we examine questions on which the Transylvanian and Romanian adolescents responded alike and in a different way from the Hungarian sample.

Only two such items (good health and travel) were found among the future expectation questions, and both can easily be interpreted and explained with reference to the specific social-political situation in Romania. The poor condition of the healthcare system could clarify why those two groups put larger emphasis on good health, and limited possibilities of traveling abroad may account for their stronger desire to travel.

Among the coping strategy items, we found four country-specific questions. Those adolescents who lived in Romania (Cluj and Bucharest) were more likely to choose the "I cry" and the "I pray and hope" as well as the "I am sad" and "I give up" options. Each of these strategies have the giving up motive, or at least the perception of barriers. It's worth noting here that Transylvanian adolescents were the most likely to cry or become sad when experiencing problems (Fig. 9.4).

The largest number of country-specific responses was found for the personal control items. In general, the Hungarian adolescents indicated a weaker sense of personal control than those living in Romania. This was the case for their future behavior (H: 7.01, T: 7.66, R: 7.76), their present learning activities (H: 1.34, T: 1.56, R: 1.53), their learning activities in the future (H: 2.57, T: 2.78, R: 2.86), and their influence on job possibilities (H: 6.90, T: 7.13, R: 7.15). Although on the personal control items

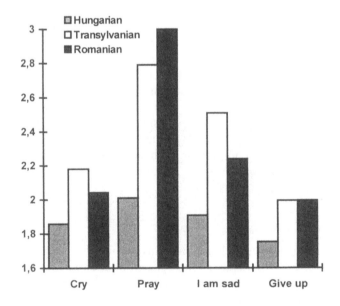

FIG. 9.4. Signigicant differences between the Hungarian (Szeged) group and the other two groups in emotion-oriented coping strategies.

cross-country differences were smaller than those found for the coping strategy or well-being items, there was a slight tendency for the adolescents who lived in a less liberal country to express a higher level of the perception that they personally controlled their lives.

Minority Status

There were some questions on which the adolescents of the Romanian and Hungarian samples responded alike, but in a different way than the adolescents from Transylvania. Only a few such questions were found, but some of these questions were rather characteristic. The most striking example is the self-esteem item ("I feel I am less worthy than others"), where the two majority groups responded almost the same way (H: 3.06, R: 3.07), but those belonging to the minority expressed much lower self-esteem (T: 2.72).

With respect to intercultural attitudes, the most interesting finding was related to preferences as to how much contact the adolescents would like to have with people in other countries (see chap. 8, this volume). The results showed the sympathy of the Hungarian adolescents living in Transylvania toward Hungarians. Their score was higher (3.69) than any other intercultural attitude in the three groups considered. The next highest (3.51) was the Romanians' attitude toward the United States. Also, the Transylvanian adolescents expressed the lowest level of desire to make contact with teenagers in another country, namely with those in Russia (1.43). The next lowest level was the Romanians' attitude toward the Hungarians (1.59). These figures show the nature and multitude of the minority problems in Transylvania: the strong attachment of the Hungarian minority children to the country that represents their language and culture, on the one hand, and the fact of being a minority in a nation that is less liked by those children who belong to the majority, on the other hand.

The other questions to which the minority children gave different answers than those belonging to the majority were found among the personal control items. The Transylvanian adolescents felt less strongly that they themselves could influence what jobs they would have, and they were more likely to believe that their behavior, their learning, and their job possibilities were influenced by their parents and by institutions. However, they felt that in the future, they would have better control over what they learn.

DISCUSSION AND CONCLUSION

We found that in almost one half of the variables analyzed, the two Hungarian-speaking samples (H and T) were similar to each other and different from the Romanian sample. So out of the three possible relations, language and culture of origin proved to be the strongest link that made two groups similarly feel and respond to the questionnaire. To approximately one quarter of the questions, the two groups living in Romania (T and R) responded alike, and in a different way than the Hungarian adolescents living in Hungary. So the country, the immediate political—social surroundings, and the quality of everyday life form the second strongest link. To about every ninth question, the two nonminority (R and H) samples responded alike. In these questions, the minority status of the Hungarian children living in Transylvania might have directly affected their responses (felt less worthy than others). Finally, there were questions where it was not possible to identify a close relation between any two samples. The most typical pattern in this category was that the mean of the Transylvanian sample was nearly equidistant between the means of the other two samples.

The questionnaire we used in this project was not designed to address the specific issue of minority problems in Europe, nor were there questions that directly explored cultural identity or minority status. However, the questionnaire turned out to be an excellent instrument for revealing some interesting phenomena concerning the role and meaning of culture, even in such a specific case as the cultural identity of national minorities. The results of this study show the strong cultural identity of a minority group not at the level of conscious declaration, but rather throughout a variety of choices that prove to be different from those of the dominant group of the country.

The Hungarian adolescents in Transylvania who participated in the survey are at least the third generation to have spent their childhood in a state other than that which represents their cultural identity; probably, their grandparents were also born in Romania. Cluj, their hometown, is quite far from the Hungarian border, and they do not have too many opportunities to travel to Hungary (under the ancient regime several restrictions prevented citizens of Romania from traveling to Hungary), so their direct communication with Hungarians living in Hungary has been minimal. Thus, our results may suggest the long-lasting effects of culture and the importance of cultural identity in personality development.

The questions we asked were not about national identity, they were simply about future expectations or coping strategies, but it turned out that the responses of the groups belonging to the same culture were very much alike, even though they lived far away from each other in different countries under different political and social circumstances. These similarities show that culture in general may play a more important role in shaping adolescents' personalities that do actual living conditions. Turning back to the question of their acculturation, assimilation does not seem to be a real alternative with such a strong and lasting sense of cultural identity. Instead, ways of integration should be sought, ways of coexistence, in which cultural variety—including the protection of minority culture—is recognized. Recent ideas of multicultural education may help this process—if adapted both to mainstream and to minority children education.

There were much fewer questions to which the Transylvanian adolescents and the Romanian adolescents gave similar responses, but some of these questions indicate the real and deep influence of the other culture. Furthermore, a more significant indicator of this double influence is that in most of the questions, whatever side they were closer to, the responses of the Transylvanians were between the two others. Being familiar with two cultures, they could bridge the differences, providing the political conditions allowed it. These similarities could be considered as indicators of possible integration.

We found few signs that would suggest that minority status in itself deeply affects personality development. Only those characteristics and attitudes were different in the minority group that could directly be related to its specific status (e.g., self-esteem and intercultural attitudes) and are influenced by intensive everyday experiences or by acculturation shock.

The similarities between the Transylvanian and the Hungarian adolescents show the strong cultural identity of these minority children, but there is another factor that accounts for these similarities as they were examined here, namely, their large differences from the dominant group of their country. The large number of significant differences between the Transylvanian and Romanian samples may also be an indicator of separation. More precisely (using the framework of Berry at al., 1992), these differences may be indicators of segregation. In this case, the distancing process is not voluntary at all, it may also be imposed by the dominant group, as was clearly shown by the negative attitudes of the Romanian children toward the Hungarians.

There are other possible interpretations of our results, or at least other factors that may also contribute to the differences found between the Romanian and Hungarian adolescents. One is the language in its narrower and technical sense. For the two Hungarian samples, the same questionnaire was used while another translation of the questionnaire was administered to the Romanian adolescents. Even slight differences of wording might have affected the meaning of some questions. However, the largest cross-cultural (in this case, cross-language) differences were found in the case of the ages that were indicated for the future expectations items, where translation differences may not play any significant role. Furthermore, the results are usually so consistent and the differences so large that they cannot simply be attributed to translation dissimilarities.

Another source of the difference found between the Transylvanian and Romanian adolescents might have been regional differences. We cannot exclude the interpretation that Romanian adolescents in Transylvania were also different from the Romanian teenagers. As is often suggested, one effect of the European unification process would be the growing role of regions as larger economic, administrative, and cultural units. In the long run, this might be true for Transylvania, too, but the economic and cultural differences between the different regions of present-day Romania are not so large that they could explain our results.

Humanist thinkers of the region have often dreamt about Transylvania as the Switzerland of Eastern Europe. There are some hopeful indicators among our results; however, if we compare these findings with those indicating the relationships of Swiss adolescents to their neighboring cultures, we may conclude that there is still a long way to go to fulfill this dream and that the educational systems of the region face a challenging task.

ACKNOWLEDGMENT

The data collection of the Hungarian samples was partly supported by a grant to Csapó (OTKT: Socialization of Hungarian adolescents in a cross-cultural context). The first draft of this chapter was completed while Csapó was a Fellow at the Center for Advanced Study in the Behavioral Sciences. He thanks the Andrew W.Mellon Foundation and the Johann Jacobs Foundation for their financial support.

REFERENCES

Berry, J.W., Poortinga, Y.H., Segall, M.H., & Dasen, P.R. (1992). *Cross-cultural psychology*. Cambridge, England: Cambridge University Press.

Prins, G. (1990). *Spring in winter. The 1989 revolutions*. Manchester, England: Manchester University Press.

10

European Adolescents: Basically Alike and Excitingly Different

Françoise D.Alsaker
University of Bergen, Norway
University of Berne, Switzerland

August Flammer
University of Berne, Switzerland

In the first chapter of this volume we discussed some of the many problems associated with cross-cultural and cross-national research, but we also argued for the usefulness of conducting such studies of adolescent development. The time is ripe to ask what the costs and benefits, so to say, of this study have been. Kohn (1987) stated rather pessimistically: "As with any research strategy, cross-national research comes at a price. It is costly in time and money, it is difficult to do, and it often seems to raise more interpretive problems than it solves" (p. 713). We agree with Kohn on the time costs; a research project conducted in 12 nations is time-consuming at all levels (not only in time, but also in energy and in communication efforts). As for the statement that cross-national research creates more problems than it solves, we argue that the Euronet project has at least provided many answers—for more than we had sensible questions. In this chapter, we summarize the main and clearest results and come back to the general issues raised in the chapter 1.

Based on the writings of Narroll (1970), we considered our samples to be *culture-bearing units*—groups of people that are under the influence of a certain set of cultural variables, but may have their own definite peculiarities. Thus, we do not claim that our samples are strictly representative of the cultures in which they are embedded, but these cultures are manifest in these samples.

On one hand, differences between the samples may possibly be explained by cultural differences. On the other hand, the results may contribute new knowledge about the culture bearing units, but may not be readily generalizable to the respective whole culture. In the same vein, we pointed out in chapter 2 that, even if speaking of the U.S. sample, the Russian sample, and so on, we did not mean that these samples were fully representative of all adolescents in their countries of origin. They were not, geographically speaking, in that they did not cover the entire national territory. Therefore, we have to be careful in assuming that differences between our samples are differences between the countries. However, we also claimed that parallels in findings in several samples that are culturally or nationally connected to another (e.g., the two Swiss samples, the two Scandinavian samples, or the Central European samples) deserve more confidence than more isolated findings. Bearing these cautionary remarks in mind, we have used terms such as the *French adolescents* when presenting results from the sample from France for matters of simplicity. Also, in the following, we discuss issues such as country profiles in the same generous way.

Although the extension of the culture concept is not always precisely definable, the extension of nationality is. As indicated in chapter 1, we take many differences between our samples to be cross-national more than cross-cultural—differences in time-use on a regular schoolday between French Switzerland and France are partly due to national institutions such as school organization rather than to cultural specifics. Also, we conceived of Europe as offering a large number of cultunits and added an American sample as a contrast. However, in most West-East comparisons, there were good reasons to pool the American sample with the Western European (including the Scandinavian) ones.

In the following, we try, in a first step, to give a picture of the different country units. In a second step, we look into the West—East dichotomy, the universality of gender and age differences, and the importance of language versus geographic borders.

THE PECULIARITIES OF THE 13 NATIONAL SAMPLES

The variables that differentiated most between the national samples were daily activities (leisure time and necessary activities) and future orientations (also called *values* here). In the following discussion, only the results significantly differentiating one country from several other countries are used in the description of the samples. That is, when we say that French adolescents use a great deal of time for meals, it means that on average, they use more time than most other adolescents in the study. Throughout, we concentrate on country main effects that are not qualified by interactions with gender and age, either because the interactions are basically ordinal or even absent.

Eastern and Central Europe

Bulgarian Adolescents. Bulgarian adolescents participated little in sports, but they reported a high percentage of time spent on leisure activities in general, especially hanging around with peers and watching television. However, in terms of future perspectives, social pleasure (leisure time and time with friends) was less important to them, whereas they reported considering social responsibility (taking care of parents and being useful to one's country) and success (earning much money, being famous, and being professionally important) as being very important. Interestingly, they were less interested in meeting compatriots than were adolescents of most other countries.

Czeckoslovakian Adolescents. Czeckoslovakian adolescents did not fall far from the overall average. They watched a lot of television, typically had a long way to school (in terms of time used), and the older adolescents reported doing many household chores.

Hungarian Adolescents. They used relatively little time for leisure activities and they did little shopping. They did not show much interest in pursuing a career (obtaining a good education and profession); however, starting a family and social responsibilities were very important to them.

Polish Adolescents. Like their Hungarian peers, Polish adolescents had little time for leisure activities. They did not consider a professional career as being very important, but they highly valued social responsibilities. However, unlike their Hungarian peers, Polish adolescents did a lot of shopping and household chores. In general, Polish adolescents were interested in having success and did not consider social pleasure to be very important in life.

Romanian Adolescents. Like their Bulgarian and Czeckoslovakian peers, Romanian adolescents spent much time watching television. Like their Bulgarian peers, they participated little in sports. Romanian adolescents also reported spending little time playing a musical instrument. Like the Polish adolescents, they highly valued success and social responsibility, but not social pleasure.

Russian Adolescents. Like Bulgarian and Romanian adolescents, Russian adolescents did not seem very interested in sports. They were generally low on leisure activities, but they were high in reading. The Russian adolescents highly valued having success in life.

Western European Adolescents

Finnish Adolescents. Finnish adolescents used much time for leisure activities, especially for hanging around with friends. They spent little time going to and from school and not that much time on homework. They highly valued a professional career and social pleasure.

Norwegian Adolescents. Norwegian adolescents had much leisure time, they were very active in sports, worked for money, played a musical instrument to a large extent, and still had time to hang around with their peers. Why? Possibly because they had a rather short schoolday, a short way to school and did little homework. Like many of their Western European peers, they highly valued a professional career and social pleasure.

French Adolescents. French adolescents reported having spent little time on leisure activities, especially on sports, television, leisure reading, and dating. They also used less time for body care, shopping, and household chores. So what did they do? They slept, had very long schooldays, and spent a large amount of time on meals. They were low on valuing social responsibility and high on valuing social pleasure. Interestingly, they were not very interested in meeting compatriots and their well-being did not correlate with control beliefs, as it did in all other countries but the French-speaking part of Switzerland.

German Adolescents. German adolescents did what one wouldhave expected French adolescents to do—they spent much time on dating. They also had much leisure time and spent much time on playing a musical instrument. They did not participate, to a great extent, in household chores, had a rather short way to school (in terms of time), wanted a professional career and did not especially value social responsibility.

French-Speaking Swiss Adolescents. They had little time for leisure activities, and they did not spend it hanging around with peers, but on playing a musical instrument. Like the French adolescents, they slept a lot and spent much time on meals. They highly valued a professional career and social pleasure, but not social responsibility. As noted earlier, well-being was not significantly related to control beliefs in this sample (as in France).

German-Speaking Swiss Adolescents. These adolescents did not report much time spent on leisure activities in general, but they still were very high on playing a musical instrument and spent much time on leisure reading. Like their French-speaking Swiss peers, they were low on body care and high on time spent on meals. Also, they did little shopping. In terms of values, like their French-speaking Swiss peers and many other Western European adolescents, they wanted to attain a professional career and highly valued social pleasure, but not social responsibility. They were not very interested in visible success, as defined in this study, nor in starting a family.

Adolescents From the United States

The American adolescents had a lot of leisure time, they were very active in sports, worked for money, but did not spend much time on leisure reading. They highly valued a professional career, being successful, and (in contrast to their Western European peers) they highly valued social responsibility. Their subjective well-being was prominently dependent on strain and control beliefs (like Hungary). In all countries, Americans were the first or second preferred as potential social partners by adolescents answering the question "How much contact would you like to have with adolescents from other countries?"

This condensed overview of the results by country does not show very distinct national profiles, except for France. French adolescents clearly differed from other samples in time-use (see chap. 4), but shared many values with their Western European peers.

What seems interesting to us, is that some of the largest differences between countries reflect differences in the institutions of the society, for example, differences in sports and working for money as a consequence of the organization of the schoolday. The three countries yielding the highest percentages of time spent earning money were countries in which adolescents reported the shortest schoolday. French adolescents, who typically had the longest schoolday, had only very little space for leisure activities. This does not mean that French adolescents would not appreciate leisure time, but there was simply not enough time left. As a matter of fact, the French adolescents had rather high scores on social pleasure, when thinking about their future. We suspect that in France, leisure activities are allocated to special days like Wednesdays (school-free day in France) and weekends.

Such differences in school organization led to the fact that European adolescents living rather close to one another (geographically speaking) had rather different lifestyles. When school occupies a large part of the day, when schools are far away from home, or when the students go home at noon and back to school in the afternoon, there is necessarily less opportunity for other activities.

Our data also confirm some striking national stereotypes or traditions. American and Norwegian adolescents could have spent their free time doing things other than working for money. That is, these differences indicate deeper value choices or traditions on the societal level. In fact, Norwegian adolescents, for example, are more or less expected to take some small jobs in the afternoon to earn some of their pocket money. Actually, girls often start already in first grade, walking around with the neighbor's dog or with a baby buggy. Another example is the German and Swiss adolescents, who also fit well in their respective cultures, showing a high interest in playing musical instruments.

In sum, knowledge about the organization of the societies to which our samples belonged, and knowledge about the cultural traditions in which they were embedded, may help interpret some of the differences among the samples, but clearly not all. Why, for example, did Bulgarian, Romanian, and Russian adolescents report doing less sports than others?

EAST-WEST DIFFERENCES: FICTIONS AND REALITIES

There was a clear gap between the four Eastern European countries (Romania, Bulgaria, Poland, and Russia) and all other countries in terms of their daily family life; these adolescents had more often reported the presence of grandparents and other relatives in the household. We speculated that living near the older generation could increase the sense of responsibility for taking care of older parents at later stages in life. The results reported in chapter 5 supported this hypothesis very clearly. Adolescents from the four Eastern countries rated social responsibility (including taking care of one's parents) significantly higher than did Western adolescents. Such differences show how living conditions and traditions are inter-twined.

As for future-oriented interests, more generally speaking, both similarities and differences were found. To mention only some, adolescents from all countries considered education and career as an important issue. However, education was more important to the adolescents from the Western countries. On the other hand, visible success seemed to be more important to adolescents from the Eastern European countries (and the United States) than to their Western and Central European peers. This gap between values for success and education is particularly interesting and may reflect somewhat naive representations about the future in countries where the previous decades have been characterized by little control over one's own personal success (see discussion in chap. 5 for more details). Indeed, it seems that relief from the former system had led these adolescents to believe rather strongly in their control (chap. 6). As for their personal development, they judged their own control higher than did the Western peers; generally, when they felt helpless, it was more often personal rather than global helplessness—helplessness that was perceived as due to the nature of things or to the system they were living in. In addition, in all domains that were investigated, the Eastern/Central Europeans indicated more of a desire than did their Western peers to actively strive for an increase in personal control. It is important to remember, in this context, that this optimistic trend was not reflected in their reports of their actual well-being. They did not score as high on well-being as did their Western peers. That is, they felt in control of their own development and they wished to become important persons; they thought they would gain control of their working place, but possibly, they still had not learned what was needed to realize success in the new societal system in which they were living.

Although responsibility for parents was more highly valued in the Eastern part of Europe, leisure activities were considered more important in Western countries. This difference also reflects the development that occurred in Western Europe since World War II. Leisure time became something like a human right and acquired a value of its own. The question is: How long will these rather large differences in values between East and West persist? A similar study in about 5 to 10 years from now could be highly interesting.

When asked about how much contact they would like to have with adolescents from the other countries included in the study, most adolescents showed high interest in having more contact with adolescents from Western countries (especially from the United States). On the other hand, there was generally low interest in meeting adolescents from Eastern and Central European countries. This result may reflect the hegemony of North America and Western Europe in the international media, especially in the entertainment industry, shaping ideals and stereotypes (chap. 8, this volume). This bias in interest was expected—most people do not often seek contact with people from cultures or countries they do not know at all—but it is somewhat sad. It may be all the more sad because the news coming through from the Eastern part of Europe is still negatively biased in the Western media, and it is not likely that this preference pattern will change very quickly.

The picture we get from these different chapters indicates that Eastern European adolescents, at least in 1992, felt they were on the way to change for the better. They were not very happy with what they had, they believed in their potential to change the situation, and they typically oriented themselves to what they believed were Western standards.

LANGUAGE BORDERS
AND GEOGRAPHIC-POLITICAL BORDERS

Another interesting feature of the Euronet study was the inclusion of samples from different countries sharing the same language (the two Swiss samples, France, and Germany) and the inclusion of a Hungarian minority population living in Romania. Interestingly, a comparison of the latter sample with the Hungarian and the Romanian samples (chap. 9) showed more similarities between the two Hungarian-speaking samples (even if the Hungarian minority had been living in Romania for three generations already) than between the adolescents living in the same country (minority Hungarians and Romanians).

The Hungary-Romania results may give some support to the hypothesis that language borders are more important than national borders. This is exactly what we did not find, however, for Switzerland. In the cluster analysis reported in chapter 4, the two Swiss samples (German-speaking and French-speaking) clustered together at the very first step. There were only two variables clearly tying together the language-defined cultures. First, the German-speaking Swiss adolescents and their German peers invested more time than did all others in playing a musical instrument. Interestingly, the neighboring French-speaking Swiss adolescents had high scores on this activity too. Second, we found French adolescents to spend much time eating, and so did the Swiss adolescents, both the French-speaking and the German-speaking ones. That is, there was no unique influence of the French culture, in the French-speaking part of Switzerland. These two examples may indicate some influence from bordering cultures at some point and spillover phenomena to each other part of Switzerland. It is, however, quite clear in this case that national units (including the institutional specifics) were more important than language units.

The Hungarian adolescents living in Romania did not only share language with their Hungarian peers in Hungary, they also shared history to a great extent. The results also show how the repression of minorities can contribute to a cementation of the culture and work against the process of integration. As an a propos, it should be noted that Romania and Hungary have just (July 1997) agreed to reopen a Hungarian consulate in Cluj— the city included in our study. This reflects a more positive attitude from the Romanian government toward the Hungarian minority during the last years.

AGE DIFFERENCES

The analyses on age effects did not yield any unexpected results. Here, again, we were more impressed by the triviality of the age differences than by the differences themselves. Some differences were associated with organizational factors that seem to be rather similar in many countries, such as advanced and specialized schools being separated from primary schools and somewhat more centralized than primary schools. This meant, for example, that older adolescents had a longer way to school than did their younger peers. Other differences reflect adolescent development. Older adolescents reported spending more time dating and hanging around with peers. A result that also showed consistency across samples was related to participation in sport activities. Younger adolescents were more active in sports than were older adolescents. This is a fact that worries many sports organizations and it was clearly confirmed in this study.

Younger adolescents were less interested in becoming successful, and they also valued social pleasure and social responsibility less than did their older peers. One may ask why there were not more differences in future-oriented interests among these age groups. In fact, most items corresponded to goals to be achieved in adulthood, and one could have expected younger adolescents to show less interest in them. Possibly these results simply reflect the norms of their respective communities.

If we assume that only the adolescents of the older age group started to feel the personal seriousness and the weight of these projected realities, we have a further possible explanation of our finding that the older adolescents indicated lower subjective well-being than those of the younger age group.

GENDER DIFFERENCES

The results from our 13 samples showed a high degree of similarity among the countries in gender differences. Where there were differences, they amazingly mirrored old stereotypes. Girls spent more time than did boys on homework, leisure reading, body care, household chores, and shopping, whereas boys engaged in more sports and watched more television.

Boys also felt generally better than did girls, they valued becoming successful in life more than girls, whereas girls valued starting a family and having higher social pleasure. In comparing themselves individually with comparable others, boys, as well as girls, believed they had more control over their own development and future workplace. Interestingly, this kind of overestimation was more pronounced in boys than in girls.

It seems that traditional attitudes are alive and well among our adolescents. Possibly, some attitudes have changed, but only at a very superficial level or only in very specific domains. The fact that, officially, women have the same political and occupational rights as men does not prevent them from being socialized according to stereotypes.

The finding that girls spend more time on homework (and leisure reading), whereas boys play sports, corresponds well with the general expectation that girls are more quiet and careful, but also more serious. The latter characteristic, combined with the new expectations that women (like men) should get a good education and have a good profession, may herald a dramatic reversal of gender roles in coming decades. In fact, in countries in which professional expectations toward women are well-established, such as Poland or Russia, more young women obtain higher education than do young men. Speculating further about changes in gender role, it is also possible that the academic domain is becoming more feminine and that the stronger gender (i.e., males) will find its new ecological niche in business and money.

CONCLUSION

Cross-cultural research is about similarities and differences. In terms of differences between the countries, we have found many, especially between the Eastern and Western clusters. However, looking into the uniqueness of our culture-bearing units, we concluded that there were no very distinct national profiles.

When all results are compared, there seem to be even more similarities than dissimilarities among our 13 samples, both in terms of absolute figures and in terms of gender and age differences, as well as in relation between variables. Well-being was related to strain, coping, and control beliefs in very much the same way in all samples. The finding that adolescents who experienced more strain than others also felt worse may seem trivial, but the universality of the finding is interesting. One could, for example, have expected adolescents in countries that have been very restrictive in civil rights and that have put a lot of strain on their inhabitants to have learned to disentangle daily problems from their own well-being, or on the contrary, to be even more sensitive to strain. Both were apparently not the case. Cultural context did not interact with any of the predictors of well-being. Thinking about next steps to take, we would suggest including predictors that may, themselves, be under the influence of the cultural setting, such as academic achievement, body image, and different interpersonal variables.

With regard to cross-cultural research in general, we have learned from the present pilot experience, that it is worthwhile to carefully choose the cultunits to be included in a project. For good reasons, Euronet started with a spontaneously emerging group of researchers and therefore, chose samples from the environment of their respective research sites. As an ideal, however, we recommend starting by defining what aspects of what cultures are relevant to the issues addressed. In order to be sure that the chosen samples really represent the cultures one has chosen to study, it also seems advisable to include indicators of culture. In addition, as a cultunit may be defined as a particular nation, indicators of institutional peculiarities in these nations should also be part of the data collection.

One may wish to select samples that are representative of the entire culture one wants to study. However, this might turn out to be unrealistic and even not optimal. Every culture is composed of subcultures, tied to religion, to political ideas, to geographical specificities, to social class, and so on. The subcultures may be larger or smaller units, and numerical representativeness may neglect some of them. If it is essential for a (large) culture to be phenomenologically heterogeneous, it would, thus, be more interesting to explicitly study the subcultures in separate samples, or more easily, to include cultural indicators that allow further differentiations in the data analysis. Therefore, we again argue for the use of the concept of culture-bearing units.

Although our results reflect the fact that all of our samples pertained to one broad culture, the Western one, there still are fine-grained differences between the countries. Traveling through Europe is easy because of so many first-order similarities, but it is interesting because of so many second-order diversities. We wonder about the within differences that could be discovered if 13 samples from different U.S. states or 13 samples from different Russian areas had been used.

In conclusion, having been planned as a comparative study from the very beginning, conducted following a common procedure that aimed at controlling variables often confounded with cultural differences, and conducted at approximately the same time in all countries, the Euronet study represents a unique set of data in the area of psychological cross-national and cross-cultural studies. It might be considered as a unique historical document, inviting researchers to collect comparable data some 10 years later.

REFERENCES

Kohn, M.L. (1987). Cross-national research as an analytic strategy. *American Sociological Review, 52,* 713–731.

Naroll, R. (1970). The culture bearing unit in cross-cultural surveys. In R.Naroll & R.Cohen (Eds.). *Handbook of method in cultural anthropology* (pp.721–765). New York: Natural History Press.

Author Index

A

Abramson, L.Y., 100, *112*
Adams, G.R., 5, *13*
Albrecht, H.T., 2, *14*
Alloy, L.B., 100, *112*
Allport, G.W., 96, *97*
Alsaker, F.D., 2, 7, 12, *13,* 20, *32,* 33, 35, *59*
Argyle, M., 116, *128*
Avery, P.G., 132, *142*

B

Bagdikian, B.H., 133, *142*
Baltes, P.B., 100, *113,* 115, *128, 129*
Bandura, A., 100, *112,* 116, 118, *128*
Barber, B.R., 133, *142*
Barker, R.G., 34, *59*
Barrera, M, 116, 117, *128*
Beck, I.L., 132, *143*
Berry, J.W., 1, 3, 4, 8, *13,* 15, *32,* 147, 163, *164*
Blackburn, T.C, 100, *113*
Blyth, D.A., 2, *14*
Bradburn, N.M., 116, *128*
Bronfenbrenner, U., 6, *13,* 116, *128*
Brown, J., 100, 106, *113*
Burger, C., 85, *98*

C

Campbell, J.D., 133, *143*
Cantril, H., 116, *129*
Chapman, M., 100, *113*
Cobb, N.J., 135, *143*
Cohen, S., 116, 117, *129*
Colletti, J., 34, 50, 59, 134, *143*
Compas, B.E., 118, *129*
Cooney, G.H., 85, 86, *98*
Costa, P T., Jr., 117, *129*
Crockett, L., 2, *14*
Csikszentmihalyi, M., 34, 47, 49, 50, 55, *59,* 68, 72, *82*

D

Dasen, P.R., 1, 3, 4, 8, *13,* 15, *32,* 147, 163, *164*
DeGrazia, S., 34, *59*
DeLongis, A., 116, 120, *129*
Dennis, J., 132, *143*
Deutsch, K.W., 132, *142*
Diener, C., 119, 127, *129*
Diener, E., 116, 117, 119, 127, *129*
Diener, M, 116, 119, 127, *129*
Dixon, B., 131, *142*
Duckett, E., 34, *60*

E

Eccles, J., 34, 50, *60,* 61, 62, 65, 67, 68, 75, 77, 81, *83*
Elmwood, J.M., 87, *97*
Emmons, R.A., 116, *129*
Erikson, E.H., 85, 97, 97, 141, *142*
Euronet, 37, *59,* 103, *113,* 119, 127, *129*
Evans, D.R., 117, *129*

F

Fabrega, H., 6, *13*
Fiore, Q., 131, *143*
Flammer, A., 12, *13,* 33, 35, 37, *59,* 65, 66, 76, *82,* 99, 100, 101, 102, *112, 113,* 115, 116, 119, 120, *129*
Folkman, S., 116, 120, *129*
Fuchsle, T., 85, *98*

G

Garton, A.F, 35, 47, 53, *59*
Gillies, P., 87, *97*
Gillispie, J.M., 96, *97*
Goulet, L.R., 115, *129*
Greider, W., 142, *143*
Grob, A., 37, *59,* 100, 101, 102, 103, *112, 113,* 116, 119, 120, 127, *129*

Subject Index*

A

Academic achievement, 174
Age differences, 11, 138–139, 172
Asia, 35
Attachment, 2
Australia, 35

B

Body, 6
  body care, 40–56, 67, 69, 73, 81
  body image, 174
Bulgaria, 167

C

Career, 86, 88–90
Cold War, 134
Compatriots, 133, 140, 141
  (*see also* Homeland)
Constraints, social, 86
Control, 27, 170
  controllability, 102–104
  control appraisal, 102, 108–109
  perceived control, 27, 99–112, 120, 125, 153–155, 159–161, 173
Coping, 120, 125, 151, 158, 160
Culture, 1–7, 16, 31, 162, 174
  cross-cultural research, 3, 4, 8, 173
  cross-national research, 4, 5, 8–9, 15, 16, 17, 29, 118–119, 165,
  cultunit (also cultural bearing unit), 4–5, 10, 174
  interest in cultures, 131–142
Czechoslovakia, 19, 94, 96, 167

D

Daily activities, 166
  leisure activities, 33–60, 71, 74, 76, 86, 166
  necessary activities, 61–83, 166
Dating, 5–6, 37, 40–56, 67–68, 70, 73, 75, 81
Developmental tasks, 86, 87, 95

E

Eating, *see* Meals
Education, 86, 88
Europe
  Central Europe, 19, 136, 138, 146
  Eastern Europe, 86–87, 94–97, 138, 141, 146, 170
  Western Europe, 86, 94–97, 170

F

Fame, *see* Success
Family, importance of, 86, 87, 88, 91
Family settings, 24–25
Finland, 168
Foreigners, 132, 140, 141
France, 62, 71, 80, 96, 168
Friends, 37, 40–56, 67–68, 70, 73, 75
Future
  future orientations, 85–97, 150, 156–157, 166, 170
  measurement of, 87–89
  representations about, 170

G

Gender differences, 11, 173
Germany, 168

---

* Results about differences between countries are spread all over the volume. Therefore, countries are listed only when results are summarized or important specialties are discussed. The same is true of age and gender differences.

*For Product Safety Concerns and Information please contact
our EU representative GPSR@taylorandfrancis.com Taylor & Francis
Verlag GmbH, Kaufingerstraße 24, 80331 München, Germany*

T - #0026 - 270225 - C0 - 229/152/11 [13] - CB - 9780805825527 - Gloss Lamination